A WRONGFUL
DEATH LAWSUIT

ISBN-13 Paperback   978-1-967903-95-5
           eBook   978-1-967903-94-8

Library of Congress Control Number: 2025920739

A WRONGFUL DEATH LAWSUIT

A True David Versus Goliath Story

JOHN SIKO

BOOK DOMAIN LLC
Publish to Perfection

REVIEWS

The book takes readers on a detailed journey through the complexities and challenges of seeking redress in the American judicial system. The poignant narrative chronicles the suffering endured by his wife and highlights the arduous process of holding a healthcare provider accountable for their negligence. It serves as a critical educational tool, shedding light on Florida's Sovereign Immunity Statutes, which often deter victims from pursuing justice by capping potential damages.

Atticus Publishing.

The book was captivating and emotionally stirring. I found myself cringing, especially during the part where the author saw his wife's last moments, with Beth's eyes and mouth open, but she could neither see nor speak. I expected the author's relentless efforts to bring justice, but I was shocked to learn that the hospital actually got away with the claims the author had raised (malpractice and negligence).

Online Book Club

The book aims to inform the public about injustices in Florida laws and the unfair advantages that health-care facilities enjoy, despite their patients suffering and even dying due to malpractice and negligence by healthcare providers. I admire the author's persistent efforts to have the hospital admit his claims that they did not provide the standard quality of care his wife deserved and acknowledge the negligence that led to her death.

Amazon

The book offers a heartfelt and thoroughly detailed account of one man's journey through Florida's complex legal and medical malpractice systems. Written by a passionate and eloquent narrator, it describes the tragic events that led to his wife's untimely death and the lengthy legal battle that followed. The author's vivid descriptions and raw emotions draw readers into his intimate and moving world.

Literary Titan.

My four-year journey through the halls of justice seeking redress from a healthcare provider whose medical malpractice contributed
to my wife's death.

CONTENTS

CHAPTER 1

The Beginning

I DIDN'T REALIZE THAT May 12, 2017, would be the beginning of my longest four years.

Returning home from running an errand, I found my wife, Beth, on the floor with Coke spilled all over the wall and floor. She told me she had slipped and fallen earlier and couldn't get up. I tried lifting her onto a chair, but she was dead weight and complained about her knee hurting.

She was hurt much worse than initially suspected, and my attempt to lift her onto the chair could have worsened her injury. I decided she needed to go to the emergency room (ER) and called 911 to have her transported by ambulance. EMS arrived, stabilized her, and agreed with my decision to take her to the ER, explaining it would take about an hour to admit her.

After waiting for an hour, I drove to the emergency room and found out she was being admitted. The nurse would call me when I could visit her.

Let me take a moment to describe an emergency room in a Florida hospital. As you enter the waiting area, it feels like you've stepped into a meat cooler; it's cold. You'll see a room full of potential patients—some in wheelchairs, some lying across two or three seats trying to sleep, others wrapped in blankets to stay warm if they have one, and some with their noses in their iPhones. If you're not wearing a sweater, you might be better off waiting in the parking lot, where it's warmer.

Upon entering, you go to the admitting desk, where the first question they ask is whether you have insurance. If you pass that test, they ask why you are there. Your case is placed in a gray folder, and you are given a wristband with your name on it; then, you are sent back into the waiting room. People who have used the ER before are smart enough to say they have chest pains, whether they do or not. They receive a red folder and are moved immediately to get an EKG; they might find something wrong with your heart.

In most cases, the EKG shows nothing, and you lose your red folder, which gets replaced with a gray one before being sent back to the waiting room to join the other patients, who are served on a first-come, first-served basis. Depending on the time of year, you may or may not be able to find a seat in the waiting area. Southwest Florida is along the migratory path of snowbirds, many of whom spend the winter here seasonally. Without a local doctor, they often use the ER as their fallback for headaches, stomach aches, or simply because they do not feel well but are unsure why.

The local saying is, "Do not get sick between November and April and go to the ER because you may face a two- to three-hour wait to be seen." If you're going to the ER, bring a book. However, you might find reading material left in the waiting area by patients who have moved to the business area of the emergency room. The available literature could include the Christian Science Monitor, the Enquirer, and other dog-eared magazines.

When called, you move from a cold, waiting room to a chilly ER area. Depending on your condition, you might be assigned a room, a gurney in the hallway, or a reclining chair. If you get a room, they remove your clothes and put you in a private gown—a male or female nurse wearing a floral blouse, checkered pants, and sneakers will visit. You don't know if they are there to draw your blood or clean up trash. It's pretty different from when Beth was a nurse. Back then, she wore a clean, white dress, polished shoes, a cap that had taken hours to starch and iron, and her nurse's pin.

Although nursing attire has evolved, it hasn't affected their professionalism, and Beth never complained about the care she received from all the nurses who treated her. They remained professional and compassionate, regardless of their attire. If you get a gurney, a curtain is pulled around the bed, and you change in the hall. You get a chair if your symptoms don't require you to lie down. Now, the wait begins again for a doctor to see you. When they arrive, they ask what brought them in today and tell the nurse to draw blood.

Typically, blood test results help identify the issue and determine if it's serious enough to warrant admission. Waiting to see a doctor usually takes about 30 to 40 minutes, and blood work results are generally available within three to four hours. Remember, no one in the waiting room can be admitted to the emergency room until someone else leaves—whether they are on a gurney or in a chair.

Beth, brought by ambulance, hurried through the check-in process, and the nurse placed her on a gurney in the hallway. After examining her, the doctor ordered an X-ray of her leg. Once again, she waits in the cold ER hallway, but Beth is lucky enough to get a blanket.

An hour later, the doctor said, "The good news is there are no fractures," and told the nurse to give my wife a 'road test.' If she passed, she could go home. The medical definition of a 'road test' is: "To assess discharge suitability criteria by the testing level of self-sufficiency, cerebellar function-gait, ataxia, ambulation, and the ability to understand discharge instructions."

The medical definition of ambulation states, "The ability to walk from place to place independently with or without assistive devices."

The ER nurse grabbed a walker and asked Beth to stand. Using the walker and putting in a lot of effort, she managed to stand but complained about leg pain, telling the nurse she was in severe pain in her left knee and couldn't take a step without the pain getting worse. I asked the nurse to see if she could walk to the bathroom without pain, but she said she had passed the 'road test' by standing up and bearing weight on the injured leg with help from the walker.

She told me there were no fractures, and pain usually occurs after a fall. I informed the case worker, who collaborates with the discharge nurse, and explained the discharge process; Beth needs to stay in the hospital for observation. She mentioned that this would be costly because Medicare wouldn't cover this type of stay unless a diagnosis indicated medical necessity. I said I was willing to pay the fee because I believed additional tests would reveal an undiagnosed condition. She told me that the hospital would not admit Beth.

The Case Worker explained that my wife was leaving because the X-ray showed no fractures, so there was no reason to keep her. I strongly disagreed, arguing that my wife could not walk without significant pain. The Case Worker reiterated that pain is expected with any fall, and she was experiencing that pain. She told me Home Health Care would be notified, and a nurse would visit in the morning to assess whether she might need physical therapy. I firmly objected to her leaving, reasoning that if the nurse couldn't walk her to the bathroom, how would I get her into the house?

I asked to speak with the doctor, but I was instead directed to the nurse to sign the discharge papers.

I only spoke with the doctor when he stopped by and said, "Good news, no fractures," and then he was gone.

The nurse had me sign the discharge papers while applying an ACE bandage to Beth's lower leg, gave her some pain medication, and, with great effort, my wife was placed in a wheelchair and wheeled out to the parking lot. Beth, suffering from intense pain, was carefully seated in the car by the two nurses, experiencing the same difficulty as when they helped her into the wheelchair.

During the four hours in the ER, Beth was never tested to see if she could put weight on her left leg without a walker or asked to take a step without help. Before discharge, a nurse's 'road test' is the final check to ensure the patient can leave safely.

If there is doubt, the nurse must notify the doctor that the patient failed the 'road test' so the doctor can reassess his decision to discharge the patient. Beth's final discharge medical advice came from the ER nurse and the Case Worker, and at no point was she told not to load bear on the leg until she saw an orthopedic doctor or was given a 'road test' as previously defined.

After carefully placing Beth in the front seat of the car, we started the fifteen-minute drive home, her still in severe pain. Once we got home, I grabbed her walker and, despite her complaints of pain, helped her out of the car. She took five steps from the car to a five-inch step at the house entrance. As she put full weight on her injured leg to step up, she collapsed into a sitting position in the doorway.

She didn't just fall; she collapsed as if a building had lost its walls. She was in severe pain, and I couldn't lift her to a standing position to reach her walker and bring her inside the house. My only choice was to call 911 for help lifting her.

EMS arrived and helped her to her feet, but couldn't move her from the doorway to the bathroom because she was unable to walk. They requested a wheeled desk chair, and she was placed in it and pushed to the toilet. After she finished, they seated her, put her back in the chair, and wheeled her to bed. Each time she was moved, she complained about the intense pain.

I asked what to do if she needed to use the bathroom at night, and the EMS personnel told me to use the desk chair to help her get to the toilet. If I couldn't get her up, I was to call EMS again for lift assistance. At 4:00 a.m., she needed to use the bathroom. I placed her on the chair and the toilet seat, and, as expected, I couldn't stand her up to put her back on the chair. As advised, I called 911 again for EMS assistance with a lift.

They arrived quickly and helped her back into bed despite her severe pain. They examined her leg, which was swollen to about one and a half times its standard size, black and blue, and hard as a rock. They said the leg looked serious, and she needed to go to the hospital. I told them she had just been discharged from the ER, where they said there were no broken bones, and the pain and swelling were just side effects of the fall. EMS explained that I was in a challenging situation because she had a problem, but who do you turn to if the hospital says everything is okay because they found no fractures?

After a sleepless night, I removed the ACE bandage applied in the ER, thinking it might restrict blood flow and cause swelling. The leg was black, and she was in pain every time she moved it. I called Home Health Care to ask about their nurse dispatch service. The Case Worker told me to contact them and said she would send a referral to Home Health immediately.

To my surprise, Home Health informed me that they had no referral for my wife and required one from the hospital before sending anyone. I explained that I already had a referral, but they stated that the protocol required Home Health to obtain a referral from the hospital before opening a case. I told them I needed someone to look at my wife's leg immediately to see if she should go back to the ER. Home Health said they would check with the hospital and call me back.

After waiting an hour without a response, I called the ER directly, explained my wife's condition, and was told to bring her back to the ER. Once again, I called 911, and EMS arrived to transport her. They noted her pain was severe and moved her from the bed to their stretcher by lifting the sheet she was lying on and sliding it onto the stretcher.

She arrived at 10:45 AM and stayed in the hall on a gurney until 2:00 PM, when a doctor finally saw her. He asked why she was there; she showed him her leg and explained what had happened the previous evening. He told me she needed an ultrasound and that I could go home since it was clear she would be admitted.

At 3:00 PM, the hospital called to inform me that the ultrasound revealed she had a fractured tibia and fibula, the two bones in the lower leg, and that she would be admitted. The swelling and bruising were so severe that the surgeon could not operate until both symptoms eased. Instead of being placed in a hospital surgical bed, she would be transferred to the HPCC skilled nursing facility and stay there until the swelling and bruising decreased enough for surgery, with the surgeon making the final call.

With time to reflect, I asked myself, "Did the ER send my wife home on Friday night with a broken leg?" After researching the tibia online, I concluded that Beth had a stable fracture, meaning the tibia probably had a hairline crack that would have been visible with ultrasound when she was first admitted. Although her x-rays of the hip, pelvis, and knee showed no fractures, her complaint of pain below the knee should have prompted an ultrasound.

Nevertheless, the ER nurse did not inform the doctor about my wife's ongoing pain and her inability to walk. Fixing a cracked tibia is very different from repairing a broken one; a broken tibia usually requires surgery, while a cracked tibia is typically stabilized with a brace for several months to limit weight-bearing until it heals. The crack in the tibia was probably why it collapsed as soon as Beth tried to enter the house and put weight on it.

Question: Was the ER negligent in sending Beth home with a broken leg?

CHAPTER 2

Rehabilitation

O N MAY 18, Beth checked into the HPCC skilled nursing facility to wait until her swelling decreased enough for surgery, with the surgeon's decision scheduled for June 1. She is in constant pain, and all HPCC can do is keep her on prescribed pain medication, which offers little relief. Beth is showing signs of depression and has expressed a desire to die rather than wake up each morning and suffer through the pain.

She is in an immobilizer and needs help whenever she urinates. On May 18, HPCC, in violation of Medicare rules regarding the restricted use of a catheter unless medically necessary, inserted a urinary catheter—an unjustified decision not based on medical needs, but rather to make things easier for the aides by avoiding the need to help her to the bathroom or change diapers—an important date.

I'll briefly mention Medicare's directive on urinary catheters and discuss it in more detail later. Medicare states, "Ensure a resident who enters the facility without an indwelling catheter is not catheterized unless the resident's clinical condition shows that catheterization was necessary, and if the resident later receives one, it is removed as soon as possible." Urinary catheters are the leading cause of urinary tract infections (UTIs).

On June 1, we talked about her surgery with her orthopedic surgeon. The surgeon showed us her fracture x-rays and gave some bad news. The fracture looked more like a shattered tibia and was so severe that it needed major surgery. Another problem was that her bones were very soft due to osteoporosis, so they couldn't support the screws required to hold the metal plate he planned to attach.

Due to the high risk of surgery failure, he advised against proceeding with the operation and recommended letting the bones heal naturally. He estimated that recovery would take 16 to 19 weeks and warned that the leg might never regain its full function. This news deeply depressed Beth, knowing she would endure another five months of suffering.

I asked the surgeon to review the X-rays taken on May 12, when she was admitted to the ER, to see if he found any evidence of a tibia fracture. He examined the X-rays and identified what he believed was an abnormality that might not have been obvious to an ER doctor. I inquired whether this abnormality could have caused the pain she experienced during the so-called 'road test' and whether the pain alone should have prompted further examination. He agreed that the pain alone would have been enough reason to admit her to the hospital for an orthopedic consult or for the ER doctor to have ordered an ultrasound in addition to the X-rays.

She should not have left the hospital on May 12. When asked why, he vaguely and off the record mentioned hospital policy that limits ER admissions. If this were true, my wife's upcoming months of pain might have been determined by policy rather than medical judgment. The surgeon ordered a custom-made leg brace, which a technician from the manufacturer would fit.

Since surgery isn't an option to repair her leg, her depression has become more evident. She isn't eating and seems confused, likely due to the strong pain medication. Her desire to die led me to contact the facility's Quality-of-Life team to address her depression. Worsening her discomfort, she now has a spastic bladder and feels the urge to urinate even though she has a catheter. The catheter might be causing this sensation, making the urge to urinate her primary concern. She isn't eating, spends most of her day sleeping, and her confusion is more noticeable.

On Sunday, June 4, I received a surprise call from her orthopedic surgeon. During the call, it was clear that he was carefully reviewing the case. He explained how the new brace would function, keeping her leg immobile to help the bones heal together. He also discussed the risks, including the high likelihood that surgery might not be successful.

On June 5, due to her ongoing pain complaints and spastic bladder issues, I contacted her pain management doctor to schedule an appointment. When reviewing her pain medications, he explained that she was already on the most potent drug he would recommend, so there was nothing more he could do for her pain. On June 6, I spoke with Beth's case manager, who expressed concern that the staff are worried about her since she is not eating and has worsened since her admission. I asked the Q Life team to check on her again and provide any recommendations they might have.

On June 6, the representative from the leg brace manufacturer arrived to measure Beth for her prescribed brace. He spent thirty minutes taking leg measurements, which involved manipulating her leg to ensure accuracy. During this uncomfortable process, Beth slept through the entire procedure, not waking up once.

Two days later, the $600 custom-made, complex brace arrived. It consisted of twelve molded plastic pieces connected by metal bars, four straps to secure the brace to the leg, and numerous adjusting screws to set it at the proper 30 to 40-degree angle. Setting the correct angle is crucial to keep the leg in the appropriate position for healing. The brace representative showed a physical therapist and me how to attach the brace correctly, emphasizing the importance of securing it properly. He also pointed out that it should be removed daily to check for sores that could develop underneath.

I immediately knew there was no way an aide would take the fifteen minutes needed to remove the mount, check the leg for sores, and then reattach the brace correctly. My suspicion proved right when I returned the next day and saw the brace was incorrectly attached. With no aide or physical therapist available, I reattached the brace myself. Many days later, I again found the brace wrongly attached and corrected it myself.

A person can have a high-tech leg brace specifically designed to help properly heal my wife's fracture. It won't work if it's worn incorrectly all the time. Another issue with the brace is that it makes sleeping difficult without medication. It limits her sleep positions and now adds sleeplessness to her urinary problems. It has also significantly reduced her mobility, making her more dependent on help.

On June 9, I talked with the physical therapist, who explained that Beth wasn't cooperating because she kept wanting to sleep. The drowsiness is probably caused by her taking Percocet and Xanax, both of which are sedatives and naturally make her want to sleep. The physical therapist mentioned she wasn't making progress; if she didn't improve, physical therapy would need to be stopped.

My next question was, "Why is she on physical therapy when she will be in a brace for the next 16 to 19 weeks?"

Wouldn't it be more practical to start PT when she is weight-bearing on the broken leg? I learned that although Beth is in the facility for the long-term care needed for her leg to heal, HPCC gets paid for sixty days of physical therapy as long as there is progress. If there isn't, Medicare payments stop. So, they are providing her with occupational therapy, which focuses on the upper body, even though that treatment wouldn't be relevant until she is out of her brace.

Her confusion has worsened; she isn't eating and keeps crying, "I have to pee." Her shouting led to her being moved to another room because her roommate complained about her screaming. Her urgent need to urinate with an empty bladder has become her most significant problem, even more than the pain. It has reached a point where staff place her on the toilet, where she tries her best to urinate but is unsuccessful.

One day, I received a call; she was uncontrollable, had taken off her brace, and was trying to walk to the bathroom. Telling her she has a catheter in doesn't help because the urge to go is still there. I scheduled an appointment with her urologist to see if he could relieve this urge to pee.

She is becoming increasingly challenging to manage and keeps trying to remove her brace so she can walk to the bathroom and urinate. I am starting to wonder whether the urge is physical or psychological in nature. The facility finally arranged a psychiatric consultation to address her agitation and depression. The doctor prescribed a new antidepressant, and there seems to be some improvement. I even brought in a Scrabble game and played it with her many times.

Surprisingly, her mind stays clear. She figures out words, does the math, and never once complains about needing to use the bathroom. Is her urge to pee physical or mental? It has become so urgent that she wheels herself down the hall searching for a bathroom to relieve herself. During the day, the nurses keep her at the nurse's station to watch over her.

We attended her urologist appointment, hoping he could diagnose her issue.

His first question was, "Why does she have a catheter in rather than be in diapers?" I told him I did not know.

He responded, "I know why; it's convenient for the attendants not to have to change her diaper all the time."

It is meant to make their job easier, not for medical necessity.

Inserting a catheter at any point will significantly increase her risk of urinary tract infection for the rest of her life. Although the catheter might cause her to feel like she needs to urinate, it is likely a psychological issue, with antidepressants being the only potential treatment.

"She feels like she needs to urinate, but there is nothing physically wrong with her that can be treated with any medication I may give her." The doctor's diagnosis crushed our hopes that the urologist could prescribe something to ease the urge to urinate.

I researched the persistent urge to urinate without any physical cause and developed a hypothesis about her condition. It seems to be a psychosomatic illness, specifically a form of Somatic Symptom Disorder, or SSD. In SSD, individuals experience physical symptoms despite the absence of any physical reason. An example given was people showing all the signs of cancer but not actually having the disease.

Medication cannot cure the illness; only management is possible. Treatment involves mental conditioning, and SSD medications may or may not be effective. The medicines currently prescribed are trying to treat a non-existent physical condition. Doctors tend to dismiss my diagnosis because they don't accept diagnoses from those with WebMD credentials.

I explained my SSD diagnosis to Beth and told her she should distract herself mentally from the urge to pee and focus on something else.

For example, when we played Scrabble for an hour or more, she didn't say, "I got to pee." She said she understood, but I doubt it will relieve her urge to pee.

Beth's persistent "I have to pee" mantra and her efforts to get out of bed to use the bathroom kept the nurses responding to her room all night. They moved her to a room near the nurse's station to better address the issue. On June 30, I noticed she was less agitated and not complaining about needing to pee constantly. Per my suggestion, HPCC had started her on Seroquel, an antidepressant that may have helped her. She is now going hours without needing to pee, so pain has become her primary concern.

I visit her for three hours every day, taking her out to the patio in her wheelchair and playing Scrabble on the terrace or in the game room. I visit around dinnertime so I can help her eat. I've been called home many nights to help calm her down when she is in severe pain or has urinary issues. I sit with her until she calms down and falls asleep.

One night, I was called in because she was unmanageable, had taken off her brace, and was sitting on the commode. No one knows how she managed to get there, which is one of the attendants' problems; she wants to remove the brace and walk to the bathroom. The constant urge to pee must be unbearably painful, and it's heartbreaking not to be able to help her. The other sad thing is that she keeps asking when she can go home. She desperately wants to go home, and I find different ways to tell her she won't be going home until she can walk again.

Let me step away from the script to clarify a Medicare issue. On July 14, 2017, HPCC informed me that Beth's Medicare coverage would end on the 17th, which meant she would have to leave or pay $275 per day because her 60 days of physical therapy had been used up. I responded that she was at HPCC for skilled nursing, not biological treatment, and that the facility needed to focus on caring for her leg brace.

Providing occupational therapy to a resident who cannot bear weight for more than 60 days seems excessive. It appears to be an attempt to take advantage of Medicare's coverage for only 60 days of therapy. Medicare covers 60 days of physical therapy if the patient demonstrates progress toward their treatment goals. By giving her PT daily for 60 days and reporting her improvements to Medicare, the facility ensures Medicare will pay for the therapy. I question how HPCC could have reported to Medicare that Beth was improving during those 60 paid days, yet her progress stopped after day 61. I submitted an appeal to Medicare.

Medicare denied my appeal. The Decision Explanation states that skilled nursing services might be necessary to improve the patient's condition, which requires the bones to fuse—something therapy cannot accomplish. To maintain the patient's condition, as the leg stabilizing brace supports, and to prevent further deterioration—that is the purpose of the brace, not therapy.

The decision to deny also stated, "Such skilled therapy services are covered when an individualized assessment of the patient's clinical condition shows that a qualified therapist's specialized judgment, knowledge, and skills are necessary for performing the rehabilitation services."

Why was physical therapy started on day one and continued for eight weeks despite knowing the patient could not bear weight on her leg for an indefinite period, which meant she would not meet Medicare's requirements for showing progress? It is this lack of progress that led to Medicare denying further coverage.

The Explanation of the Unfavorable Decision discusses the issue as 'skilled nursing facility services.' It also states that to cover post-hospital care in a skilled nursing facility (SNF), Medicare requires patients to receive medically necessary and reasonable skilled nursing services on a daily basis. Only inpatient care in an SNF can provide those professional services.

"Coverage for skilled therapy inpatient services does not depend on a beneficiary's potential, but rather on their need for skilled care." If therapy does not depend on potential, then how can a lack of progress justify discontinuing Medicare coverage for skilled nursing? Beth meets Medicare's criteria for requiring 'skilled nursing.'

I also disagreed with the decision, "The medical record does not support she could derive that additional benefit from a SNF level of care for further improvement, restoration, or to prevent or slow further deterioration of the beneficiary's current status."

The added benefit of SNF-level care is that the surgeon orders daily checks of the leg for blood clots or sores. Only by preventing these issues can the patient continue to improve as healing progresses.

I didn't submit the second appeal to Medicare because it was no longer necessary. I've noticed that Beth's memory has worsened recently. Beth has been calling me more often at night, saying she doesn't know where she is and asking why she can't go home. I'm uncertain if this is dementia or just a different UTI.

She also appeared dehydrated, so I performed a skin turgor test, which involves lightly pinching the skin to see how long it takes to bounce back, and I concluded that she was dehydrated. I informed the charge nurse that I believed Beth was dehydrated. The nurse then performed a turgor test, which confirmed my diagnosis. She told me they would give her more to drink, but it is clear she is not drinking enough of what they are currently providing, which is causing her dehydration.

It became clear that her dehydration was worsening, so I asked the nurse to place her on an IV to rehydrate her. She agreed and said they would start one. However, when I visited the next day, she wasn't on an IV. I asked why and was told the nurses tried four times to insert an IV, but her veins kept collapsing. No one was able to insert the IV, so they stopped trying and focused on increasing her fluid intake. Beth continues to show more signs of confusion and remains lethargic. I went to the PA assigned to the floor and explained that Beth's dehydration was worsening and that HPCC needed to send her to the ER. She told me the ER would just put in an IV and then send her back.

I said, "If she is dehydrated, rehydration is the reason for sending her to the hospital."

Instead of rehydrating her in the ER, the facility chose to do nothing. I kept insisting that her BUN level in her blood work was high, which usually indicates dehydration. She isn't drinking, her skin doesn't respond to turgor testing, and she needs to be transferred to the ER. The nurses ignored my suggestion and said they would find a nurse who could insert the IV for rehydration at HPCC. Eventually, after significant effort, a nurse inserted the IV line. Rehydration began on July 27, but it was clear that it had started too late.

On July 28, Beth had an appointment with her orthopedic surgeon for an X-ray of her leg to monitor its healing progress. Notably, her bones had healed well, and the doctor removed her brace. However, the nurse at the doctor's office noticed that Beth was unresponsive and had fallen asleep in her wheelchair. The nurses struggled to get her onto the exam table because she was weak. They realized that a concern needed to be addressed by HPCC.

The surgeon wrote a script permitting Beth to bear weight on her leg so she could begin rehab. I then discussed with him the hospital's failure to identify the tibia fracture during her initial ER visit. I will address this later. When I returned to the HPCC, I gave the nurse's station the doctor's script indicating her now being in a weight-bearing status for rehab. When I left her, all she wanted to do was sleep, and again, I informed the staff she was dehydrated.

On Saturday, July 29, I received a call from HPCC at my home, informing me that they found Beth unresponsive and were administering an IV while waiting for the facility doctor to arrive. Two hours later, I was told that HPCC had rushed Beth to the ER. When I arrived at the ER, the doctors were working on aggressive rehydration, but she remained unresponsive. She finally started to respond after the second bag of saline.

She was also diagnosed with a UTI and pneumonia, which led to her hospital admission. The UTI and dehydration likely caused her confusion. HPCC called to ask what to do with her belongings, and I told them to leave them there since I expected her to return after discharge.

On August 1, the case manager informed me that Beth was to be discharged from the hospital and inquired about her discharge plans. I told them to return her to HPCC, the facility that sent her to the hospital, but the case manager then said there was no bed available for her. A bed hold form, as required, was supposed to be sent by HPCC with her hospital admission forms, but HPCC did not include the document. The bed hold form states that I could keep the bed by paying a $100 bed hold fee for the days she was hospitalized, which I would have gladly paid.

The Case Manager, off the record, told me she heard HPCC did not want her back because she required too much attendant care. So, after spending eleven weeks in rehab, and now that effective rehab therapy could begin, they no longer want her. Not readmitting a resident is a practice AARP calls a 'nursing home eviction,' and it is a practice against which AARP has filed suit.

The case worker and I looked for another rehab facility with an available bed. We found one, but it was like moving from the Hilton to Motel 6, and it wasn't my first choice if I had other options. HPCC, part of the hospital system, could hire experienced staff by offering good wages and benefits. The new facility, which I will refer to as FMR, was primarily staffed with aides from Haiti or Jamaica.

They were kind people, but the experience needed improvement due to the high turnover among aides. Beth immediately noticed the change in environment and felt even more depressed. She has only thirty days left on Medicare for room and board, as well as physical therapy. Medicare payments for physical therapy restart after a recipient has spent three days in the hospital.

On August 13, I visited FMR to check on her physical therapy progress and noticed they were only doing upper-body exercises without focusing on improving her mobility. I asked why the therapy wasn't aimed at helping her walk again, and I was told, according to the hospital discharge documents, that she was non-weight-bearing. I informed them that she has been weight-bearing since July 28.

A review of the hospital documents shows she was non-weight-bearing, and the hospital records match the information provided by HPCC when Beth was sent to the ER. FMR told me she was sent to the ER by HPCC with incorrect details, as the doctor's orders permitting her to be weight-bearing were left out. When I asked for a copy of HPCC's transfer documents to the ER, the facility refused. Either HPCC or the hospital provided incorrect patient status information, which caused Beth to miss ten days of urgently needed weight-bearing exercises, leaving her with only 15 days of PT remaining.

At FMR, she kept complaining about needing to pee even though the catheter was in place. The head nurse asked me why she had the catheter. I told him I knew of no medical reason, and her urologist believed it was only for the convenience of HPCC's aides so they wouldn't have to change diapers or help her to the bathroom. The urologist concluded there was no medical issue requiring a catheter. The nurse also informed me that Beth might experience difficulty urinating once the catheter is removed. It had been in for over two months, and her bladder had been inactive during that time, which caused her muscles to weaken.

Like her urologist, he also told me she would face frequent urinary tract infections for the rest of her life. I told him I was aware of the risks associated with catheters, but I had to assume HPCC placed the catheter for medical reasons. He asked if I objected to him removing it since we both agreed there was no medical need for it to stay. The catheter had been in for an estimated 90 days when it was removed.

That was when I researched how to use catheters. Every website, including Medicare's, emphasizes that catheters should only be inserted when medically necessary. If necessary, a catheter should be removed promptly due to the risk of urinary tract infections. Initially, I suspected that HPCC may have committed medical misconduct by using a catheter that wasn't medically justified.

On August 16, 97 days after she fractured her tibia, I assessed her condition. She still experiences constant pain from physical therapy and often feels the need to urinate, even though FMR has removed the catheter. She is growing more depressed and has once again expressed a wish to die rather than endure the ongoing, debilitating pain every day.

She can dress without the brace, but she still isn't eating and has lost eleven pounds. She has no idea when her bones will heal, but she knows she will be in constant pain until they do. Medicare expires in fifteen days, and she needs to switch to home health physical therapy or pay a $300 daily fee to stay at the facility.

On August 28, her Medicare coverage ended, and she left FMC to begin physical therapy at home. She feels relieved to go because the nursing home environment made her more depressed. She was around many others in wheelchairs, many with declining health, knowing some would never leave. She is still far from walking without pain and often feels the urge to urinate.

In summary, her rehab has shown limited progress in restoring her to her pre-fall condition, and I understand she will probably never regain the quality of life she had before her fall. She now attends physical therapy two or three times a week at home. A few days before leaving FMR, she fell and severely bruised her tailbone, which was a serious injury. I asked FMR to send her to the ER, but they discouraged it since she would be leaving rehab soon, and I could take her to the ER if needed.

I did, and the hospital admitted her for intractable back pain. She stayed five days, and they couldn't lessen the pain. The doctor told her that a bruised tailbone is painful and might take up to two years to heal. The medical team could only prescribe pain medication, and the bruising would eventually heal.

She will start physical therapy at home three times a week, provided by a Home Health Agency. Although the therapist spends most of her time filling out reports, she still manages to give Beth an effective workout during their sessions. Beth will never walk again without a walker, and I worry about her falling when I am not home. I am now thinking about moving her to assisted living.

CHAPTER 3

CMS 20068

CONSIDERING I MIGHT have a medical malpractice claim, I searched online for regulations related to the use of an embedded catheter. I found what I thought was the Holy Grail—a rule that confirmed my belief that I had a lawsuit. The principle is explained here and will be referred to as CMS 20068 in the story.

Title: Urinary Catheter or Urinary Tract Infection Critical Element Pathway issued by the Department of Health and Human Services, Center for Medicare & Medicaid Services. Form CMS 20068.

Critical Element Decisions:

Based on observations, interviews, and records review, did the facility provide quality and adequate services, treatment, and care according to current standards of practice and the resident's comprehensive assessment and care plan to:

Ensure that a resident entering the facility without an indwelling catheter is not catheterized unless the resident's clinical condition indicates that catheterization is necessary.

Ensure that a resident entering the facility with an indwelling catheter or who later receives one is promptly evaluated for removal, unless the resident's clinical condition requires that catheterization continue.

Ensure a resident receives proper treatment and services to prevent urinary tract infections.

Has the staff involved the resident or their representative in developing a care plan, including whether interventions reflect their preferences and choices, and discussed the risks and benefits of a urinary catheter? Failure of HPCC to follow Medicare mandates regarding the use of an indwelling catheter will form the basis of our medical malpractice lawsuit. As a Medicare facility, HPCC is required to adhere to these mandates.

CHAPTER 4

Malpractice Case

THERE MIGHT BE reasons to pursue a lawsuit based on off-the-record talks with Beth's orthopedic surgeon. From our discussions, I understood the following statements:

A review of Beth's original knee X-ray revealed an abnormality on the left side of her knee. Her complaint of pain below the knee, combined with this abnormality, suggests a possible stable tibia fracture. Based on the X-ray findings and her pain, she should not have been discharged from the ER on May 12. Conducting a standard 'road test' before her release could have confirmed that she was fit to go home.

When Beth put her whole weight on her left leg while entering the house, what was a possible stable fracture turned into a multi-fracture of the tibia. He reviewed the statements and agreed they could be accurate, but he would not sign off on them because he needs to work with this community. I agreed with his position and his reluctance to sign off on it.

Confident that there was a legitimate malpractice claim against the hospital, I reviewed the nursing home's actions to verify if I had the necessary documentation to pursue a case against HPCC. I called the HPCC administrator to inform him.

On July 29, HPCC told me they had taken my wife, who was unresponsive, to the emergency room due to severe dehydration. I had recognized and reported this condition multiple times to the HPCC nursing staff. They agreed that Beth was dehydrated and planned to start an IV for rehydration. When I returned to the facility and did not see my wife with an IV, I asked the charge nurse why. She responded that the staff tried to insert an IV, but her veins kept collapsing, so they stopped and decided to hydrate her orally.

Blood work showed that her BUN level continued to rise, and I informed the charge nurse that she needed to go to the ER for rehydration. After our talk, a nurse was found who could insert an IV and start an IV drip, but it seemed too late. She was rushed to the ER three days later, dehydrated and unresponsive. Dehydration was a condition the facility was aware of but chose to ignore.

He responded, "I will review the actions of the staff."

After I was discharged from the hospital, the Case Manager told me she wouldn't be returning to HPCC because they no longer had a bed for her. I was told I needed to find a rehab facility elsewhere. When I called the nursing supervisor to ask why Beth wasn't returning, I learned about the bed-hold policy.

Notice upon transfer—when a patient is transferred out of the facility, nursing will provide a copy of HPCC's Bed Hold Policy in the transfer packet and contact the patient or their representative to discuss the Bed Hold Policy. The Business Office will contact the patient or their representative the next business day to confirm the bed hold status.

I told him that HPCC had never contacted me, as per policy, and that if HPCC had sent a bed hold form with the patient, the Case Manager would have given it to me. She told me no bed hold form came with Beth and asked if the facility had contacted me about how to ensure her bed would be held for her return. I reassured her that I had not been approached, and I assumed she would return there since she had transferred out of HPCC due to their negligence.

The final decision was that the facility would not take her back, and my only option was to find another facility. This new facility would be unaware of her condition or the procedures performed in the last seventy days at HPCC. The administrator stated that the facility had followed all the Bed Hold Policies and would review the process further to see if improvements could be made to the notification system. I then asked him to send me a copy of the records that accompanied Beth to the ER from HPCC on July 29 to check if a bed-hold policy form was included with the documents. He said he would not grant my request for a copy of the transferred records.

I received a letter from HPCC's Administrator and Risk Manager, who said I had received the bed hold form. I told her I never received the document because, according to the hospital's Case Manager, no record came with Beth's transfer to the hospital, which violated HPCC's Bed Hold Policy. She insisted that the staff notify me.

I repeated that the only notification I received was, "What do you want to do with Beth's clothing?" to which I replied, "Hold it at the facility, assuming she would be returning." She said I had declined to sign a bed hold form, which was false because it would have been foolish not to sign the paper since she had just spent seventy days at the facility. Not signing the form would have required me to arrange another rehab to receive her after hospital discharge, which I did not have.

A copy of the transfer forms I requested would show whether a bed hold form, per facility policy, was included and whether the hospital was aware that Beth was now weight-bearing. This information would reveal if HPCC were negligent in not providing a bed hold form and in failing to inform the hospital that Beth was now weight-bearing for physical therapy.

After reviewing the actions of the hospital and nursing home, I concluded I had enough evidence to file a malpractice lawsuit and drafted the following summary of my findings. I argue that the medical staff at the hospital emergency room was negligent in their duty to provide proper medical care on May 12, 2017, by failing to recognize a broken tibia. My case is based on the following procedures, or lack thereof.

The ER discharged my wife after her fall at home, even though x-rays showed no fractures above the knee, despite her severe pain and inability to walk without pain. The ER discharge nurse's failure to perform an adequate 'road test' on my wife, as the doctor requested, contributed to her injury. Although she was in significant pain, the test involved her standing while supported by a walker. My request for the nurse to walk her to the bathroom to see if she could walk without pain was ignored.

The medical description of a 'road test' states: "The test assesses discharge suitability criteria by evaluating the level of self-sufficiency, cerebellar function, gait, ataxia, ambulation, and the ability to understand discharge instructions."

Ambulation refers to the ability to walk independently from one place to another, regardless of whether you use assistive devices.

The Case Manager acknowledged my repeated emphasis that my wife could not walk without pain, repeatedly saying, "The pain is just the expected result of the fall."

The nurse again ignored my request to see the doctor. The discharge instructions didn't mention that my wife shouldn't put weight on her leg until she saw her doctor, and the ER nurse's failure to include this led to my wife collapsing when she put weight on the injured leg. She collapsed but didn't fall, as stated in the ER readmittance information.

My argument, supported by her orthopedic surgeon's opinion, is that my wife may have had a stable tibia fracture that could have been detected with an ultrasound, preventing it from turning into a shattered tibia when she put weight on it. Performing a proper 'road test' would have revealed that my wife did not meet the standard criteria for walking, and the nurse should have informed the doctor. Notifying the doctor could have raised suspicion of a fracture below the knee, prompting him to order X-rays of that area or request an orthopedic consultation.

I argue that an ultrasound of the lower leg could have detected the suspected stable tibia fracture before it turned into a shattered, broken tibia. A stable fracture would have required immobilizing the leg for some time, but rehabilitation could have been done at home rather than in a skilled nursing facility. The tibia shattering caused severe swelling and bruising, which was evident twenty days after the incident when her orthopedic surgeon examined her. She spent those twenty days in a skilled nursing facility on strong pain medication, which provided little relief.

My argument, supported by the orthopedic surgeon, is that my wife should never have been discharged from the ER without further examination of her leg when she complained of ongoing pain. We believe her tibia was fractured at the time of discharge. In summary, the ER at the hospital failed to perform a proper 'road test' before discharging my wife, which resulted in her suffering months of debilitating pain in a skilled nursing facility and the risk of permanent damage to her future mobility. Due to their negligence, the hospital should be held accountable for its actions.

Case Summary: The hospital emergency room did not perform a standard 'road test,' despite multiple requests, before discharging my wife. Shortly after leaving, she collapsed when exiting the car at home. She was later readmitted to the ER with a shattered, inoperable tibia and fibula fracture. Due to the ER's negligence, my wife will undergo very painful rehab for the next four to five months with severe leg damage that could have been prevented if a simple one-minute 'road test' had been done before her discharge. In short, the hospital sent my wife home with a broken leg.

I sent this summary to several attorneys, expecting to easily hire a firm to handle this case. How mistaken I was.

CHAPTER 5

The Plaintiffs

On August 15, 1936, Beth was born in Akron, Ohio, but she grew up on a farm in western Pennsylvania. Her mother was a retired registered nurse, and her father managed a meat processing plant in town. After graduating from high school, she entered the nurses' training program at Columbia Hospital in Pittsburgh, a three-year in-hospital program where she lived in the hospital dorm. It was during her training that she met me. After serving three years aboard a U.S. Navy destroyer with two tours in Korea, I attended Duquesne University on the GI Bill. I was only 23 years old, having joined the Navy right out of high school at seventeen.

My friends and I heard about a bar where nurses hung out, so we decided to check it out. That's where we met, and even though I wasn't the one she wanted to go home with, I ended up taking her back to her dorm. We hit it off, and the rest is history.

She graduated in 1957 and immediately began her career as a nurse in the operating room. She became so skilled at her duties that she was one of the few doctors specifically asked to assist during surgeries.

I graduated in 1958 and took a job with Dan River Mills in Danville, Virginia. The position led to a long-distance relationship, as I traveled back about once a month after an eight-hour drive. I spent only nine months in Danville before moving to a new role in Montgomery, Alabama, as a plant industrial engineer, which made our long-distance relationship last even longer than just the drive.

Our wedding plans were already set, and on August 1, 1959, we got married. We quickly packed a trailer, hooked it up to a car her father gave us, and drove to Montgomery. We got married on a Saturday, and I had to return to work the following Tuesday. We spent our wedding night at a cheap motel in Cincinnati, Ohio.

Montgomery marked a significant change for both of us. As Northern Catholics, we felt out of place in the new environment. Being a Yankee was challenging, and being Catholic was unfamiliar to the Southern Baptists. Beth quickly found a job in the hospital's ER, working the 3:00 to 11:00 evening shift. She quit that job after she was followed home one night and ran inside in fear. Afterwards, she moved into the new field of industrial nursing, thanks to my help in securing a position at the plant where I worked.

The employees liked her, and the nurses' station became a popular gathering place. During the Easter holidays in 1960, we decided to take a honeymoon trip to New Orleans. On the drive down, Beth experienced what was not her only miscarriage. It happened in a service station restroom and was very traumatic for us.

We enjoyed our time in Montgomery, where we bought our first home—a yellow brick ranch house with pink shutters. It cost only $13,000, which was a lot at the time. Since I had just graduated from college and was working my first job, I earned $70 a week for a 45-hour workweek. Later, I took a new job with a higher salary of

$412 a month, so a $13,000 expense was significant, but we managed to make the mortgage payments with both of us working.

We also learned about the Southern perspective on segregation; although I experienced it in Danville, this was Beth's first time seeing it. She had a strong connection with the women of color working in the plant, despite the white workers looking down on them. Many employees resented her treatment of the 'colored folks.' Our introduction to Montgomery's view on African Americans happened one Sunday.

The Reverend Abernathy, a colleague of Dr. Martin Luther King, announced that Black participants would organize a demonstration march on the Capitol Building to protest the city's discrimination practices. So, from a church where they dressed in their Sunday best, hundreds of people gathered outside, waiting for the march to begin. At 2:00, when the march started, the protesters left the church, and the crowd began to attack them and throw objects at them.

I saw four Allied Van Line trailers parked near the Capitol building. When the riot started, the doors of those trailers opened, and horse-mounted state troopers rode into the crowd with long sticks in their hands, swinging them to disperse the people. Then, the fire department arrived and sprayed water to break up the chaos. The Black individuals then retreated into the church; eventually, everyone went home. I was taking pictures of the scene when one of the rioters approached me, asking if I was 'one of those Yankee newspaper photographers.' I told him I was just a regular Alabama redneck with my best southern accent, and he moved on.

In Montgomery, we got our first dog. I went to the local dump to toss out some trash, and I found this puppy in the garbage. I decided to bring it home and surprise Beth. It was the first of many.

Our time in Montgomery ended in November 1960 when I was laid off and started looking for a new job.

One of the companies I applied to was RJ Reynolds Tobacco in Winston-Salem, North Carolina. In summary, I mentioned my job experience with Dan River. The Director of Industrial Engineering at Dan River was a good friend of the Director of IE at RJR. He provided me with an excellent recommendation, and RJR hired me immediately in December 1960. We sold the house in Montgomery and moved into a second-floor rental in Winston-Salem, where we had a family with a kennel in the backyard to accommodate Hooker, our dog.

The dog house had a light bulb burning constantly to keep it warm. One night, the bulb slipped off its bracket, fell onto the straw on the floor, and started a fire. We managed to get the dogs out and put out the fire without needing to call the fire department. The new dog house did not have indoor heating.

With her background in industrial nursing, Beth got a job as a plant nurse at the main cigarette factory. Once again, she became popular among the workers, especially the Black employees, because they knew she was a Yankee. Beth was a smoker, and they often brought her cigarette packs directly from the production line. I remember her first day on the job.

She got on the interstate highway, and with her poor sense of direction, she turned right instead of left, heading toward Greensboro, North Carolina, before realizing she was going the wrong way. Once again, we experienced segregation, but now the restrooms were integrated, which was a big step forward for RJR. I was still called a Yankee, but I kept telling people I had to travel north to get to North Carolina, having come from Alabama.

We bought our second home for $33,000. It was a brick ranch; all homes in Winston-Salem were built with brick because the clay in North Carolina was ideal for making bricks, which made them inexpensive. The house was in the countryside, and we relied on a well for water. A month before we moved out of the rental, the husband of the couple had a heart attack. I heard the wife scream and ran downstairs to find him on the floor, unresponsive. I did my best with artificial respiration, but he died when the EMTs arrived.

During our time in Winston-Salem, Beth experienced her second miscarriage, which left her deeply distraught and led her to develop anorexia. We ran all the necessary tests to find out why she couldn't conceive and found no known risk factors. Then we shifted our focus to adoption and contacted the local Catholic agency. They carefully examined our background; the intense questioning worsened Beth's mental health.

Before finalizing the adoption, I was offered a promotion and transfer to a Del Monte plant in Lockport, NY, just outside Buffalo, which was a valuable opportunity. It would be only three hours from her home and four hours from mine, so I accepted. In February 1969, we sold the house and moved.

By this time, we had gone through four dogs and believed we had purchased a purebred Basset Hound. However, when we took it to the vet, he told us it wasn't a purebred but a mix. Soon after, the people we bought it from said the mother was a purebred Basset Hound, but the father was not, although he did come from a reputable neighborhood.

Since we couldn't keep a dog in our new rental in Lockport, we took her to her parents' house on the way north. Her father later told us that we had forgotten to mention that the dog was pregnant, which we were unaware of at the time. Because the dog was part basset, he had no trouble finding homes for the puppies.

We bought a house in Lockport, and Beth started working as a school nurse, adding a new role to her resume. I became the plant manager within a few years, and Beth shifted into a new field—geriatrics. After a quick trip to the ER, Beth experienced her third miscarriage. Her depression and other issues worsened, and we decided to give up on having children. Then, against all odds, at ages 42 and 45, she became pregnant; this one was a keeper, born in July 1978, though it was not an easy birth.

I received a call at work and rushed home to take her to the hospital, nearly causing an accident along the way. After several hours of labor, she was moved to the delivery room, and I went in with them. As the labor progressed, I saw the doctor struggle with the delivery. I realized there were serious problems when the nurse pressed on Beth's stomach, trying to push the baby out.

After the delivery, we looked at our baby, a boy, and the nurse took him out of the delivery room. Later, we discovered that the umbilical cord had wrapped around his neck, and he had inhaled meconium. After a day in intensive care, the baby was fine, and he came home with us on time.

However, Beth's health problems persisted. We planned a trip to Hawaii for Thanksgiving in 1981, and she had a doctor's appointment two weeks earlier. He detected a lump in her breast, and she underwent a mastectomy, with chemotherapy scheduled for the following week.

She decided to delay starting chemo until we got back from Hawaii. She kept up her exercises while on the islands, and we had a wonderful time, even though we knew she would begin chemo once we returned home. Months of weekly chemo and using a cold cap to prevent hair loss went smoothly; thirty years later, she is still cancer-free.

Medical problems continued when she saw her doctor in the summer of 1953, feeling very ill. She entered the doctor's office and was then taken to the hospital by ambulance, where her temperature soared to 108 degrees.

When I saw her the next day, she was covered in ice in the intensive care unit, where she stayed for three days. She spent three months in the hospital with a low-grade fever, but the medical team, including every specialty available, couldn't determine the cause of her illness. Finally, she was discharged home, where her fever broke, and she never experienced the symptoms again.

After enduring harsh Buffalo winters for 25 years, we became snowbirds. We spent many years vacationing in Florida, and in 1996, we purchased a condominium in Fort Myers. As a golfer, I discovered that the area has one of the few courses you can walk, which was the deciding factor in where we would settle. Beth was a charge nurse on a 3-11 shift at a nursing home, overseeing 25 patients with Alzheimer's. Little did we know then that this facility would later have a profound influence on our lives. She also volunteered with hospice, sitting with patients as they approached the end of their lives.

CHAPTER 6

Hip Surgery Lawsuit

Beth started having problems with her left hip replacement, and the doctor decided it needed to be replaced. The surgery went smoothly, and she was placed in bed with a Velcro-fastened stabilizer to keep her leg secure. During the night, she kept calling the nurse to report severe pain in her leg. The traveling nurse, unfamiliar with hip replacements, would administer pain medication instead of taking the necessary steps—loosening the Velcro and readjusting it.

Beth clearly noticed the leg swelling, and the nurse needed to remove the restraint. When the doctor arrived in the morning, he became angry when Beth complained about the pain and saw that the nurse hadn't loosened the restraint. By then, it was too late, and Beth had suffered severe nerve damage to her foot. It was clear I had a valid hospital malpractice case. As a novice, thinking I could file a complaint with the hospital and resolve the issue, I sent the following letter to the hospital administrator.

Re: Formal Complaint—Postoperative Nursing Care: On October 19, 1999, Dr. Smith (not his real name) performed my hip revision surgery at LM Hospital. At 3:00 PM, I was moved from recovery to a room to begin the recovery period. Soon after arriving, I complained about the pain in my leg while in the immobilizer. The pain worsened throughout the day, and the nurse on duty informed the head nurse. She administered the prescribed pain medication.

Later in the evening, I told the duty nurse that the pain in my leg had worsened, and my foot was numb and cold. She touched my foot and said it didn't feel cold. The pain and numbness persisted throughout the night, and I updated the duty nurse about my discomfort. At 6:30 AM the next morning, Dr. Smith was informed about the pain and numbness in my foot. His assistant immediately removed the immobilizer, which lessened the pain, but the numbness remained.

When the numbness continued for several days, Dr. Smith referred the patient for a neurology consultation. He diagnosed nerve damage, likely caused by the leg immobilizer being too tight for an extended period. From my nursing experience, I knew restraints should be loosened every two hours and readjusted to prevent swelling.

When a patient reports an extremity feeling cold and numb, it indicates reduced circulation to that area. When I experienced pain, numbness, and a cold foot, the immobilizer should have been loosened, circulation checked, and the immobilizer reapplied. The duty nurse failed to follow any of these procedures. The nurse did not readjust the immobilizer from when it was applied on October 19 until it was removed on October 20.

I am currently experiencing severe foot pain and numbness, which are interfering with my hip replacement therapy and recovery. The success of the hip revision surgery may have been affected by poor judgment during post-operative nursing care—specifically, not loosening the immobilizer when I reported the pain. Dr. Smith also agrees with the neurologist that the immobilizer's tightness was probably the cause of the nerve damage.

He remains optimistic that the damaged nerves will regenerate and has been prescribed vitamin B6, along with other medications, to speed up the process. However, three weeks after surgery, the pain and numbness persisted. This formal complaint documents my dissatisfaction with the postoperative nursing care I received at the hospital. Further action will depend on the expected nerve recovery within a reasonable timeframe after my hip replacement rehabilitation.

I thought sending a letter would persuade the hospital to consider settling the matter. I received a letter from the administrator thanking me for writing and saying they would investigate the complaint. It then became clear that I needed professional help.

I contacted a local malpractice attorney and explained the situation using the above letter to detail the incident. He said I had a case but couldn't take it because Dr. Smith was his friend. Instead, he referred me to an attorney in Tampa, who gladly accepted the case. So, on February 21, 2001, a claim was filed against LM Hospital.

To better document the pain and suffering my wife experienced, I kept a post-op timeline from October 19 to January 29, 2000. Reviewing this timeline emphasizes the severity of her nerve pain. On October 28, I contacted Dr. Smith for the first time, describing how intense her pain was, and he prescribed Neurontin, a seizure medication known to help with nerve pain. The pain persisted, and while doing her walking exercises, she experienced no sensation in her foot; it felt as though it had gone to sleep.

I contacted the doctor and told him the pain was still as severe, so he increased the medication dose. He was hopeful that the nerve would heal and asked to be kept updated. Her pain still bothers her at night, making it difficult to sleep. When she walks with her shoes on, she feels a stabbing pain that persists all day without relief.

It is now clear that she is suffering from severe depression. She was looking forward to her hip surgery to relieve the pain she experienced before the replacement. She fears she has only traded her hip pain for even worse foot nerve pain. She increasingly depends on pain pills to get through the day; the medication only eases the pain and doesn't eliminate it.

Dr. Smith continues reassuring her that the nerve will regenerate, but he also expresses concern. He mentioned that he has never seen a case like this before, despite having performed over 8000 hip replacement surgeries. Her debilitating pain persisted, so she was referred to a neurologist for an NCV nerve test. While Dr. Smith confirms the hip surgery was successful, the NCV test shows she did suffer nerve damage. He believes the sensory nerve will regenerate, but his experience suggests recovery happens at about one inch per month.

Her nerve damage extends for eighteen inches, meaning she will face at least eighteen months of ongoing nerve pain. During a visit to the neurologist, and without us asking, he mentioned that Beth had sustained nerve damage caused by the immobilizer being too tight. He said he couldn't do anything to repair the nerve damage since only nature can heal it, and all he could do was try to manage the pain.

I could talk about what Beth experienced because of the nerve pain from hospital malpractice, but I will focus on the hip replacement lawsuit case.

LAWSUIT SETTLEMENT

The case starts with our attorney gathering all the nursing notes for the relevant days, while the hospital attorney opposes us at every turn. In 2001, my wife was called for a recorded deposition that lasted over an hour. The deposition frightened her because she didn't know what to expect or if she could answer all the questions correctly. She did okay, but the thought of doing it again worried her. Then, the hospital attorney also took Dr. Smith and us through a deposition.

The doctor supported our claim that the nursing staff did not follow his protocol, which resulted in nerve damage. Additionally, we presented a letter from the neurologist, whom Dr. Smith called in to evaluate Beth's nerve injury, whose opinion stated, "Left peroneal neuropathy—most probably secondary to compression from immobilizer."

Our case was scheduled, with the next step being a court-ordered mediation between the plaintiff and the defendant's attorneys. We waited for the hospital attorney to set a date for the mediation. We left for Buffalo in June 2002, and in July, we were notified that the session was scheduled for August, which meant we would need to fly back to attend.

Mediation exists for that purpose, but it's a sham. I will explain the entire process later, as it relates to our current lawsuit. We requested $200,000; the opposing attorney then went into another room, where they probably watched television for about fifteen minutes, and returned with a $10,000 counteroffer. There is a mediator, earning $600 per hour with a three-hour minimum, who moves between rooms to facilitate each party's proposals and responses.

The negotiation ultimately focused on our demand for a settlement of X and the hospital's offer of Y. Since mediated settlements are confidential, I cannot specify the amounts; however, the payment was in the high five figures. It all boiled down to whether we wanted to go to trial for a potentially larger amount or accept their offer. Afraid of going to trial, Beth decided to take the hospital's proposal.

The release stated, "for consideration of Y, the receipt and sufficiency thereof acknowledged, the undersigned now release and forever discharge LM hospital and continue with legalese." After deducting contingency fees and expenses, Y was reduced by $28,408. No amount of money will ever compensate her for her suffering and the pain she had to endure until the nerve regenerated.

CHAPTER 7

Search for Attorney

I STARTED SEARCHING FOR a law firm that promotes itself as experienced in medical malpractice. My first contact was with the MM law firm, which states it will secure the best settlement. Their motto, displayed on television at least five times a day, is "MM for the People."

I said, "What the hell?" I am a person, so I called them. My call was answered by a secretary who asked what I was calling about, and I told her it was a medical malpractice case. She wondered who the defendant was, and I told her it was the hospital. She said she would check with an attorney and, in two minutes, was back, telling me the firm was not interested in the case. Why wasn't I one of MM's people? I soon learned they weren't against me, the people, but against the not-to-be-mentioned word 'hospital.' MM didn't even offer me my free consultation as advertised.

I received a name from the attorney service and sent my case description. After waiting two weeks for a response, I started a new search. Using the details of Beth's case, I began by searching the internet, focusing on practices in the immediate area. Surprisingly, none of the firms wanted to take on the case once they learned it involved a lawsuit against the hospital. I then expanded my search across the entire state of Florida and encountered the same response—either they declined the case over the phone or did not respond to my inquiry.

I personally interviewed a local attorney and discussed the case with him, as well as an attorney who specializes in malpractice lawsuits. They declined to take the case and sent me a letter explaining their reasons. Here are parts of that letter.

Thank you for contacting our office regarding your wife's potential medical malpractice case. As we discussed during our meeting, recent legislation enacted in Florida—primarily influenced by physicians' lobbying efforts—has limited the types of cases we can handle. These laws significantly increase the costs and time required for lawyers to investigate or pursue any medical negligence claims. Additionally, our rules mandate that the patient must prove, through expert witnesses, that the defendant's standard of care was below what other doctors would provide.

In your wife's case, we agree that the emergency room physician should not have discharged her after telling her she couldn't walk without pain. However, and often more challenging, we also need to demonstrate that this deviation from the standard of care directly or indirectly caused the injuries the patient claims resulted from treatment.

In your wife's case, her injuries resulted from the fall that initially brought her to the emergency room, not from the staff's delay in admitting her to the hospital. The information gathered about your wife's situation has been reviewed against the legal requirements mentioned above and our experience with previous cases. We have determined that her case does not meet our current criteria for recommending further action. Therefore, we cannot pursue her case.

Please understand that this does not mean she has no potential claims. This decision reflects our office's opinion, and you have the right to, and should consider, consulting other counsel.

I decided to keep looking for other counsel based on the latest recommendation. During my research, I found the main challenge of filing a lawsuit against a hospital, which can be summarized as 'Florida's Sovereign Immunity Statutes.' Below is a summary of these statutes.

CHAPTER 8

Sovereign Immunity

SOVEREIGN IMMUNITY REFLECTS the principle that the 'King can do no wrong.'

It is an ancient principle based on the idea that courts have no authority to impose judgments or verdicts on the king, as the king establishes the courts. Sovereign immunity is a legal doctrine that shields a sovereign entity, such as a hospital or nursing home—considered a state agency—from being held liable for civil torts committed by its employees or agents unless the sovereign entity explicitly agrees to be sued.

Tort law aims to hold parties accountable for negligent acts and provide compensation to those who have been harmed as a result of such acts. Sovereign immunity is an exception that fully shields individuals acting in their official capacities from tort liability.

Government immunity was established when Justice Oliver Wendell Holmes stated in 1907, "A sovereign is exempt from suit because there can be no legal right as against the authority that makes the law on which the right depends." In other words, since it creates the law, it is not subject to it, which undermines the law's fairness and impartiality. In a 1945 Supreme Court opinion, the Court declared that sovereign immunity is 'embodied in the Constitution.'

However, no legal scholars have definitively located where this doctrine is 'embodied' in the Constitution. In Marbury v. Madison in 1803, it was stated that "the very essence of civil liberty certainly consists of the right of every individual to claim the protection of the laws whenever he receives an injury." Despite this, states are passing more restrictive laws regarding damage limits.

Florida attempted to abolish sovereign immunity in 1969, but after a year, pressure from school boards and insurance companies led lawmakers to only partially implement it. Many lawyers refer to sovereign immunity as the 'Free Kill Law.' Medical negligence injuries affect more than one million Americans each year and are the third leading cause of death in the US, following only cancer and heart disease. Taxpayers partly fund so-called 'public' hospitals, which are protected by sovereign immunity, yet they also receive millions in private insurance annually, similar to other hospitals. There is no good reason to treat these 'public' hospitals differently in terms of protection.

However, Florida has waived sovereign immunity to allow for defendant substitution. In torts committed by state entities, especially hospitals and nursing homes, Florida's waiver of sovereign immunity enables plaintiffs to seek damages from the state government. However, it restricts the payment of judgments or claims to $200,000 per person. Our case falls under the 2019 Florida Statutes, Title XLV, Torts, Chapter 768, Negligence, Section 768.28, which details the waiver of sovereign immunity in tort cases, recovery limits, and restrictions on attorney fees.

The main drawback of finding an attorney is that: "No attorney may charge, demand, receive or collect, for services rendered, fees above 25% of any judgment or settlement." By setting a cap on fees, an attorney can only collect up to 25% of the total amount. This restriction decreases the number of cases filed against the state. It is often difficult for plaintiffs to find an attorney willing to work within these limits. The caps leave plaintiffs with valid claims without representation because an attorney can collect up to 40% contingency fees for lawsuits not involving the state.

A firm will invest the same amount of time, money, and effort in representing a client with a million-dollar case as it would in representing a plaintiff suing the state, where the maximum award is $200,000 with a slim chance of winning that amount, along with a maximum contingency fee of $50,000. Moreover, as I have observed, hospital attorneys who are on a substantial hourly retainer tend to prolong the case to occupy as much of the plaintiff's attorney's time as possible by slow-walking it toward a conclusion.

Under sovereign immunity, the hospital might, during a procedure, remove the healthy right kidney instead of the failing left one. The patient endures years of pain, racks up huge medical bills, and ultimately dies of kidney failure. Even though the hospital commits medical malpractice, its maximum liability for this malpractice is $200,000.

In its pure form, sovereign immunity completely shields the sovereign from legal liability, preventing injured parties from pursuing compensation. In medical malpractice cases under negligence law, sovereign immunity and the related concept of defendant substitution can provide considerable protection for physicians acting on behalf of a state or federal government.

Medicine is a complex field, and the Florida approach clearly demonstrates how modern sovereign immunity impacts the practice of medical malpractice law. While Florida has chosen, for policy reasons, to allow its local governments to be sued as defendants in medical negligence cases, thereby enabling plaintiffs to recover damages from the state, the state has also imposed limits on those damages through monetary caps.

Sovereign immunity explains why firms weren't eager to pursue my case against the hospital and nursing home.

Florida's medical malpractice laws do not favor patients; they favor insurance companies, hospitals, and doctors. The laws in Florida make it very difficult to pursue a medical malpractice case. It is costly, and the maximum attorney fee, based on a settlement of $200,000, is $50,000. This amount depends on being awarded the highest amount allowed under sovereign immunity, and the chances of receiving the maximum award are very slim, as court-ordered mediation is a common practice in such cases.

It is now the attorney's responsibility to assess whether taking the case is financially viable. Sovereign immunity faces growing criticism, and most academic opinions oppose it. While it has not prevented effective remedies for unlawful acts by state agencies, it has limited claims arising from their actions. In fact, at least four Supreme Court justices have been willing to eliminate the doctrine for some time.

My search for an attorney to represent us expanded to include all Florida malpractice law firms. After numerous rejections and waiting for responses to my case description, I finally received a positive reply. I was contacted by a firm we refer to as LGF in Tampa. After a fifteen-minute discussion with the managing partner, he decided that LGF would take the case. On September 5, I received a letter welcoming me and including several forms to sign and return.

Thank you for choosing our firm to represent you in your potential medical malpractice claim. A file has been opened, and we need some or all of your medical records. We will review the records and any other relevant information you provide. If we determine that you may have a valid claim, your documents will be forwarded to one or more medical experts for review and evaluation.

After reviewing the records, our experts will advise us on whether we can obtain a declaration of facts supporting your claim. Communication is crucial to your case, and we're happy to answer any questions you may have. Please email them to us. (Remember this statement.) Keep in mind that medical malpractice cases are often lengthy, costly, and time-consuming. Your cooperation will be vital in deciding whether to pursue your claim.

I returned my signed documents to LGF for their signature and to get a copy for my records. LGF still has not returned the signed documents as required by law, despite my repeated requests. The contract details will be provided later when I receive my copies.

I'll briefly explain the contingency agreement. Although the Florida Constitution limits contingency fees to a maximum of 25%, lawyers representing clients in medical malpractice cases can charge more than this with the client's consent. LGF informed me of their plan to set a 40% contingency fee and may petition the court for approval to exceed the limits of Rule 4.4-1.5.

To secure representation in a sovereign immunity lawsuit, I had no choice but to accept the 40% contingency fee and sign the agreement. Later, I found out that my contract was invalid because the law requires that my consent form be notarized. The Rules of Professional Conduct mandate that a lawyer charging a contingency fee in a medical liability case give the client a copy of the fee limitations outlined in the constitution, which I did not receive.

Florida Statute 768.28 states that Florida attorneys handling claims against state agencies are limited to a contingency fee of 25%. The statute questions the 40% contingency fee outlined in the contract with LGF. The court would unlikely rule that the legislature's power to limit attorneys' fees paid from a claims bill award is unconstitutional because such authority affects access to the courts. Contingency fee arrangements are 'the poor man's key to the courthouse' and ensure every citizen's right to access our courts.

Subsection 768.28 (8), which establishes a cap or 'ceiling' on contingency fee contract compensation, has been upheld by the Florida Supreme Court as a constitutionally permissible limit on attorneys' fees. The right to contract for legal services is a fundamental constitutional right that requires strict scrutiny and cannot be restricted by subsequent legislation attempting to limit this contractual right. Will my signing a contract agreeing to a 40% contingency fee bind me to that, or does the legislature's rule that claims against state agencies cannot exceed 25% nullify that contract?

The goal of medical negligence lawsuits is to compensate the injured plaintiff, discourage negligent practices, and uphold justice. Only 15% of medical malpractice cases are reviewed, and data from malpractice insurers show that fewer than 1% of all filed cases end in a verdict favoring the plaintiff. In most cases, attorney and administrative costs eat up the awarded amount. Litigation remains expensive and inefficient.

In an appeal, a withdrawing judge called the 25% attorney contingency fee 'draconian' and said it unconstitutionally interferes with the contract between lawyer and client. Limiting contingency fees for attorneys could restrict access to the court for many people who otherwise could not afford legal help. However, the Florida Supreme Court has ruled that restrictions on attorneys' fees are a constitutionally acceptable exercise of legislative authority and do not impair contractual obligations.

Sovereign immunity is frequently mentioned in this context and relates to the specific lawsuit. LMHS is one of the hospital systems in Florida governed by these laws. Below is the defendant's response to the question, "Describe all policies which you contend cover you for the allegations outlined in Plaintiff's Complaint."

LMHS and HPCC are public healthcare systems created by a special act of the Florida Legislature, Chapter 63–1552, Laws of Florida Special Acts. LMNS is an independent special district under Florida law. As government entities, LMHS, its employees, agents, and related entities are protected by the Florida Waiver of Sovereign Immunity Act, Section 768.28, and are subject to liability limits.

CHAPTER 9

Lawsuit Investigation

LGF WILL BEGIN collecting information to support a lawsuit by obtaining Beth's hospital medical records and X-rays from her ER visit. LGF will have its medical experts review the X-rays to determine if they can identify the same anomaly her surgeon noticed. LGF mentioned I should email any questions or additional information. On January 2, I sent these details to my attorney.

One significant consequence of my wife's broken tibia, caused directly or indirectly by HPCC, is her increased risk of urinary tract infections (UTIs). These infections resulted from HPCC's actions upon her arrival at the facility. After breaking her tibia, she was placed in a leg immobilizer, which made it difficult to use the bathroom without assistance from CAs. To avoid needing help, HPCC inserted a catheter for her to urinate.

After a few weeks, she reported feeling the urge to urinate despite having a catheter in place. We visited her urologist to see what he could prescribe to help manage her issue. His first question was why she was using a catheter instead of diapers. He emphasized that the longer she kept the catheter, the higher her risk of developing frequent UTIs. I told him that HPCC had inserted the catheter without explaining the reason for doing so.

The urologist explained he understood why the procedure was performed; it was for HPCC's CA's convenience, so they wouldn't need to spend time escorting her to the bathroom or changing her diaper. However, a measure taken by HPCC for their ease could result in Beth having frequent UTIs for the rest of her life.

The warning from her urologist has proven true. She has had five UTIs since leaving HPCC, each requiring hospitalization. Based on a review of Beth's medical records, do we have a valid claim against HPCC?

On March 1, I sent the following: I am still waiting for the promised case progress reports.

Per your September 5th letter, 'We feel that communication is vital to your case' and 'we are happy to answer any question you may have.'

My previous questions may have upset you because I still haven't received the case update I asked for. Not seeing a response, I checked the Florida law website for options to get case updates. They recommended sending information requests by 'certified mail' with a receipt requested. On May 4th, I sent the first of several certified mail requests.

Many requests for case updates have received the response, "You will get back to me with answers to my questions." Refer to your latest email of April 13, stating that I would get an update next week.

It has been three weeks since the following week passed without any answers, and I am requesting responses to the question below. Your September 5, 2017, introduction stated that LGF had started a file for your preliminary review of the medical malpractice cases.

Referring to the 'Statement of Client's Rights,' you, the client, have the right to ask your lawyer at reasonable intervals how the case is progressing and to have these questions answered to the best of your lawyer's ability. Inquiry: How are the Medical Malpractice cases going?

LGF responded that our expert is currently reviewing your medical malpractice case. Please allow our firm and our expert enough time to thoroughly examine all aspects of your potential claim so we can provide the best possible representation. The nursing home malpractice case is entering a new stage, known as NOI, or Notice of Intent, to notify the defendants. Once it is sent, we will update you. Our office will contact you once our expert has finished their review and provided us with a report on your medical malpractice case.

An NOI (Notice of Intent) is a letter that raises a legal issue with someone and notifies them that you intend to file a lawsuit. It informs the other party that you are no longer trying to settle the case and will leave the final decision to the court. You do not need to threaten court action for it to qualify as a notice of intent to file. The NOI states: "Please be advised that according to Chapter 400, Florida Statutes, Elizabeth believes you are a prospective defendant in a case involving violating her resident's rights and negligence."

Elizabeth intends to sue you and anyone else legally connected to you over her rights as a resident and the care she received. She was a resident at HPCC from May 18, 2017, to July 29, 2017. There are many other legal details, but the main point is that, under Florida law, the parties must first participate in a pre-suit mediation to discuss liability and damages. I will explain the mediation process later.

During a call on March 8, I was told that LGF is still reviewing the case and that my attorney will keep me informed. I suggested that instead of emailing, we set up a monthly conference call to discuss the case's progress. She agreed. After speaking with her for the first time, six months into the case, I expected to be more impressed with her knowledge.

A review of her credentials on LGF's website shows she is listed as a Litigation Associate with a BA in Political Science. She later earned a law degree and has experience representing lenders in the foreclosure industry. This background is not very impressive for her to be representing me in a medical malpractice case. A follow-up email informed me that the defendant received the NOL on April 16.

I received a letter from LGF on May 31 regarding my nursing home claim. I am attaching the Pre-Suit Interrogatories and Pre-Suit Request for Production directed to you, which you are legally required to answer. Interrogatories are questions that must be answered under oath and can be used in court.

Please complete your suggested answers on the enclosed working copies. Be as specific as possible in your questions and answers. The final answers to the interrogatories must be filed with the Court within thirty days of the date on the certificate of service; therefore, I ask that you return your draft answers promptly.

Interrogatories: These are questions that the defendant sends to the plaintiff to answer. The defendant may submit up to thirty questions, and each answer must be at least one sentence long. The law requires that both the plaintiff and defendant share information about the facts of the incident, the plaintiff's claims, and the defendant's potential responses to those claims.

To fulfill the prompt request, I immediately began the process. There were 23 questions, most of which requested information they already possessed, and others that would not influence the case. By law, the opposing counsel has the right to ask these questions, and it is my duty to answer them regardless of their relevance. Gathering the records would take over thirty days for the plaintiff to respond with all the requested information. These questions, and many similar ones, will be used by the plaintiff's and defendant's attorneys throughout the litigation.

A list of the names, addresses, and specialties of all hospitals, physicians, and other healthcare providers, including dental and psychiatric care, visited over the past five years, along with a brief description of the treatment provided by each. Copies of all medical, dental, psychiatric, and hospital records in your possession from the last three years. Elizabeth has held positions with the names and addresses of all employers for the past five years. Copies of Elizabeth's tax returns for the last five years.

Provide Elizabeth's educational history by listing the schools she has attended over the past five years. Include the current names and ages of Elizabeth's children, along with their addresses at the time of the alleged incident. Offer a detailed account, including specific dates, of each injury and illness Elizabeth has experienced over the past ten years. Please list the names and addresses of the doctors Elizabeth has consulted regarding her health, and specify the purpose of each consultation.

What are the names and addresses of all hospitals where Elizabeth was a patient, including her hospitalization dates? Apart from the alleged incident, has Elizabeth ever filed a lawsuit or claimed money, damages, or compensation from any person, company, or organization? (In response to this question, I answered yes, indicating I had filed a lawsuit in 2001 alleging medical malpractice against the parent company of HPCC, the subject of this case.) Please list all medical and hospital expenses Elizabeth incurred or paid, including the date of each expense, the name and address of the recipient, and the dates payments were made.

Please list the name and address of each person known or believed by you, your attorney, or other representatives to be: A. an eyewitness to the occurrence described in the Pre-suit Notice, and specify their location at that time; B. not an eyewitness but who may have knowledge of the facts on which the negligence allegations in the Pre-suit Notice are based, and specify their location; C. not an eyewitness but who has or may have knowledge of the facts on which the damages allegations in the Pre-suit Notice are based.

These questions were answered briefly while still meeting the requirements for a thorough response. I provided a detailed answer to the following question. What you are about to read has already been covered in other questions and will probably be discussed again later. Therefore, I will give a summarized version of my detailed response.

Q: Describe each act or failure by the defendant that you believe led to negligence and caused the incident.

A: The catheter was placed for convenience to prevent aides from changing her diaper or helping her to the bathroom, and it was left in place well beyond the duration recommended by Medicare guidelines. This exposure increased Elizabeth's risk of frequent urinary tract infections. Severe dehydration forced Elizabeth to be rushed to the emergency room in a non-responsive state, requiring rapid rehydration to restore her consciousness. HPCC knew she was dehydrated, but did not have a nurse on staff who could insert an IV.

My response to the Pre-Suit Interrogatories was sent to LGF on June 4th for review of my suggested answers. I requested this review based on research showing that the court allows a party to consult with their attorney when answering interrogatories, enabling counsel to help their client carefully craft the responses. This collaborative approach can help reduce any potentially damaging effects of the client's answers.

On June 15, I emailed LGF. Since I haven't heard from you, I assume the interrogatory answers I submitted are acceptable and that you don't need any additional information from me. Please confirm this. I received no response. On June 27, I sent another email. Since I have not received any comments on my pre-suit interrogatories, have you forwarded my answers to opposing counsel as they are? No response.

Fed up with the lack of response to emails, I sent the following certified mail letter to LGF again on July 10.

I find it hard to understand how a firm claiming, "We feel that communication is essential to your case," can be reluctant to communicate.

I refer to two recent emails that have yet to be acknowledged or answered, a task that could have been handled with a simple reply. Instead, I am once again reminded of the Florida Bar's recommendation that if firms do not respond to requests for information sent through regular channels, the same request should be made by 'certified mail.'

I am seeking answers to these questions about my nursing home claim: Were my suggested Pre-Suit Interrogatories submitted to opposing counsel as written, and if so, when were they submitted? Also, when must opposing counsel respond to the Pre-Suit Interrogatories?

On August 6, I emailed the managing partner after not hearing back about my 'certified letter' information request. When a client has to request case information by 'certified mail' because answers cannot be obtained through regular channels, I must assume the system is broken. LGF received the last certified mail request for information on July 11, and I am still waiting for a response as of today.

Based on the email above, I received a call to arrange a conference call with my attorney for August 7. I made a list of questions, hoping her verbal answers would address my concerns. Not surprisingly, they did not; the following summarizes our conversation.

Question: Were my suggested pre-suit interrogatories sent to opposing counsel as written?

Answer: Yes.

Question: Is it advisable to review them with me before sending, since they were labeled as suggested draft answers?

Response: The answers appear to be appropriate and will be forwarded without modification.

Question: When were they sent?

Answer: The answers still need to be sent to opposing counsel.

Question: Why? You instructed me on May 31 to submit my answers promptly, as they were due to opposing counsel by June 30. I sent my responses to you on June 4. You are now telling me that, as of August 7, you still need to submit them.

Answer: I was out of town, but I will get them out tomorrow. The rest of the call went downhill from there. I requested we hold a monthly telephone conference so I could ask my questions directly and hopefully get an answer.

I received an email from the managing partner asking whether my questions had been answered. I responded that I had the chance to discuss my questions with her on Tuesday, August 7, but I wanted more detailed answers. For instance, on June 3, I sent expedited answers to the Pre-Suit interrogatories to be forwarded to opposing counsel, meeting a 30-day deadline.

However, on August 7, 65 days after I submitted my responses, she informed me that she still needed to send the interrogatory answers to opposing counsel. I do not know when she would have submitted them if I had not called. I asked my attorney to hold a monthly case update call. I suggest you establish such a practice.

I'll bring this up at our next scheduled attorney meeting. Thanks for your feedback. Trust me, it helps.

It didn't help because, as of November 19th, the monthly case progress calls scheduled for October 10th still have not taken place. To address this, I scheduled a conference call for November 20th. I then sent her a list of questions I wanted to discuss.

I called on the 20th, only to be told by her secretary that I was off her schedule and that she was on the phone. I repeated that I had confirmed I would call and asked if it was necessary to change the date via email. I instructed the operator to inform my attorney that I had set aside the time and date for our call and to have her call me when she finished her call, before 4:00 p.m. When I didn't receive the callback I requested, I gave her another chance to answer my questions via email with a Wednesday deadline. Still not hearing from her, I knew it was time to take corrective action.

On November 26, I emailed the managing firm's partner and told him it was time to end my relationship with my attorney. We have no client-attorney rapport, and I no longer trust her work. I provided details about the missed call mentioned above and informed him that, in previous lawsuits, my attorney had always given me at least monthly updates on the case's progress. I requested that my attorney-client relationship be terminated and that my case be reassigned to another attorney from the firm. He responded that my case had already been assigned to someone else. I am now starting over with my second attorney.

He informed me that opposing counsel had received the answers to the interrogatories, and the next step was to proceed with mediation. These answers relate only to the nursing home lawsuit, and I will discuss the mediation process later.

CHAPTER 10

Wife's Deterioration

Beth returned home from her rehab at FMR at the end of August when her Medicare coverage expired. She still felt the urge to urinate and couldn't walk without a walker. Most of her day is spent in bed, suffering from daily debilitating nausea that begins first thing in the morning and persists most of the day. While she can move from one place to another, her primary destination is now the bathroom, which she visits multiple times every hour.

Her daily mantra continues to be "I got to pee." When she tries to do so, little or no urine comes out. The pain must be excruciating, but no medication can alleviate the feeling. The only web-listed remedy was exercise, which she was unable to do, and pelvic exercises. As for nausea, she underwent many tests, and the medical professionals could find no physical explanation for her sickness.

She started physical therapy at home three times a week. The sessions went well, but several had to be canceled because of her nausea. She remains very unsteady on her feet, and in November, during one of Florida's hurricanes, she fell. It was impossible to get EMTs to take her to the hospital because of the weather.

The next day, EMS transported her to the ER, where she was again diagnosed with a severe UTI. The culture grew a bacterium that the hospital could not identify, so they consulted the CDC to determine its identity. It was confirmed as sepsis, and the only way to treat it was to insert a PIC line in her arm and administer the antibiotic intravenously for ten days.

The hospital initially thought that a home nurse could administer the shot daily, but this proved impractical. The Infectious Disease Medical Department instructed me to take Beth to the ER so that hospital staff could administer the infusion. To free up a hospital bed, she was moved to a nursing rehab facility where they could complete the daily injection.

Again, let me digress here. After the infectious disease, the doctor told me to take Beth back to the hospital. I received a letter from the hospital informing me that her admission was on observation status. I would be responsible for 20% of her hospital bills since Medicare does not cover hospital stays under observation.

I again objected, explaining that Beth had been readmitted to the hospital at the infectious disease physician's request so a medical procedure could be performed. I clarified that she was admitted based on medical need, not observation status, and that Medicare should cover her stay. It was covered. Do you remember the ER case worker telling me the hospital wouldn't admit Beth on an observation basis?

On November 10, 2017, she was admitted to the WC rehab facility so the nursing staff could administer the daily antibiotic. The medication cost $1192 for ten days, which I had to pay because it was not on our prescription drug plan formulary. A rule of thumb is that each day spent in bed is equivalent to losing three days of physical therapy. She began occupational and physical therapy twice daily to recover the ten days lost during the infusion.

The $254 daily room charge for her 21 days in the facility was covered by Medicare because she met the requirement of staying three nights in the hospital, making her eligible for coverage. However, the $875 physical therapy costs were self-paid because she had exhausted all her Medicare physical therapy benefits at HPCC. In early December, she was discharged and returned home to continue receiving in-home physical therapy.

She continued to experience daily nausea, which limited her ability to participate in physical therapy on some days. Starting in March 2020, she received occupational or physical therapy seven times at home. Wanting to get her out of the house, I rescheduled her treatments with a physical therapy unit at a PT facility. She then received another twenty-two days of occupational and physical therapy, but it did not significantly improve her walking ability. After the last sessions, they told us that her current condition was likely the furthest she would progress, so there was no reason to continue her therapy.

Hearing this diagnosis only worsened her depression. She rarely went outside, except for her Thursday hair appointment and our trip to Perkins for dinner. The strange thing was that her nausea usually lasted from early morning until around three o'clock. Whenever she went to the hospital with severe nausea, they could never reproduce it while she was a patient. She would leave the hospital feeling okay, but be sick the next day.

She had undergone a brain scan, multiple endoscopies, blood tests, and even had her gallbladder removed, but couldn't find any physical reason for her constant nausea. We also tried four one-hour hypnosis sessions to see if they might help relieve her nausea. As a licensed hypnotherapist, she enjoyed the sessions, but they did nothing to ease her symptoms.

I researched online to match her symptoms with a possible cause and found a condition that fit her presentation. I suspected her nausea was psychosomatic. It was previously described as a somatic symptom disorder, where a person feels nausea despite having no physical cause. Since nausea could not be reproduced in the hospital, I suspected it might be environmentally triggered, especially since it returned when she went back.

To test my belief that her home environment might be a factor, I observed that her frequent trips to the bathroom increased her fall risk when I wasn't there; I considered removing her from the house. To confirm that her nausea was a physical issue and to ensure help was available if she fell, I placed her in an assisted living facility for a thirty-day trial.

Surprisingly, the change reduced her daily nausea; therefore, modifying the environment confirmed my SSD diagnosis. As a side note, her gastroenterologist agreed that I had made a diagnosis that the medical community has been unable to solve. He even presented the case at a gastroenterology symposium in Baltimore.

However, the urge to urinate persisted, and she became disruptive at the facility because she constantly called for a CVA to take her to the bathroom. The frequent calls created a situation that could prevent her from becoming a full-time resident. She returned home after the thirty-day stay, but her nausea returned, and trips to the bathroom remained as frequent as ever. I then decided that her only option was to have her return to the assisted living facility full-time.

Having long-term care insurance, I expected no trouble getting approval for Beth to move into an assisted living facility. I was wrong. I knew there was a ninety-day elimination period before long-term care benefits began. Still, it was clear that her hundred days in rehab under Medicare counted toward her ninety-day elimination period, since Medicare-covered days are included in the elimination period.

When the long-term care policyholder requested proof of completing the ninety days, I provided her with Medicare's statement, which showed that she had used all her 100 days and was no longer eligible for Medicare benefits this year. The insurance company told me that the Medicare document was not acceptable and that they required itemized monthly bills from each rehabilitation facility. The information request asked all the rehab facilities she stayed in to provide a list of her costs, including her room, medications, the facility's license, and a copy of the current Minimum Data Set Assessment. The MDS is a document that the nursing home must complete at least every three months.

The facilities submitted the documents they believed the insurance company needed, but they were told the forms had to be more specific and that corrected copies should be sent in. The facilities told me this was nothing new because dealing with the insurance company was a pain in the ass. Eventually, the company received all the necessary documents and approved her stay.

Before determining if the facility met the insurance companies' requirements, the assisted living facility needed to prepare a new set of documents demonstrating its nursing facility's compliance with all the insurance company requirements, along with submitting a current MDS.

Aside from the necessary documents for the facility, Beth also had to undergo an evaluation by an insurance company nurse to determine if she was unable to perform two of the six activities of daily living (Bathing, Continence, Dressing, Eating, Toileting, Transferring). She met that requirement, the facility provided all the required documents, and she was approved to cover her monthly assisted living costs.

The facility accepted her back because I was willing to pay an extra fee for CNAs to make trips to her room to quiet her down when she called for them to take her to the bathroom. Her room cost $3,360 per month, plus an additional $375 for medication dispensing, $221 to assist her to the dining room, and $265 for extra care, totaling $4,314 per month. I also furnished the room with a bed, dresser, chair, and table for $2400. Her long-term care insurance covered her room and service costs.

She adapted well to her new home, spending time watching TV and steadily working on 'word unscramble' puzzles. We played Scrabble several times a week, and she had no trouble forming words and earning points. I made sure to join her for dinner every night. However, she was becoming increasingly disruptive, screaming for help to pee, going out into the hall looking for me, and showing more dementia-related symptoms.

At the end of August 2018, I visited Beth at the assisted living facility. It was raining, so I started running for cover as I exited the car. Then it happened: I heard my knee pop, followed by a sharp pain, and I managed to limp to Beth's room. I sat down and explained what had happened; she thought it might be a pulled muscle. When I tried to stand up to leave, I couldn't, so I called for an aide to bring me a wheelchair and contacted EMS to take me to the hospital.

After spending three hours in the emergency room and undergoing X-rays, the doctor informed me that nothing was broken and suggested I see my orthopedic doctor the following day. I was given crutches and had to take a cab at 12:30 AM to get back to my car at the nursing home, which was five miles away. I managed to drive the car and got home around 1:00 AM. The next day, I saw my orthopedic doctor, who suspected I had a torn meniscus.

An MRI confirmed his belief, and surgery is scheduled for September 6. I underwent arthroscopic knee surgery, relying on my neighbor to drive me to and from the surgery center. He stayed on call as I endured the pain from waking up from anesthesia. Two days later, I began my eight weeks of rehab. Since it was my left knee during those eight weeks, I was able to drive and make my daily trips to see Beth.

The urologist explained that a medical issue likely to become more common due to prolonged catheter use is her developing urinary tract infections (UTIs). From her August admission to the assisted living facility through December, she had three UTIs, two of which required hospital stays of three and four days.

Every time she visited the hospital, her condition worsened, and she grew weaker. Her mobility declined, and she never seemed to recover after each visit fully. Confusion and memory loss are common symptoms of a UTI, and it became clearer with each visit that her short-term memory was deteriorating.

In November, I began to notice a change in Beth's behavior. When she entered the facility, she used to spend hours doing Word Scrabble puzzles, but now she complains of constant pain, and all she wants to do is sleep. I also get reports from her neighbor and the staff that she is beginning to leave her room and wander the halls, calling for me. Her neighbor has my phone number, and whenever she was being unruly, he would call me. I, ten minutes away, would rush over to the home to calm her down.

It is now clear that she is in the early stages of Alzheimer's and will eventually need to move to a memory care facility. In February 2019, a room became available, and she was transferred to it. Her condition had worsened- not her memory, but her strength. She complained of constant pain and wanted to sleep all day. Interestingly, her last nursing job was at this same memory care unit, where she served as the charge nurse for twenty-five Alzheimer's patients. The monthly cost for room and services in the memory care unit increased to $6413.

She adjusted to her new room and continued watching TV and doing her word puzzles. We even played a few more games of Scrabble. She was also able to use her walker to reach the bathroom when she needed to urinate and no longer had to call the caregiver for help. She could dress herself, change her ileostomy, and walk to and from the dining room for meals.

She adjusted well for a month, but then she started showing clear signs of decline. Her memory got worse, and her ability to walk declined. It was clear she was sick, so I decided to take her to the emergency room. She was diagnosed again with a severe UTI and was admitted.

Between November and April, the local hospitals operate at 120% capacity. During this season, 'snowbirds,' or visiting northerners who have no local doctor, often use the emergency room as their primary source of care. All the emergency rooms are full; patients fill every gurney in the halls, and many sit in chairs waiting to see a doctor.

She was transported to the hospital by ambulance, placed in an ER room, and stayed overnight while waiting for a bed in the main hospital. She remained hospitalized on IV antibiotics and magnesium due to low magnesium levels. Although her other blood tests showed abnormalities, they did not treat blood deficiencies, and she was eventually transferred back to the facility.

When she returned, she was in the best shape she had been in for months. Even the staff commented that she was more alert and had more energy than they had seen since she came to memory care. Physical therapy was scheduled to start the following week. However, her condition worsened two days after returning from the hospital. She gradually became more confused and was losing her ability to walk.

The therapy was started, but she was too weak to participate. She could no longer stand or walk and became dependent on the CAs or me to help her to the bathroom and to get dressed. I told the nursing staff I thought she might still have her UTI and asked them to take a urine sample and get it tested. The first test came back negative, and I was confused about why her condition had worsened so quickly.

On April 10th, I put her to bed, and she was almost unresponsive. I hesitated before deciding what to do next when I received a call at 11:00 PM saying that Beth had fallen and had a significant bump on her head. They asked for my permission to take her to the emergency room, and I gave my approval.

Once again, the hospital ER was crowded, and her ambulance transport secured her a bed because they needed the equipment to diagnose her condition. She again had a severe UTI. Her doctor told her that it appears the antibiotic prescribed for her two weeks ago was not the right one to treat such a severe infection.

She had a mastectomy on her left breast, so the nurse should not draw blood from that arm. To make matters worse, as nurses have described, she has tiny veins, making it nearly impossible to draw blood. Usually, the nurse must call an intravenous specialist to insert a line for blood draws. Her UTI and other blood work results required her to be admitted to the hospital as soon as a bed was available. So, once again, she spent the night in the emergency room.

She wasn't planning to return to the memory care unit, so I informed them that she would be leaving. I only had one day to clear out all the furniture from the room because those items belonged to me, and the unit didn't want to keep them. Her room rent would keep adding up if the furniture stayed, so I spent the day hauling the furniture to the back of my SUV to store it in my garage.

Her UTI was severe, and she faced additional complications from multiple past UTIs. Upon hospital admission, she was in third-stage kidney failure, which progressed to the fourth stage by discharge. She also struggles to maintain a healthy magnesium level, possibly because her kidneys are filtering out too much of this essential mineral. The main issue being treated was the UTI, and she experienced a constant urge to urinate due to the infection.

Because it was a problem, her condition made her needs more urgent and persistent. Her ongoing need to use the bathroom necessitated a move from a two-person room to a single room closer to the nurse's station, allowing staff to reach her more quickly. She kept trying to get out of bed to go to the bathroom, which she wasn't supposed to do, so the hospital assigned a sitter to her room to prevent her from doing so.

The search began to find a skilled nursing facility with a bed available for her. Rehabilitation beds are limited, and we have contacted several facilities to ask about open spots. Medicare will now cover her stay for the first 20 days of rehab, and her secondary insurance will pay for the next 80 days.

The hospital noted in her medical reports that she would go to a skilled nursing facility after discharge. Therefore, she could not return to her memory care room because they are not a skilled nursing facility and had already filled her space with another resident. It then became Beth's caseworker's responsibility to find skilled nursing facilities with available beds in their memory care units.

She found two options, WC and MC, who could take her. She mentioned that MC had a representative at the hospital I could talk to about sending her there. This representative might be similar to a lobbyist who walks the hospital halls to identify patients being discharged and who may need a rehabilitation facility. I should note that MC was a for-profit facility, while WC was not, so I suspect the representative might be earning a commission from the facility for patients referred by her.

I evaluated the facility to see if it was suitable for Beth's care. The building wasn't impressive because it needed resurfacing of the parking lot and more landscaping. However, it was unique, featuring a large bird enclosure with six tropical birds in a cozy lobby. I spoke with the Admissions Director, explained my situation, and she informed me that since her doctor at the hospital was also MC's doctor, he was aware of her condition. After touring the facility, I was impressed and agreed to have her transferred there for rehabilitation.

On April 25th, Beth was moved from the hospital to MC and assigned a bed in the memory care unit because she kept crying out, "I have to pee."

She was the only person in the two-person bedroom. I initially wanted her to go to the dining room to eat, but after observing many people in memory care, I thought the dining room was too depressing, so I arranged for her meals to be delivered to her room. I found meals to be my most considerable dissatisfaction with the facility.

I usually visit for a few hours around noon and in the evening. I found that the lunch delivered to the room at 1:30 and dinner at 7:00 are generally cold. I have accepted that she will have to live with this situation.

She was evaluated and began occupational and physical therapy two days after her arrival. I found the therapist to be very professional, but Beth was difficult. All she wanted to do was sleep, and when they came to take her for OT and PT, she said she couldn't do them because she was too sick. Not participating in PT defeats the purpose of rehab, and if she continues to refuse therapy, they will report that she is not making progress, and Medicare will stop covering her stay.

Medicare covers the first eight days at no cost, during which her progress is evaluated. If progress is observed, Medicare covers 80% of the costs, and my secondary insurance covers the remaining 20%. If there is no improvement and I need her to stay, I will cover the full amount.

On April 29th, I received a letter informing me of my daily cost. My 20% share of the expense would be $171 per day, making the room's total price $853 per day. MC listed the services covered by Medicare (room and board, therapy, medications, wound care, incontinence products, special nutritional items, tracheostomy care, ostomy care, oxygen, special mattresses, x-rays, laboratory tests, nursing services, activities, social services, and physician visits) with no cost per service shown.

I will not discuss fees until the first in-service meeting, which reviews her progress and determines if she qualifies under Medicare's criteria for continued coverage. Whether she has met the requirements doesn't matter, as I had no choice but to keep her in the facility at $853 a day while I searched for a different placement. The nonprofit WC fees were $254 per day, and PT cost an additional $40 to $50 daily, totaling $304.

To add to the costs, hundreds of dollars' worth of medications still in the prescription bottles used to treat her in memory care at BD were considered unacceptable by MC and could not be used because all medicines must come from MC's pharmacy. The same applies to the Pampers I supplied, which are the diapers provided by MC.

On Thursday, May 2, at 11:00 PM, I visited Beth just as they were about to take her to OT. She was in bed and as weak as she had been recently. The therapist helped her into a wheelchair and took her to rehab while I stayed in the room. At 1:00, I started walking toward the rehab area, only to meet her and her PT therapist coming up the hall. She was in her wheelchair, and the therapist had her push herself along the hall by manually turning the chair wheels.

I then took her back to her room for lunch. As usual, the aide had already brought her lunch, which was cold and unappetizing. Once again, she did not eat; she only drank a little of the soft drink I got her and said she was feeling sick and needed to go to bed. I dressed her in her nightgown, put her in bed, and left.

When I got back at 6:00 PM, she wasn't in her room. I found her sitting in her wheelchair in the empty dining hall, with an untouched meal before her.

She said, "Get me out of here." I told her I'd take her back to the room after she ate.

Again, she commented, "I cannot eat this crap; I must lie down." I took her back, dressed her in pajamas, and put her to bed. She complained of being sick and so weak that I had to lift her legs into bed. She couldn't move in bed and asked me to turn her onto her side.

I got upset and told her, "You can do it by yourself," but it was apparent she couldn't. I told her she should be sitting up; all she wanted to do was sleep. I left in a huff, thinking she was trying to get sympathy.

When I got home, I felt terrible about leaving and wondered if she was truly sick and exhausted. I decided to go online and research fifth-stage kidney failure, discovering that all her symptoms matched. It then struck me that she was dying. Beth isn't saying she is sick to avoid doing physical therapy, but because she genuinely is.

All I could think about was my next move. Should I call hospice for another consultation, start looking for a long-term care bed, and ask MC to do a respite blood workup to confirm my suspicion that her kidneys were failing and she was dying? I spent a sleepless night staring at the clock, waking up at 5:00 AM, and then spent the next hour trying to decide her future and my options.

My options are limited. If it is confirmed that Beth has kidney failure and she is not in a rehab facility, she will lose Medicare coverage and have to pay out of pocket at $853 daily until I can find a long-term care bed for her. This process could go on indefinitely. Should I contact hospice to see if they have a bed available at their facility?

My last hospice representative mentioned that Beth, a former hospice volunteer, might get priority for admission. Should I tell MC about my dying belief now or wait until the Care Conference on May 9th? I headed to the golf course for a 7:00 tee time with all these thoughts on my mind. Again, my playing partners sense that something is wrong, but I haven't shared my troubles with them. I have chosen to keep my family issues to myself.

On May 9, I conducted my review and planning meeting to decide Beth's ongoing treatment. I have participated in similar meetings at other facilities where the facility administrator and two therapists discussed her occupational and physical therapy. The therapist shared updates on her progress and provided a projected timeline for her to reach her therapy goals. I asked questions about her therapy progress and agreed to meet again in two to three weeks.

The meeting at MC was utterly different. After waiting an hour, only the Social Services Director came to see me. He then looked at his laptop for five minutes, which showed that Beth was making progress, with no extra comments about her goals for the coming weeks. He emphasized that she was making progress. Those two words, 'making progress,' help the facility continue to collect its $852 daily from Medicare and my secondary insurance for the next

100 days. Informing Medicare that Beth is making progress ensures they will continue to cover the daily costs.

I asked him to clarify what the $852 daily fee covered. He said the room costs $325 a day, and physical therapy is $100; I would need to discuss the remaining $225 with the business manager. He implied I shouldn't worry about the rest of the costs because Medicare and my secondary insurance would cover them. I told him I cared because if Beth had to stay beyond the 100 days, I would pay the full $852.

On June 17, I visited a newly built care facility that has one memory care room. I liked the facility and went back to MC to find out when physical therapy expected Beth to be able to use a walker, which is necessary for transferring to the memory care unit. PT estimated she would reach that goal in two to three weeks. Based on that, I paid the $1500 down payment to the facility and scheduled an occupancy date for June 3. However, when Beth was rushed back to the hospital, the need for a memory care room no longer mattered.

CHAPTER 11

Medical Malpractice Case

THE HOSPITAL MALPRACTICE case is less promising than the nursing home case. LGF hoped to base its claim on the ER doctor's failure to notice the break on the X-rays and a review of the ER dictation. My initial review of the case began when I read the 'Emergency Room Dictation' and started to notice contradictions in the statements made there.

Statement: "XR of the left knee was reviewed by a radiologist, and I found no fracture or osteopenia. Additionally, the patient complained of pain radiating from the knee down her leg, but no scans or X-rays were taken below the knee." I responded that if the patient complained of leg pain, why weren't additional X-rays taken?

Statement: "At 7:40 PM, Pt could ambulate in the department." This statement is false, and she was not ambulating, as documented by her inability to walk to the bathroom at the time of discharge.

The statement: "The Pt was informed of her results, and her diagnosis of pelvic contusion" is also false. Our only encounter with the attending physician was when he told us, "Good news, there are no fractures," and then he left. Since a recording attendant was not present, he wrote this statement himself.

Statement: "Pt is agreeable and verbalizes understanding" is partly true in that I understood what the case worker was saying, but I strongly disagreed with her being discharged. The patient's complaint of pain was responded to by saying, "She has no broken bones, and the pain she is suffering is normal pain experienced with a bad fall."

Statement: "Results were reviewed as displayed above" is false. The only review of the results was the 'good news' statement, and I never got a chance to ask the doctor why, with no broken bones, my wife is experiencing severe pain below the knee.

Statement: "The Pt was given a treatment plan." The caseworker would immediately ask Home Health Care to call my wife in the morning, but that was never done.

Statement: "At 8:06 PM, Pt was able to emulate with some difficulty," another false statement. The patient was moved, with great difficulty, from the bed to a wheelchair because she could not walk without assistance. The nurse recognized the patient's pain and applied an ACE bandage below the knee.

The final diagnosis was a pelvic contusion, which no longer accurately describes the condition identified when she returned to the ER the next day.

Statement: The referral to counseling was that 'the pain is normal to fall pain,' and she would contact Home Health to set up a physical therapy schedule. I responded, "How will she do PT when she cannot stand up without pain?" I disagreed with the discharge plan, but she would still be discharged despite my objection.

The scribe did not personally observe the comments made by the physician. The treatment, procedures, and medical decision-making were discussed with the patient. Information was not discussed with the patient.

Statement: On page 19, the report first states that 'Pt needs to be assisted with ambulation.'

The initial information I received about the case came in an email sent on July 17, 2018, stating that LGF's expert had reviewed the medical records and believed the radiologist might have missed the fractures on the ER x-rays. He informed LGF that radiologists often overlook this type of fracture.

X-rays taken on May 12 and 13 were not sent to our office and have been re-requested by the radiology department. Our expert will review these and make a final decision about your claim. My understanding is that LGF's expert based his assumption on reading the records rather than the X-rays, which I believe he can only do by viewing the X-rays.

On September 10, LGF informed me that their medical experts needed assistance in determining whether the ER doctors had missed the tibia fracture on the X-rays. Based on my previous lawsuit, which I will document for you, I told them that we might spend too much time and money trying to prove a subjective point and should focus on an objective issue. I am not trying to act as my own lawyer, but the attached narration might be helpful.

In 2002, Beth settled a medical malpractice lawsuit with the hospital corporation involved. In that case, we did not pursue damages from the primary doctor. Instead, we sought damages due to negligence by the nursing staff, showing they failed to follow the standard post-operative hip replacement surgery protocol. Their failure caused permanent nerve damage to Beth's foot.

Since your medical experts cannot agree that the ER doctors missed a tibia fracture on the x-ray or that they should have performed an ultrasound of the lower leg, the facts remain that the final tibia fracture was not caused by the doctor's oversight but by the ER discharge nurse's negligence. The discharge nurse did not conduct a proper 'road test' as ordered by the doctor and repeatedly requested by me.

Requests for the nurse to see if my wife could walk to the bathroom without pain were ignored, as was my request to see the doctor, being told the doctor had released her. The nurse did not instruct Beth not to bear weight on the leg until she saw an orthopedic doctor. The discharge nurse had trouble getting my wife into the car without her complaints of pain, and I asked how I would get her out of the vehicle. The nurse said she should be able to walk the short distance, again not emphasizing that she did not bear weight on the leg.

When I asked the Case Worker to admit my wife to the hospital for observation, she refused, saying it would be 'too expensive.' When I told her, "My wife is in obvious pain when she tries to walk," I was told, "This is just normal pain associated with a fall." The actions of the nurse and Case Worker were the main reasons my wife shattered her tibia and had to return to the hospital the next day.

The negligence of the discharge nurse and Case Worker listed above is clear and does not require expert review. I am confident that the discharge protocol can be obtained from the hospital.

Regarding the hospital visit, claiming my wife's return was due to a fall is incorrect. She did not fall but collapsed. A fall means 'to move to a lower position under the effect of gravity,' while collapse means 'to fall suddenly or cave in due to the loss of support,' which is what happened when her tibia shattered under her weight. She would have fallen on the floor, but that did not occur. When she tried to step up the 5-inch ledge from the garage to the house, her leg gave way as soon as she put weight on it, causing her to sit down.

This collapse, rather than a fall, was apparent from the ultrasound image taken when she returned to the hospital, which showed a complete shattering of the tibia instead of just a simple break that would result from a fall. A basic fall from a standing position to lying flat would not have caused such severe damage to the tibia. Her orthopedist explained that the shattered tibia probably resulted from a stable tibia fracture that broke when she put weight on the leg. He believed she should not have been discharged from the ER without further testing. I recommend that LGF investigate the objective nursing malpractice rather than the subjective claim that the doctors should have seen the break on the X-rays.

Medical negligence is defined as "A doctor or hospital is liable for medical malpractice in Florida if the healthcare provider failed to provide reasonable care, skill, or treatment of the patient." This can include "a hospital nurse failing to respond to a patient in distress."

I also informed LGF that they created the case file on September 5, 2071, and now, a year later, the firm still has not decided whether there is a malpractice case. LGF stated that they are carefully working on the matter and will follow up on my suggestion to review the ER discharge protocol.

On October 18, I sent the following message to LGF. Building on my argument that the ER discharge protocol is a more promising basis for pursuing a malpractice lawsuit, I share my experience. On Monday, the urgent care clinic referred me to the ER with what was suspected to be a heart problem. After numerous tests, they found no cause for my dizziness and unsteady gait.

The doctor said he would discharge me, pending the nurse's performance of a 'road test.' When the test was finally done, I failed because I still had an unsteady gait. The nurse informed the doctor, and he admitted me to the hospital. I am providing this background to support my claim that my wife's ER nurse did not follow proper protocol and should have notified the doctor when she saw my wife could not walk without pain. I had vertigo.

The second episode involves my request to the Case Worker for her to be admitted for observation because my wife could not walk without pain. Her telling me it was not hospital policy to admit on an observation basis because it would be too costly to the patient was false. Upon discharge, my Case Worker gave me a 'Medical Outpatient Observation Notice' to sign, saying, "You are a hospital outpatient receiving observation services that require further time and reevaluation to determine the severity of your illness and whether you require hospitalization."

The case worker attending my wife's ER visit was mistaken when she said it was not hospital policy to admit on an observation basis. It would be very costly for me if they admitted me on an observation basis, since Medicare only covers 80% of the cost. I would have to pay the remaining 20%, which my secondary insurance would cover.

Additionally, I received a GH treatment survey. To re-examine the ER nurse discharge protocol, I am submitting the survey questions for your review and consideration.

Did you understand your main health problem before leaving the emergency room? Did you know what symptoms or issues to watch for after you left? Was someone there to tell you to make a follow-up appointment with a doctor? Did anyone ask if you could follow up on this? During your visit, did doctors and nurses provide you with as much information as you wanted about the X-ray results? During the emergency room visit, how often did the nurses explain things in a way you could understand? How frequently did doctors and nurses listen carefully to you? Did the doctors spend enough time with you during the visit? In my wife's case, the answer was no to all of them.

On October 31, 2018, I received a letter from LGF regarding my medical malpractice case.

Thank you for selecting our law firm to represent you in a potential medical malpractice case. I have come to truly understand the profound personal impact that medical negligence can have on the lives of those who healthcare providers improperly treat.

You should recognize that a medical negligence claim is different from other types of lawsuits. When suing a doctor or other healthcare provider for malpractice, the injured party must show, with expert testimony, that the provider deviated from the accepted standard of care by improperly providing or failing to provide proper medical care and treatment.

Additionally, the law required testimony from qualified medical experts to demonstrate that the deviation from the prevailing standard of care directly caused or contributed to the injuries sustained.

Florida law requires that, to testify as an expert witness in a medical negligence claim against a healthcare provider, the expert must have a background, skills, and training similar to those of the potential defendant healthcare provider.

Our experience shows that establishing the medical and legal aspects of a medical malpractice claim requires a thorough review by qualified medical experts of all relevant medical data and documentation, often at a significant cost. It isn't easy to get doctors to testify against other doctors, and we usually need to consult out-of-state specialists, which increases the expenses.

Unfortunately, after reviewing the medical records, we were unable to find an expert willing to confirm that a failure in the applicable standard of care occurred. Our emergency room expert examined the documents and stated that the radiologist should have reviewed the imaging during the May 12 emergency room visit. The CT scans and X-ray taken on May 13 showed an injury that was not visible in the May 12 imaging.

We consulted an emergency room expert, as you suggested, to determine whether the 'road test' discussed applied to the emergency room nursing staff in this situation. While emergency room nurses often perform a 'road test' for patients with respiratory issues before discharge, no similar application or mandatory pre-discharge test was given to patients with ambulatory problems.

This contradicts my experience of taking a 'road test' to see if I could walk without difficulty. The nurse informed the doctor when I couldn't, and he admitted me to the hospital.

Instead, she directed us to the nurse's notes from May 12, which stated that at 7:25 PM, "Patient was able to pull herself up out of the stretcher and assume a standing position with the walker. The patient could take steps and walk with a walker, but complained of pain with each step. The patient's husband states she cannot walk with a walker, and he wants to see the doctor." (As stated, it never once mentions that the patient could bear weight on her injured leg.. Her ability to ambulate depends on the walker supporting her, so the validity of the 'road test' is questionable.)

The doctor confirmed this, stating that the patient could ambulate with some difficulty, and discussed mobility and care with the case management team. (The doctor never returned to see the patient and relied solely on the nurse's notes as his progress report, and he never observed her attempt to walk. Additionally, when discussing mobility care with the case worker, why was the patient not informed not to weight bear until she saw her orthopedist?)

The emergency room nurse later noted at 8:06 PM that the patient's husband wanted her to try to use the restroom with the help of a walker. The patient stood up with the aid of a walker and asked, "Where are we going?" I explained that we were going to try to walk to the restroom. The patient states, "I can't; it hurts too much."

Applied an ace wrap to the patient's left knee, where she reported pain. The patient said, "Make it tight." She refused to walk with a walker and told the provider that it was too painful. (The nurse's notes repeat my earlier description. She was discharged despite the patient's report of intense pain.)

The nursing expert emphasized that, in these cases, the emergency room nurse's responsibilities—and the applicable standard of care—were well-defined, including the need to notify the doctor about the ambulatory issues. As the doctor diagnosed a pelvic contusion, there was no reasonable basis for the emergency room nurse to override the doctor's discharge instructions.

Instead of blaming the discharging nurse, the malpractice charge states that the nurse provided accurate information about ambulatory issues to the doctor. The fault should be on the doctor for failing to properly follow up on the nurse's notification of the patient's pain during ambulation.

The Florida Medical Association supported the passage of medical malpractice laws in the state of Florida. These laws have made it more difficult for claimants to file medical negligence claims within the limited timeframe established by current statutes. The complex procedural requirements of Florida's medical malpractice laws have provided significant protection for doctors and other healthcare providers.

It has created significant barriers for individuals harmed by negligent medical care. These legislative changes have partly shifted the balance between the costs of pursuing a medical negligence claim and the potential benefits to the claimant. The statutory limits on damages mean that the expenses and risks of pursuing medical malpractice cases often outweigh the potential compensation if a claim is filed.

Unfortunately, this means that qualifying medical malpractice cases often cannot be taken on a contingency fee basis. The situation you described has been reviewed, taking into account the factors mentioned above and my experience. Sadly, your case does not meet our law firm's criteria for proceeding. As a result, we are unable to represent you. Our decision not to continue representing you is based on several factors, including financial considerations. This does not mean you are not entitled to sue or that your claim lacks merit, only that it does not meet our firm's criteria.

If you want to pursue this matter further, you should contact another attorney promptly. Based on all the information provided above, I agree with LGF's decision not to continue pursuing this claim. The case may have merit, but the cost of seeking it heavily outweighs the potential monetary benefits if the outcome is in our favor.

CHAPTER 12

First Mediation

MEDIATION ENABLES TWO parties in a dispute to discuss their issues and concerns and make decisions about the conflict with the assistance of a mediator. A mediator cannot decide who is right or wrong or tell you how to settle your dispute. In mediation, you can find solutions that work for both you and the other person involved, addressing some or all of your concerns.

Now, why were we at mediation? The defendant had three options after receiving the claim. First, the defendant could have rejected the lawsuit, which they did not do; otherwise, we wouldn't be here. I can conclude that the defendant recognizes that the incidents described in the Pre-Suit interrogatories are factual and did occur.

Option two was that the defendant could make a settlement offer. Again, I conclude that the defendant did not exercise this option because the plaintiff might have accepted a settlement offer, which would have eliminated the need for mediation. Option three is that the defendant can offer to mediate, in which liability is admitted. The defendant chose option three.

Mediation mainly advantages the defendant. In this case, the defendant's maximum liability is $200,000 due to sovereign immunity. Therefore, the defendant's primary goal in mediation is to reduce the liability so that the plaintiff cannot receive the full payout unless they proceed to arbitration.

Participating in required mediation offers benefits, such as lowering damages and reducing the obligation to pay additional legal and mediation costs. Although the defendant admits fault and must pay damages, they plan to negotiate for the lowest possible amount.

The mediator has experience with personal injury cases and is familiar with nursing home disputes. Since he cannot participate in the case, his expertise does not apply to it. The mediator's role is to facilitate a fair agreement between conflicting parties.

What criteria does he use to decide what constitutes a fair deal? Without a medical background or enough knowledge to judge the severity of the defendant's negligence, how can he determine what is a fair agreement?

Mediation took place on March 20, 2019, in Fort Myers. Since I had Beth's 'power of attorney,' her presence at mediation was not necessary. I met with my attorney, who had driven down from Tampa for the first time.

I discovered that my attorney used to work in a family law practice alongside his wife. I wondered how someone with a background in family law could handle a complicated lawsuit involving sovereign immunity.

The mediator introduced himself and clarified that his only role was to pass settlement offers between the parties. He would have no opinions about the case but would act solely as a messenger. His fee was approximately $600 per hour, with a minimum of three hours.

The mediation expenses were to be split evenly between both parties. Although we are in mediation because the defendant did not choose option one or two described above, the plaintiff remains responsible for paying half.

Opposing counsel entered the room with a registered nurse specialist from the hospital. Their counsel read from a written report that summarized the nursing home's stance, stating it was not liable for the incidents in the complaint because it had followed the advice of the doctor, who was not an employee but a subcontractor.

I stated that I had a contract with the facility and expected them to provide Beth with competent medical care. I observed that the incidents described in the suit resulted from nursing and staff incompetence, rather than the doctor's.

Mediation figures are confidential, so the numbers used are hypothetical. The process description is not privileged because it can be found on many websites. We made a settlement offer of $200,000, which is the maximum cap under sovereign immunity.

Opposing counsel said they would consider it and then left the room. The mediator accompanied them to get their response to our offer. After about fifteen minutes, the mediator returned with a counteroffer of $1,000. We lowered our settlement demand to $165,000, which they responded to with an offer of $3,000.

The mediator told us that the defendant's parent company would not accept a six-figure settlement offer. We then agreed to lower our offer to $95,000 to see if they would be willing to settle the case in mediation. Again, the mediator took our offer next door and returned with a counteroffer of $7,000. At that point, I decided that mediation was no longer a viable option. I was prepared to end the session and pursue binding arbitration.

The mediator was paid about $1,800 for the two hours he spent moving between rooms, and all I received was his expenses plus those of my counsel for the trip from Tampa. It became clear that the opposing counsel had no intention of settling the case in mediation. Florida law requires parties to a lawsuit to attend court-ordered mediation in good faith. The defendant did not adhere to the good-faith mediation principle and was there only because the court ordered it.

This phase marked the end of the mediation step in the lawsuit process. According to my counsel, the next step was to prepare the necessary documents to notify opposing counsel that we intended to proceed with arbitration.

Arbitration occurs when there is a reasonable initial basis for a medical negligence claim after completing the pre-suit investigation. Either party can request an arbitration panel to determine damages, rather than going to court. (According to my attorney, the parties must agree to arbitration via contract and not proceed to trial.) If the opposing party accepts, this acceptance creates a binding obligation to follow the arbitration panel's decision unless a settlement is reached before the panel's ruling.

My attorney said he would start the process immediately by requesting arbitration and keep me informed. Since mediation ended on March 20, I inquired on April 11 and 18 whether my attorney had notified opposing counsel of our intention to go to arbitration, but received no response. Frustrated with my attorney's lack of action, I considered firing him and seeking new counsel. I called the law firm where I initially submitted my case to see if they might be interested in taking over my case.

I talked with an attorney who explained how difficult it is to fire someone. It involves dividing any settlement funds to determine each person's share. Finding a new attorney to take over the case would be hard, especially in a sovereign immunity case. Because it's so tough to change attorneys, I decided to stick with the one I have.

On April 26, I resumed using certified mail to ask whether my attorney had started the process of serving a request for voluntary arbitration on the opposing counsel. When a client must go back to requesting case updates by 'certified mail' because emails go unanswered, I have to assume the attorney has such a heavy caseload that he cannot find the time to answer a simple yes or no question.

It may be helpful for the client and the attorney to resolve this issue by seeking representation from a different attorney. My departure would decrease the attorney's caseload by one client, giving him more time to respond to other clients' inquiries—your decision.

On May 2, I called my attorney and spoke with his secretary, who inquired about the reason for my call. I asked whether the opposing counsel had obtained the necessary documents for binding arbitration, and they had.

The notice of intent to go to arbitration is not just a letter stating this within the legal system. Like all legal proceedings, you cannot take any action you want. The Summons is a 19-page document sent to the nursing home and its parent hospital. It must be served on the defendants by the sheriff and states the following: YOU ARE COMMANDED to serve this Summons and a copy of the Complaint in the above-styled cause upon the defendants.

The Defendant must serve written defenses to the Complaint on the Plaintiff's Attorney within 20 days after being served with this Summons and must file the original of these defenses with the Court Clerk before serving them on the Plaintiff's Attorney, immediately afterward. If the defendant fails to do so, a default will be entered against them for the relief requested in the Complaint. On April 29, 2019, the summons was filed with the court.

There are 15 pages titled 'COMPLAINT AND DEMAND FOR JURY TRIAL.' Comes now, through the undersigned counsel, Plaintiff Elizabeth, who files this complaint against the Defendant, alleging general allegations, which include 36 specific allegations of noncompliance and negligence. Additionally, the nursing home's Summons asks that DEFENDANT SHALL PRODUCE THE FOLLOWING ITEMS AND MATTERS, and then describes 64 items and matters.

At the deadline for the defendant's response, I emailed my attorney to ask whether opposing counsel had responded to the summons. On May 20, without receiving a reply to my email, I called the Clerk of Courts directly. Since the defense counsel was supposed to file a response with the court, I inquired whether the court had received it. The Clerk told me they had no record of the summons being served on the defendants, which contradicted the secretary, who had told me it had.

I immediately called LGF, spoke with the same secretary, and asked why the summons hadn't been served. She thought the Sheriff had served them.

I said, "What do you mean you thought they were served?"

"Didn't you get a notice from the sheriff when they had been served?" she asked. She said she would look into it, verify if they had been served, and call me back. When I didn't hear back, I contacted the Court Clerk, who informed me that the summons was served on May 22. The warrant issued to the defendant is useless unless the sheriff actually serves the summons on the defendant. I couldn't understand why a law firm would prepare a 54-page subpoena, submit it to the court on April 29, and not serve it until May 22.

On June 12, the defendants responded to the summons by filing a MOTION TO DISMISS, MOTION FOR A MORE DEFINITE STATEMENT, and MOTION TO STRIKE. Filing this motion to dismiss is a common practice for defendants.

The plaintiff initiates a lawsuit by submitting a complaint to the Clerk of Court and serving a copy of the summons on the defendant. Instead of responding to the complaint by admitting or denying the allegations, the defendant replies with a Motion to Dismiss (MTD). The MTD is supported by the defendant's argument that the complaint is inadequate or improper.

In our case, the defendant states, "Now moves this court to enter an order dismissing the Plaintiff's Complaint, and enter an order requiring the Plaintiff to plead with more specificity and enter an order striking a portion of the Plaintiff's Complaint as follows." The defense lists 14 items it considers vague and in need of more clarity, which is another way the defendant slows down the progress of the suit. The plaintiff must respond to the motion.

'Defeating the motion to dismiss is crucial because your entire lawsuit could be dismissed if you lose.' Therefore, your written response to the MTD will be essential.

Since I had not received a copy of the defendant's written defense, which was filed on, I paid a $7.00 copy fee and purchased a copy of the MTD. It listed 14 items that the defendant disputed, which I decided to respond to myself.

On July 5, I emailed my attorney to ask if he had prepared an opposition memorandum for the MTD. I responded to all 14 points raised by the defendant in his motion. No response followed. On July 7, I emailed him again to ask about the court's deadline for submitting a response to the MTD. Still, I received no reply. On July 19, my attorney emailed me asking for my answers to the MTD. It seems I was supposed to be the one preparing those answers.

However, on July 8, 2019, addressing this MTD became irrelevant due to the plaintiff's death.

CHAPTER 13

The Ending

O N Tuesday, June 11, I received a call from MC informing me that Beth was in atrial fibrillation, had low blood pressure, and was sent to the ER. When I arrived at the ER, I found the waiting room full and the hallway filled with people on gurneys and chairs, but Beth had her own room. The initial urinalysis indicated she again had a UTI. However, more concerning was that her GFR kidney function was 13.9, with a count below 15.0 indicating fifth-stage kidney failure, and her creatinine level was 3.33, with 1.06 being the high end of the normal range.

These results indicate that her kidneys are not functioning, so she will be admitted to the hospital. However, a rare situation for this time of year is that the hospital is operating at 120% of its bed capacity. She will need to spend Tuesday night in the ER and hopes a bed becomes available tomorrow.

A bed became available at the hospital on Wednesday evening, and she was moved to a room. Once again, she complained about needing to pee even though bladder scans showed her bladder was empty. The hospital fitted her with a new type of catheter that sits outside her body and works by suction, specifically designed to address issues with embedded catheters.

The hospital is currently treating her UTI with antibiotics and IV fluids to support her kidneys' function. She will receive this treatment over the next five days, with blood tests taken twice daily. Her kidney function has improved to 32.0, but is expected to decrease again after the treatment ends. A positive development was that our son, who lives in London, was in town and able to visit her. Little did he know this would be the last time he saw his mother alive.

She screams, "I have to pee," which drives the nursing staff crazy every day. Tranquilizers and antipsychotic medications haven't been enough to resolve her constant urge to pee. She also isn't eating, and her mental and physical health are deteriorating.

On Friday, June 13, I had a hospice consultation to determine if she was a candidate for hospice care. Their representative confirmed she met the criteria for hospice admission since she is in end-stage Alzheimer's and will soon experience kidney failure. I signed the papers on Saturday to approve her transfer to the hospice facility.

A delay with a hospice bed postponed the move until Tuesday, June 18, when a bed in the house became available. Just like in the hospital, she immediately started her "I have got to pee" mantra once she was in the hospice bed. The hospice staff placed an indwelling catheter, but she continued to cry out. Telling her to pee because she had a catheter did not ease her feelings. After trying different depression medications, they finally managed to calm her cries but could not stop them entirely.

Hospice will stop many prescribed medications and only provide her with mood stabilizers and pain relievers.

As hospice states, "Hospice care is designed to meet a resident's physical, emotional, and spiritual needs. You acknowledge that hospice care is focused on providing comfort, pain relief, and symptom management."

She now sleeps most of the day and isn't eating.

She is dying. On Saturday, she developed a fever of 101 degrees for the first time, which could be a sign of a potential infection.

She isn't eating or drinking much; her breathing is raspy, and she keeps saying, "God, please make me better" or "I have got to pee."

The catheter remains in place, but there's little urine in the bag, which could suggest possible kidney failure, and she might have another UTI. We won't know for certain because hospice doesn't perform blood tests. Their focus is to keep her comfortable and pain-free. I visit her twice daily, and it's becoming increasingly complex to watch her suffer.

I suspected Beth again had a severe UTI. Although I understand hospice will not treat the infection, I asked the nurse to take a urine sample for testing to get more information.

On June 25, I met with the social worker at the hospice to discuss Beth's upcoming stay at the house.

The nurse told me they had stabilized her, and she was no longer yelling, "I got to pee," and "God, please help me get better" nonstop. However, it will still take another week to decide whether she stays in a hospice house or moves to a continuing care facility.

Beth keeps telling me, as she has many times, "I am sorry to put you through all this suffering, and it is all my fault." Her apology was heartbreaking, and I reassured her I didn't mind spending time with her.

Her condition continues to worsen. On July 2, she didn't recognize me during my first visit. Her kidney function is beginning to fail, and the nurse told me she is nearing the end of her life. It is becoming more challenging to watch her decline each day.

Today, July 3rd, after playing golf, I visited and spoke with the PA. She told me they are changing her medication to help calm her down again. She mentioned she would be sleeping more when I saw her.

When she wakes up, she instinctively screams, "Nurse!" or "God, please help me."

These outbursts are what they are trying to control or eliminate. Beth does not realize she is screaming and cannot stop the impulse. The PA told me her urine output is decreasing, which may indicate her kidneys are failing. Hospice attempts to estimate the resident's time to live, and Beth falls into the days-to-weeks category.

My day usually begins at midnight when I go to bed. If I am not asleep within half an hour, I get up and read until two o'clock. I wake up at 5:00, getting my usual four to five hours of sleep each night. I read the paper, have a healthy breakfast, and try to be on the golf course by 7:00. I play every day.

On Sunday, I head out to the back nine alone. Golf is my peaceful moment, where I have the course to myself and reflect on Beth's upcoming death. I haven't told any golfers that Beth is in a terminal condition. I am very private about her situation and don't want to be asked the daily question, 'How is your wife doing?' I have prepared and uploaded her obituary to the email, and it is ready to send. When the time comes, they will all be notified immediately.

My July 4 visit showed that Beth repeatedly said 'nurse,' and she no longer recognizes me. The PA told me that a brain scan from April revealed swelling in the cerebral cortex, probably causing her to repeat the exact words constantly. The medical team has been trying different medications over the past few weeks to stop this screaming.

However, this brain scan shows that no medication will cure this condition, and the nurses will prevent all attempts. I will reduce my daily visits from twice to once a day, as she no longer recognizes me. We are now on a death watch.

During a July 5 visit, I found Beth awake with her eyes wide open, but she was not actually seeing. She emits a continuous groan with each breath until she falls asleep. Her mantra has shifted from "nurse" to "God, please make me better," alongside the now-present groan. The nursing staff has learned to recognize this and no longer responds to her cries since they are unable to do anything.

I've decided to reduce my visits from twice a day, each lasting three hours, to just fifteen minutes. She no longer recognizes me, and when I look directly into her eyes and talk to her, she doesn't respond. She has stopped eating and is only getting liquids through a mouth swab.

The nurse told me it takes fourteen days without eating to die and ten days without drinking. She is dying, but the process is slow, and eventually, her kidneys will fail and shut down her vital organs, ending the death process. It is now just a matter of time.

Today, I asked the administrator if hospice could use her wheel-chair, walker, crutches, and portable toilet, and they gladly said they would welcome my donation of them. They would use all the items within the hospice community, including patients receiving home hospice services. Donating these items shows that Beth will never use them again and that they will be of greater help to others who need them.

Hospice informed me that Medicare payments for her hospice stay have ended, and her remaining care will now be paid privately. Paying isn't an issue because Beth has long-term care insurance that covers the $175 daily charge. It makes one wonder how those need-ing skilled nursing services can afford to continue receiving them.

It becomes clear that dying can be costly, which might impose a significant financial burden on many caregivers.

I saw a caregiver move from his northern home to Florida to care for his mother. He sold his house and belongings to pay for the move, and now he has no possessions left to sell to cover the costs of keeping his mother in a long-term care facility. Death costs more than life.

For example, Beth's rehab facility would have charged her $15,392 per month for a skilled semi-private room or $16,247 for a private room before she transferred to the hospice. I realize this is a for-profit facility, but moving to such a facility might be necessary to get the help your loved one needs due to bed shortages. Many people don't realize the importance of long-term care insurance until they are too old to qualify for a policy. For many, aging isn't always a blessing, as it often brings health problems that accompany it.

After my volunteer shift at the library on Saturday, I visited Beth. When I entered the room, I saw that the nursing staff had covered her with a new, warm blanket, knowing she was always cold; I understood this was a gesture she appreciated, even though she couldn't say it. Also, as usual, the TV was playing 'Easy Listening' music loudly enough for her to hear. She was lying on her back with her mouth and eyes open, her breathing labored but no longer groaning with each breath.

When she was awake, she would repeat, "Please, God, make me well," not realizing that even God couldn't help her now. I bent down to kiss her, but she wasn't seeing anything despite her eyes being open. I sat with her for an hour, holding and squeezing her hand, but she gave no response.

For the first time in her presence, I cried tears of sorrow. I told her I loved her, and she tried to speak, but no words came out. I left when she closed her eyes, hoping I would soon get a call that she had passed away.

On Sunday, I received an email informing me that new test results were available on Beth's MyChart page, a site that shows all the latest test results within 24 hours of being taken. The urine culture results indicated a growth of 100,000 CFU/ml of Enterococcus faecalis and Candida tropicalis; in other words, she has a severe urinary tract infection.

Hospice will not treat the condition that will eventually cause her kidneys to shut down. Today, she showed more significant lung congestion, but she continues to hold on to life. In the evening, I received a call saying Beth's breathing had become shallower, so I rushed over to spend some time with her. After half an hour with her, she seemed to breathe easier, so I left.

I received the call I expected at 5:30 on Monday, July 8, 2019. Beth died around 5:15, bringing an end to three years of pain and suffering. When I arrived, I went into room 18. The lights were on, and Beth was in bed, covered with a rose-colored blanket over her shoulders. Even in death, the staff remembered that she always felt cold, and she would have appreciated this gesture. I held her hand, which was still warm, and talked to her for fifteen minutes. I kissed her forehead and then went to the nurse's station.

They had her rings in a bag, and I signed for them. The only other item she had was her favorite foam pillow, which I said I would take with me. I signed the form for the cremation service to pick up the body. I went in one last time, held her hand for a minute, kissed her again, and then left. She died twenty-four days before our sixtieth wedding anniversary and thirty-nine days before her eighty-fourth birthday. Sixty years of togetherness ended as I walked out the door.

I emailed one of my golfing friends to let him know I wouldn't be at golf today and that I would email him later to explain why.

Not playing golf would have upset Beth because she told me, "I never want you to miss a round of golf because of me."

I had preloaded her obituary into an email and sent it to all the recipients. The next step was to call the newspaper and inquire about getting her obituary into tomorrow's paper. I can see that the newspaper's obituary section is a profit center. The obituary cost $394.30, and an additional picture was $30. I spent the next hour figuring out how to take a picture of an image, load the photo onto the computer, and email it to the newspaper.

I received assistance from the computer tech support, the camera tech support, and the girl at the newspaper before successfully transmitting her picture. I then contacted Social Security, the prescription drug plan, and the insurance company to report Beth's death and update their records. My next task was to meet with the cremation society to sign the necessary papers and submit the obituary for publication.

Elizabeth found peace when she passed away at Hope Hospice on July 8. Born Elizabeth (her birth name) in Akron, OH, on August 15, 1936, her family later moved to DuBois, PA. After finishing high school in DuBois, Beth earned her nursing degree from Columbia Hospital in Pittsburgh and began her career in the operating room.

She worked as an emergency room, industrial, school, and geriatrics nurse and was licensed to practice as a registered nurse in five states. Beth was also a Certified Hypnotherapist, earning her certification in 1998. She finished her career at the Lakes Nursing Home in Fort Myers.

She and her husband moved to Fort Myers from Buffalo, NY, in 2000, where she volunteered at Hope Hospice and the Friends of the Library and became part of the Catholic community. She is survived by her husband of 60 years and her son, John Alan, who lives in Dubai, UAE. The U.S. Navy Burial at Sea Program will hold a memorial service for her and her husband's ashes when he passes.

The rest of the evening was spent reading responses to the emails. It was also the first day of my new routine. For the past three years, I visited Beth every day at noon and 5:00, whether she was in the hospital, rehab, assisted living, memory care, or hospice. I always made a point to be there for lunch and dinner to eat with her or feed her. I will miss those daily visits.

On Tuesday, my computer crashed and was down for the entire day, making it impossible for me to respond to people messaging me about Beth. I also had an appointment with the cremation society to sign sixteen forms, including death certificates, cremation agreements, and other necessary documents for the service.

I was expecting to pick up her ashes, but I was told that the cremation wouldn't be finished for up to fifteen days, so the medical examiner and the doctor can sign off on the cause of death. I won't be able to bring her home for another two weeks.

Regarding the cause of death, my diagnosis is that her repeated UTIs over the past years led to kidney failure, which caused her vital organs to shut down. I attribute this to the defendant's decision to embed a catheter, despite all medical advice stating that catheters should only be inserted when medically necessary and should be removed as soon as possible. The catheter remaining in place for over seventy days was the primary contributing factor to her frequent and severe UTIs.

I look forward to holding the defendant accountable for their malpractice. My issue is that my knowledge from WebMD doesn't qualify me to make a diagnosis.

On Wednesday, I started golfing again. I wasn't looking forward to the 'Sorry about your loss' message, but surprisingly, it wasn't as complicated as I expected, and I had no trouble accepting their condolences. I also fixed the computer issues, and my life began to feel more normal. On Thursday, July 11, I sent the following email to my attorney reporting her death.

Elizabeth passed away on Monday, July 8, in hospice. The confirmed cause of death, based on a hospital urine analysis, was a severe urinary tract infection (UTI) that caused her kidneys to shut down. The UTI and many others she had before HPCC, which involved a catheter, directly contributed to this.

They're leaving it in for an extended period despite Medicare's mandate to nursing homes that 'a catheter will not be inserted unless medically necessary and removed as soon as possible.' To quote the CDC, "UTIs are the most common type of healthcare-associated infections and are most often caused by the placement or presence of a catheter in the urinary tract." To quote further, "'repeated UTIs' will lead to kidney failure."

The weekend has arrived, and it's time to clear out Beth's belongings. First, her beautiful clothing collection will be donated, and it's hard to imagine that all of it will be hung on racks at the Salvation Army store. Her diamond ring will be shipped to New York to be sold at auction, and her hearing aid will be donated to a center in Minnesota. Next, she needs to dispose of hundreds of dollars' worth of medications and supplements. Now, what should be done with her collectibles, teapot collection, Mickey Mouse figurines, and baskets?

When Beth bought them, she believed her son would want to keep them after she passed away. However, times have changed, and items she once thought would be valuable to him are now just clutter that he isn't interested in taking. He is collecting valuables for his children, who will see them as clutter when the time comes.

When I pass, my son should sell the house furnished, and I recommend that these items stay with the property and become someone else's responsibility to handle when they leave. This experience highlights the importance of organizing my estate so my son won't have to go through the same disposal task.

On Tuesday, July 23, I went to the cremation society office to pick up Beth's ashes and the death certificates. As she wanted, I didn't miss a golf day because of her; I played nine holes before picking her up. Eighty-two years of life and sixty years of marriage now fit into a 5" x 7" x 9" white corrugated box holding her ashes.

The package was heavier than I expected. The cremation society put the parcel in a blue shopping bag for me to carry her out. The bag is nice, but it bears the cremation society's name, so I don't think it's a bag you'd find at a grocery store checkout. I placed the load on the front seat and fastened the seat belt for the last time on the drive home to the house she had longed to return to over the past three years.

I attached a picture to the box and placed it in a prominent spot in the living room. She will stay there until my passing, at which point my son will put us both in a container and ship us to Jacksonville, Florida, where the US Naval Base is located. We will be taken out on a naval vessel and buried at sea.

Today is August 1, the day we got married sixty years ago. I have the same anniversary card I give her every year, just changing the year. Now, I am trying to decide what to do with the card. This was the day we hooked a trailer to a 1956 Buick that her father gave us and started our marriage by driving to Alabama. Who could ever imagine what events would unfold from that day? She fell twenty-four days short of receiving that card again with the number sixty written inside.

Two weeks after our anniversary, on her birthday, August 15, she would have turned eighty-three. In 1989, she saw a giant stuffed dog in a toy store window in Montgomery and fell in love with it. Naturally, I bought it for her birthday, and the dog has traveled with us to all our destinations for the last sixty years.

It sat in our bedroom when she was home and moved with her to the assisted living facility during her stay there. Now, it's my job to pack it up and donate it to the Salvation Army to see if they can find a child who could use it, not realizing they're getting a sixty-year-old dog. The dog's passing marks the end of Beth's memories in the house.

CHAPTER 14

Wrongful Death Lawsuit

R EADERS MAY FIND this hard to believe, but Beth's death now turns a promising medical malpractice case from a strong plaintiff's position into a clear victory for the defendant. The attorneys know they could settle this matter within months of Beth's death, but the defendant's retained lawyer will drag it out for years.

In mid-July, I received an unusual text message from my attorney, sent from his personal phone instead of his work email. He complained that he didn't like the way I asked questions and said he had gone to law school, expecting to be treated differently, since his questions were more demanding than simple requests.

A request for information is still a request, even without a 'please' prefix. Since we both have law degrees, you understand that "The attorney works for the client, and the client works with the attorney." You might be more familiar with the law, but I have greater knowledge about the case. My expertise and presentation in arbitration—if the case ever reaches that stage—could significantly impact your compensation. Please keep me informed about the case's progress, and I will avoid sending a flood of questions.

However, I have a quick question. Did you receive the death notice I sent? It's been five days since I sent it, and I haven't heard back from our attorney. It would be appropriate for the attorney to call the client's spouse, update him on the next steps, or at least offer his condolences. He has spent over two years on her case and has not acknowledged her passing. I am gradually building an adversarial relationship with my second attorney.

I received an email from my attorney asking, "Are you planning on hiring an estate lawyer?" I responded, "No, because she had a will and I was the executor, so why would I need an estate lawyer?" His subsequent email states,

"I must hire an estate lawyer to proceed with the claim," I answered. Not to be critical, but why didn't you send the second e-mail before the first? You don't ask me whether I have hired an estate attorney, but you should tell me I need to hire one.

You are supposed to be my legal advisor. Besides what's above, why didn't you call or email to inform me that the case changed from medical malpractice to a wrongful death suit as soon as you learned about Elizabeth's death? Does this mean the current lawsuit has been resolved, or does the case need to be reopened?

On Monday, June 22, I called my attorney or the managing director and was told they were out of the office. I asked them to return my call when they got back. My call was to set up a conference call to address several questions that had been requested via email.

On Tuesday, after receiving no callback, I emailed and warned about filing a complaint with the Florida Bar. I explained that I cannot obtain case information when I ask by email, phone calls go unanswered, and I have to send certified mail to receive responses. I also included a list of questions I needed answers to. Additionally, I asked if they were sure they could handle my case. The last question annoyed them, and they told me that LCF was dropping my case.

Their email also said, "In response to your threat, please seek new counsel." It further stated, "You are free to do whatever you feel is best for you; he also suggested setting up a telephone conference with your lawyer next time so he can answer all your questions instead of threatening the attorney. Threats break down the trust factor essential to the attorney-client relationship." I responded.

Before I explain my email, I want to note that it is not easy for an attorney to withdraw from an ongoing litigation case. It is uncommon for an attorney to file a Motion to Withdraw from a lawsuit. While a client can dismiss a lawyer at any time for any reason or no reason at all, the opposite is not true. Lawyers are expected to see each matter through to its conclusion. The Law Governing Lawyers states that even when a cause exists, a lawyer may still be prohibited from withdrawing if they believe the harm caused by withdrawal would be significantly greater than the harm to the client if the representation continues.

However, the client's consent must be fully informed, meaning the client has been advised and thoroughly understands the consequences of the lawyer's withdrawal. The client should have the opportunity to refuse permission to withdraw. An attorney must give the client adequate notice of their intent to withdraw and explain the implications of this action. Lawyers should document conversations and consultations with clients regarding the withdrawal of their services.

Failing to obtain the necessary permission and protect the client's interests could lead to potential malpractice liability and disciplinary sanctions against an abandoned client. An email notifying me that a Motion to Withdraw has been filed with the court does not follow the proper procedure for informing the client as outlined above. I visited the court and obtained a copy of the Motion to Withdraw filed on July 2, 2019.

COMES NOW counsel for the Plaintiff, Elizabeth, and hereby files this Motion to Withdraw from representing the plaintiff. For similar reasons, it is stated that the attorney-client relationship between the parties has deteriorated to the point where counsel for the plaintiff can no longer effectively represent her. (My answer is that they have yet to represent me effectively since receiving the MTD on June 12. Nor have they communicated with me since that date.)

Plaintiff and their counsel need to communicate more effectively about the progress of the litigation. An impasse has been reached in the attorney-client relationship. Counsel can no longer adequately represent the plaintiff due to this fundamental breakdown in communication.

They certify that a true and correct copy of the previous document was given to Elizabeth on July 2, 2019. Once again, this is not accurate. The only notice I received was a notation at the bottom of the email, informing me that a motion had been filed. I was required to visit the Clerk of Court to obtain a copy of the Motion to Withdraw, which I was supposed to receive from my attorney. I welcome their withdrawal, but finding another attorney to handle a litigation case is a significant challenge. I will explain this problem later, in my response to the email.

Yesterday, I called you and was told you were out. I specifically asked the operator to have you call me back on Monday, the day I made the call. The purpose of the call was to set up a conference call, as you suggested in your last e-mail. You do not return calls or answer e-mails; I have to resort to certified mail to get responses. It is only reasonable to expect a client's attorney to call the new plaintiff immediately after learning of your client's death.

In two years, I have spoken with you only once by phone. In a previous message, the managing partner assured you would make monthly progress calls, but you never followed through. If I need to resort to threats to get you to respond, so be it. Before officially filing the Florida Bar complaint, I gave you a 'heads-up.' I am willing to work with you, but I expect you to keep me updated on case progress as you promised.

For example, after our mediation on March 20, 2019, you stated that you would promptly begin the process of voluntary arbitration, and you filed the necessary paperwork on April 23, 2019. According to your secretary, the summons, along with the arbitration filing, was served on the defendants. However, when I asked you for their required response, my requests were again ignored. After calling the Clerk of Court, I learned that the summons was served on May 21, 2019.

Opposing counsel filed an MTD on June 12, 2019, and it has not been responded to as of July 23, 2019. The promised monthly calls would have kept me updated on this matter without needing to threaten you to discuss it. I am not firing you, but that is your decision if you choose to leave. I'd be happy to speak with you before you leave, if you'd like.

I called my attorney after receiving the above e-mail and explained why I made the threat. I referenced item 9 on the 'Statement of Client's Rights'; you, the client, have the right to ask your lawyer periodically how the case is progressing and to receive answers to these questions to the best of your lawyer's ability.

As a law degree holder, I ask more questions about legal procedures than the average client, but humor me. I reminded him that petitioning the court to drop a client near the end of a lawsuit is a complex process. He agreed with my points, answered the eleven questions I asked, and realized he should have kept me better informed. He said the firm would review its decision to drop me as a client.

The next day, I was told that after reviewing yesterday's conversation, my attorney agreed to improve communication and that the firm would continue to represent me. I don't feel good about threatening a formal complaint against the firm, but my frustration apparently achieved the results I wanted. Hopefully, we are back on solid footing with our attorney-client relationship. He also informed me that LGF had filed a motion to rescind the Motion to Withdraw that was previously filed with the court.

It would have been interesting if this matter had gone before a judge, where the attorney would have needed to justify their withdrawal motion. The law states there are specific reasons an attorney can withdraw from a case, especially one that has progressed this far, and a client seeking case update information is not among them.

After expressing my complaints and objections to the firm's withdrawal, it seems unlikely that the court would have granted the motion. We had a court date scheduled to discuss this motion, but the attorney's attempt to rescind it canceled the hearing. Questions I asked.

Q: Did you answer the MTD?

A: No, a response may not always be suitable. As attorneys, we purposefully take specific actions to help our clients. There is no set timeframe for responding to an MTD, as the defendant's counsel must schedule a hearing with the judge to obtain a ruling.

Q: After hearing about your client's death, why didn't you call to inform me of the next steps?

A: I asked if you're hiring an estate lawyer because you need to open an estate if any distributions from the lawsuit were made.

Q: Have you filed the client's death with the court?

A suggestion of death should be filed after you are appointed as the estate's representative. You will then become the plaintiff.

Q: Does this now qualify as a wrongful death case?

Potentially. I do not understand this answer because attorneys have told me that the wrongful death case is added as a new claim. I am waiting for clarification from my attorney. In addition to the above email, my attorney noted that I am sorry for the loss of your wife. It has been fourteen days since I told him about Beth's death; this is the first acknowledgment.

A formal estate is required for all wrongful death cases in Florida because a deceased person cannot file a claim. This estate is a legal entity created to hold assets, including settlement proceeds from the case. I will be named Beth's representative. The estate is the entity that files the wrongful death lawsuit in court, with a court-appointed personal representative—me in this case—who has the authority to pursue the case on behalf of the estate.

Whenever a person's death results from the wrongful act or negligence of another individual or company, Florida law requires the case to be filed as a wrongful death claim. Beth's case of nursing home negligence meets this requirement. A wrongful death claim is a civil lawsuit in which a family member sues to hold someone responsible for their negligence that caused the family member's death.

Florida law states that a wrongful death claim must be based on conduct that constitutes a wrongful act, negligence, default, or breach of contract. The conduct underlying the claim must have caused the death, and such behavior must have given the injured person the right to pursue an action and recover damages if death had not occurred.

Two instances of wrongful death occur in this case: first, when a physician or mid-level provider prescribes and inserts a catheter without medical necessity, as outlined in CMS20068, and ignores the potential consequences, leading to death; and second, when the provider's actions contribute to the fatal outcome. A wrongful death claim is filed against HPCC nursing home for providing care below the expected standard.

I assert that HPCC was responsible for the negligence mentioned earlier, supported by HPCC's knowing violation of CMS 20068, as previously explained, in their placement of a 'urinary catheter' without any clinical indication that catheterization was necessary. Additionally, HPCC violated all other requirements related to catheter use outlined in the directive.

I argue there was no reason other than the facility's convenience for Beth to have a catheter inserted. The facility should have known Medicare's directive that a catheter should not be inserted unless medically necessary. They also should have known that violating the Medicare mandate could expose the resident to urinary tract infections. These infections would likely increase the longer the catheter remained in place.

As previously mentioned, Beth suffered from multiple UTIs severe enough to require hospitalization. Doctors know that repeated UTIs can eventually cause kidney failure. A urinalysis was performed at the hospital before her death, revealing that Beth had a severe UTI, which contributed to her kidney and vital organ failure.

Again, after receiving my $700 bill for hospice, the long-term care insurance company refused to pay it. They required a current MDS, which hospice is not obligated to provide, and my informing them of this did not satisfy the insurance company. They wanted a letter from the hospice confirming what I had just told them. The company also requested a Medication Administration Record or a medication list if the MAR was unavailable.

Once again, I explained to the company that hospice care focuses on providing comfort, pain relief, and symptom management, so the record of medications or medical history would be irrelevant. They did not accept my explanation and insisted on a MAR. Finally, the hospice sent a letter stating they did not need to complete an MDS and listed the medications given to Beth. Even though they received an itemized bill and all the other requested documentation, the insurance company will need fifteen business days to review the claim.

I paid them $1600 a year for the past twenty years for Beth's insurance, and it takes over a month to approve a $700 bill. Despite the delays in approval and payment, the insurance was worth the cost. The long-term care payments for the assisted living facility and hospice totaled $40,800. Over the past twenty years, I have paid approximately $29,000 in premiums, so the insurance has proved to be worthwhile. Paying an annual premium of $ 1,600 was much easier than covering the reimbursed $40,800 out of pocket.

Our original lawsuit sought damages under the Survival Statute, which applied when the claim involved medical negligence; however, the claim for damages shifted to the Wrongful Death Statute after Elizabeth's death. The following explains why this change is necessary.

Under previous statutory laws, a plaintiff could bring two separate claims: one for negligently caused death and another for pain and suffering. At one point, a plaintiff was able to seek damages under two different statutes simultaneously.

The ability to file two claims was based on the Florida legislature amending the survival statute to state, "No action for personal injuries and no other action shall die with the person, and all actions shall survive and may be instituted, maintained, prosecuted, and defended in the name of the Personal Representative of the deceased."

Under the original provisions of Sec 200.023, along with Florida's survival and wrongful death statutes, if a nursing home violated a resident's rights and the resident later died from unrelated causes, the decedent's estate would still have a remedy under Chapter 400 for the wrongful conduct through the survival statute and could pursue a wrongful death action.

In 1973, the legislature restructured the system by enacting the Florida Wrongful Death Act. This law merged the survival action for personal injuries resulting in death with the wrongful death claim into a single process, but only if the illegal conduct caused the death. It eliminated all claims for the pain and suffering of the decedent from the time of injury until death.

Thus, when a personal injury to the decedent results in their death, no personal injury action shall survive, and any such action pending at the time of death shall be dismissed. This suit is filed under Florida Statute 400.023, which states, "Any resident whose rights are specified in this part are deprived or infringed upon shall have a cause of action against any licensee responsible for the violation. This action may be brought by the Personal Representative of the deceased resident's estate when the cause of death resulted from the deprivation or infringement of the decedent's rights."

The suit initially sought damages under the Survival Statute in a medical malpractice case. After Elizabeth's death, it shifted to a wrongful death claim seeking damages under the Wrongful Death Act. The damage caps are the same for both claims.

In merging the previous two steps, the legislature transferred the damages items, including the decedent's claim for pain and suffering from the date of injury to the date of death, to the new statute. As a result, a claim for the decedent's pain and suffering was replaced with a claim for the survivor, with the explicit intention that any recoveries should benefit the living rather than the deceased.

A 1975 Supreme Court of Florida opinion on wrongful death actions stated, "When a personal injury to the decedent results in their death, no action for personal injury shall survive, and any action pending at the time of death shall abate. The primary difference is to merge the steps and transfer pain and suffering damages from the decedent to the survivors. The legislature intended that a separate lawsuit for death resulting from personal injuries cannot be a survival action, but in a consolidated form under the Wrongful Death Act."

Under the old law, there was a separate survival action for a decedent's pain and suffering. This allowed claims for both the decedent's pain and suffering under the survival act and the pain and suffering of the survivors under the Wrongful Death Act. The court ruled that the Wrongful Death Act effectively consolidates these claims and transfers pain and suffering claims from the decedent to the survivors.

CHAPTER 15

Arbitration Prep

VOLUNTARY BINDING ARBITRATION is a legal dispute resolution process that parties involved in a claim can voluntarily choose to use to settle their disagreements. Any party engaged in a noticed lawsuit may propose submitting to voluntary binding arbitration (PVBA) to resolve their case without proceeding to court. The defendant admits liability, and the arbitration process seeks to determine the claimant's damages.

A three-person panel oversees arbitrations. Under the Wrongful Death Act, the law caps what the panel can award in a sovereign immunity case at $200,000. Florida's statutes allow the plaintiff to recover more than this limit if the state legislature approves it through an official act.

I don't believe this case will go to arbitration, but I cannot assume the claim won't proceed to PVBA. Since the damages awarded by the arbitrators may depend on my presentation of the medical malpractice incidents, I have prepared the following description of each.

You have reviewed most of this case before, but it is new to the arbitration panel. I need to demonstrate that non-medical catheter insertion and dehydration, which did not respond, contributed to Beth's death. Repeating the explanation of the events supporting our medical malpractice claim will happen frequently with different audiences throughout the story.

My primary concern is HPCC's use of an embedded catheter without an apparent medical necessity. Shortly after arriving at HPCC, the doctor inserted an indwelling urinary catheter without providing medical justification or explaining potential future health risks to my wife or me. The medical community is aware that indwelling urinary catheters (IUCs) can lead to complications.

One of the most common and serious complications of urinary catheters is a urinary tract infection (UTI), known as a 'catheter-associated urinary tract infection' or CAUTI, which can progress to urosepsis and septicemia. These infections occur frequently because a urethral catheter introduces organisms into the bladder, promoting colonization by providing a surface for bacterial adhesion and causing mucosal irritation. A urinary catheter is the most significant risk factor for bacteriuria, which usually happens in patients with a catheter in place for 2 to 10 days.

A CAUTI is the most common hospital-acquired infection in hospitals and nursing homes, accounting for approximately 80% of all conditions contracted in these settings. A CUTI is considered a complicated UTI and is the most common complication associated with long-term catheter use. CAUTIs may occur at least twice a year in patients with long-term indwelling catheters who require hospitalization.

They are linked to higher risks of urosepsis, septicemia, and death. Urosepsis can arise from a urinary tract infection (UTI), escalate to systemic sepsis, and lead to death from severe UTIs. Mortality rates are more than three times greater in people with catheters compared to those without. Confusion or unexplained fever may be the only signs of a catheter-related CAUTI.

Beth exhibited extended periods of confusion, which the nursing home should have suspected might be caused by a CAUTI. In an earlier record of septicemia, she was hospitalized on November 8, 2017, with a severe UTI. The culture identified the growth as septicemia, a condition that cannot be treated with regular prescription drugs. The standard treatment involved inserting a PIC line into her vein and administering ten days of antibacterial medication at a rehab facility.

Sepsis is a life-threatening condition caused by your body's response to an infection. Your immune system usually protects you from many diseases and disorders, but it can sometimes overreact to an infection. Sepsis occurs when the immune system releases chemicals into the bloodstream to combat the infection, resulting in inflammation. It is more common in seniors, especially those with invasive devices like intravenous catheters. The most common condition that causes sepsis in seniors is urinary tract infections.

Staff convenience often results in the use of indwelling catheters, which many government agencies, including Medicare, strongly oppose. The reasoning is that it is easier for nursing homes to insert a catheter rather than regularly assisting patients out of bed to change their sheets and clothing, use a bedpan, or walk to the bathroom, and change their diapers. Nursing homes should never justify the use of catheters with these reasons. Many medical facilities still perform unnecessary urinary catheterizations.

Although urinary catheters are commonly used and their risks are well-known, patients are rarely asked to sign a written consent form that explains both the benefits and potential complications.

Additionally, patients are often not verbally informed of the possible issues associated with catheters.

It is well-known that, in some cases, repeated UTIs can lead to kidney failure. Repeated UTIs often develop into pyelonephritis, which is inflammation of the kidney. This inflammation significantly damages the renal tissues, causing kidney injury. Chronic kidney disease usually shows no obvious symptoms in its early stages. Without prompt diagnosis, chronic kidney problems can progress to kidney failure and ultimately result in death.

The above explains why indwelling urinary catheters should not be used. The following documentation indicates that the nursing home acted recklessly by failing to adhere to Medicare's mandated guidelines for the use of indwelling urinary catheters. (Here, I quoted the mandates in CMS 20068)

In summary, HPCC needed a written baseline care plan to present to the resident or their representative. Although the resident had no clinical condition requiring an indwelling urinary catheter, HPCC inserted one without discussing it with the resident or their representative.

A contributing factor to Beth's death was persistent, severe urinary tract infections (UTIs), which ultimately caused her kidney failure. According to her urologist, the documented harmful effects of an indwelling urinary catheter, implanted by HPCC in reckless disregard for Medicare procedures, contributed to her repeated serious UTIs, which eventually led to her kidneys failing and resulted in her death.

To cite the CDC, "UTIs are the most common type of healthcare-associated infections and are mostly caused by the placement or presence of a catheter in the urinary tract."

Over the last two years of her life, she made twenty-seven trips to the hospital for suspected UTIs and was admitted twelve times with severe UTIs. The CDC further states, "Repeated UTIs will lead to kidney failure."

The second charge addressed dehydration. On June 18, 2017, Beth was admitted to HPCC from the hospital for skilled nursing while recovering from a fractured tibia. At admission, her BUN level was 15. In July, a turgor test I performed showed Beth was dehydrated, which the nursing staff confirmed. Efforts to get her to drink more did not improve her dehydration; she needed IV rehydration, a procedure approved by the charge nurse.

The nurse couldn't start the procedure because Beth's veins kept collapsing, and HPCC didn't have a nurse qualified to insert an IV. As her BUN level rose, indicating severe dehydration and a possible UTI, I asked the PA to send her to the ER for rehydration, but she discouraged it. Eventually, HPCC found a nurse who could insert an IV to start rehydration, but it was too late.

Beth had been experiencing confusion, memory loss, fatigue, and weakness for weeks. In elderly patients, these symptoms often indicate dehydration or a urinary tract infection.

Every UTI results from dehydration, which can also contribute to the development of UTIs. In elderly patients, especially those residing in nursing homes, regular monthly urinalysis is crucial to prevent infections. On July 28, during a visit to her orthopedic surgeon, the nurse noticed Beth was limp and kept falling asleep in her wheelchair. They realized she had a medical issue and advised me to notify HPCC upon her return. However, HPCC did not respond to my attempt to inform them about their concern.

On July 29, I received a call from HPCC informing me that Beth was found unresponsive and was rushed to the hospital emergency room. Upon arrival, ER doctors began aggressive rehydration with intravenous fluids. She was also diagnosed with a UTI and pneumonia and stayed hospitalized for four days. The stay resulted from HPCC's failure to follow standard procedures to prevent resident dehydration.

Dehydration occurs when the body loses excessive amounts of water. This disrupts the functioning of organs, cells, and tissues, resulting in severe problems. If not treated quickly, it can result in shock or unresponsiveness. Severe dehydration symptoms are a medical emergency and require immediate care from a healthcare professional.

Seniors should receive prompt treatment, even if they show only mild signs of dehydration. Symptoms of mild to moderate dehydration include drowsiness, fatigue, weakness, and disorientation, all of which Beth experienced before her hospital admission. Dehydration can also lead to vital organ failure. Beth was unresponsive for at least three hours or more.

There is concern about why the staff did not take Beth to the ER when they found her non-responsive instead of waiting for the doctor to tell them what to do. A non-responsive state happens when a person fails to respond to any stimuli. While in this state, the brain does not get enough oxygen to maintain its normal functions.

Among all organs, the brain is the most vulnerable to oxygen deprivation. Prompt medical care is crucial to restore oxygen levels, making quick transport to the ER even more vital for Beth. If a condition reduces oxygen flow to the brain, it could result in brain hypoxia.

The outlook for brain hypoxia depends on how long the brain is without oxygen and whether the oxygen supply has been entirely cut off. If the brain experiences only a short period of low oxygen, symptoms may subside once it receives sufficient oxygen again, and the patient can recover completely. More often, patients will have memory problems.

Furthermore, we do not know how long Beth's oxygen may have been cut off while she was in a non-responsive state, but we do know that once she regained consciousness, she experienced short-term memory loss. Dehydration is a significant cause of decreased mental clarity and memory problems, especially as you get older. It can cause significant changes in glucose levels and blood volume, particularly when severe. These changes are strong enough to cause confusion, memory issues, and other symptoms similar to dementia.

Extreme or prolonged dehydration can lead to severe cognitive problems, delirium, permanent brain damage, or death, according to the Mayo Clinic. These are early warning signs indicating that brain damage might be developing if dehydration is not treated promptly. I believe the facility ignored notices through Beth's representative and blood tests showing she was dehydrated, and that there was no nurse on staff capable of inserting an IV for rehydration. I also contend that the delay in transporting Beth to the ER probably increased the time her brain was deprived of oxygen, contributing to her later short-term memory loss.

My final concern, which I am unsure is relevant here, relates to what has been called 'nursing home eviction.' On Saturday, July 29, 2017, Beth was rushed by ambulance to the emergency room at the hospital, unresponsive due to severe dehydration caused by HPCC's negligence.

On August 1, after a four-day hospital stay, she was denied re-entry to HPCC because no bed was available, and I had not signed a 'bed hold' form, which had not been sent to the hospital, per HPCC policy. After spending 60 days at HPCC and being rushed to the hospital due to their negligence, she was refused re-entry. A review of HPCC's census for that date shows many Medicare beds were available, and she was not readmitted because she required too much care. I had only one day to find another nursing home to accept Beth.

I want to cite an article titled "Feds Seek to Stop Illegal Nursing Home Evictions." It states that discharges and evictions are the primary reasons for the annual complaints that state ombudspersons receive. The report listed reasons a facility can legally evict a resident, and Beth did not meet any of those. The CMS states that once someone becomes a resident, "it should be rare for that facility to say later that it cannot meet that individual's needs."

The AARP said, "We appreciate that CMS plans to examine and mitigate the illegal discharge—or dump—of federally funded long-term care facility residents." In another AARP article titled 'Nursing Homes: Stop Dumping Patients,' they provide an example of a resident who had been in a nursing facility for a long time and was sent to the hospital for evaluation. When the hospital cleared her to return the same day, the nursing home refused to take her back.

This demonstrates what the AARP states: "The problem of patient dumping is one of the most troubling complaints of nursing home residents throughout the country." This is a form of abuse by nursing homes that discharge these patients, especially Medicaid patients, to free up beds for residents they consider 'better.' The following quotation in the same article directly relates to Beth's situation.

To increase profits by reducing staff, unscrupulous nursing homes attempt to illegally evict residents who need the most care and require the most staff time.

One such practice is hospital dumping, where a facility temporarily discharges a resident and then refuses to readmit them after they're medically cleared.

According to HPCC's 'Resident Handbook,' the resident or their designee can hold the bed if the resident is transferred to the hospital, provided the procedure outlined below is followed.

When a patient is transferred out of the facility, nursing will include a copy of the Bed Hold Process in the transfer packet and call the patient or their representative to verbally inform them that HPCC will contact them to discuss the Bed Hold. I did not receive a copy, nor was I verbally informed of this.

CHAPTER 16

Attorney Dissatisfaction

O N AUGUST 13, I emailed my attorney to remind him that it had been three weeks since our last conversation, during which he promised to provide updates on the case. I sent nine questions asking for case updates that he could respond to either by email or during a conference call he suggested. As of August 26, I was still waiting for a reply to my email.

I have reached my wits' end with my current attorney and have started contacting other law firms to see if they would be interested in taking over my case. Despite my attorney's promise to keep me updated, he has failed to do so. I understand that changing attorneys this late in the process is complicated, but if a new attorney is willing to handle all involved parties, I will consider making a move.

Still waiting to hear from my counsel, I spoke with a local attorney about taking over the case. We talked for forty-five minutes—more than all the time I've spoken to my attorney in two years. He explained the implications related to my case. He said it's tough for another lawyer to step into an ongoing litigation. Ultimately, it depends on how long it would take for a new attorney to get up to speed, and the fact that sharing the damage award makes it not financially practical to take the risk.

The reasoning is that the fired attorney will have a lien or claim against the case to recover the fair and reasonable value of the time he spent on it; this lien may take the form of a percentage of the damage award. So why invest time in handling the case properly if he has to give up a significant fee to the earlier lawyer?

He told me that his biggest complaint about the legal profession is that an attorney doesn't respond to clients' repeated emails, phone calls, or answer their questions. He said their lack of response is frustrating and prevents clients from working as a team to resolve issues. I told him I felt like I was in the dark and was constantly begging for updates on the case's status.

He once again reiterated what I already knew: "An attorney must return a client's calls promptly." He wished me luck with my current counsel but said he was not interested in taking the case. He told me that I should not be looking for an estate attorney, but rather a probate attorney.

Following my attorney's advice to find an estate attorney, I spent weeks trying to locate one, only to realize I was wasting my time and risking the ninety-day deadline to file as the new plaintiff in the lawsuit. He then referred me to a probate attorney, whom I contacted and scheduled an appointment with for the following week.

He advised me to stick with my current counsel and hope for the best. Even though my attorney has violated many of the Rules Regulating the Florida Bar related to Diligence and Communication, there's nothing I can do about it. According to Rule 4-1.4 Communications, it states that:

Keep the client informed about the status of the matter. Respond quickly to reasonable requests for information. Please discuss with the client how their goals will be achieved practically. Effective communication between the lawyer and the client is crucial for successful representation.

The lawyer's regular communication with clients helps reduce the likelihood that a client will need to request information about the representation. When a client makes a reasonable request for information, it should be responded to in a prompt manner. If a quick reply isn't possible, the lawyer or a staff member should acknowledge receipt of the request and inform the client when they can expect a response.

It's acceptable for the Florida Bar to establish these rules, but the client has little real recourse if the attorney chooses to ignore them. Suppose the client questions the attorney about disregarding the rules. In that case, the response might be, "If you aren't happy with my representation, then find a new attorney," even though doing so is nearly impossible.

CHAPTER 17

Probate

O N AUGUST 29, I met with a probate attorney, a hire I need to make to keep the lawsuit active. An estate includes everything of monetary value; in Beth's case, since she has no assets in her name, it will be the damage award from the lawsuit. Since she is no longer alive, her estate receives all the money, and I now serve as her representative. The medical negligence case automatically becomes a wrongful death case upon her passing.

To qualify as a wrongful death case, proof of fault is required. It involves a situation where the decedent did not die immediately from the negligent act of the nursing home but experienced severe pain before passing away. The following elements must be established for a wrongful death case:

Duty of Care: The defendant owed a duty of care to the deceased and breached that duty to the plaintiff.

Causation: The plaintiff must demonstrate that the defendant's actions directly led to the wrongful death. Remember, this is a vital element in pursuing a wrongful death claim. HPCC had a 'duty of care' to prevent injuries to the plaintiff while under their supervision. By willfully neglecting Medicare mandates related to the insertion of an indwelling catheter, which likely caused severe and painful urinary tract infections, HPCC failed to meet its duty.

I argue that the medical records demonstrate the elements of negligence by a 'preponderance of evidence,' showing that her wrongful death resulted from the defendant's negligent and willful omission.

On the internet, I researched "What Are the Main Duties of a Probate Attorney?" Every will must go through the probate process. In our case, I do not have the original will; I only have a copy of it. There is no other option than to treat Beth as having died 'intestate,' meaning she died without a will. All community property passes to the spouse, regardless of whether a will exists.

The primary duties of the probate attorney are first to file the probate petition to appoint someone as the personal representative, which would be me. He must then publish a notice of filing the petition for letters in a newspaper of general circulation.

Creditors then have 120 days from the date of issuing letters to file a creditor's claim in the probate to receive payment. In Beth's case, there are no creditors, but the timeframe still applies. The probate process lasts six months because the personal representative must wait 120 days for creditors to file claims. After that period, a notice and petition for final distribution are filed.

To reach 120 days, the client's attorney must sign and file the partition with the court. The court then schedules a hearing, which usually takes place about 40 days later, depending on the court's schedule. If everything is in order at the hearing, the court approves the partition, admits the will to probate, and issues letters testamentary to the personal representative.

At this stage, the 120-day period for creditors to file claims begins. I cannot shorten this timeframe because it is a legal requirement. An attorney is necessary because probate procedures are very complex. Due to these complexities, a process that usually takes two to three months could extend to eight to twelve months.

If the original medical malpractice case had been settled before her death, none of the probate procedures mentioned above would have been necessary. The settled funds would have gone directly to her without involving probate. Her death does not lower the damage cap but does increase the litigation costs.

On July 29, I met with my probate attorney, who explained the probate process to me. He will prepare the documents to present to the court, appointing me as Beth's personal representative. The document preparation will take approximately one week, but court approval may take up to four months. Once I am appointed, a notice must be published in the newspaper stating that anyone with a debt claim against Elizabeth should submit it to the probate attorney. The appointment as personal representative and the lawsuit can proceed concurrently.

My attorney did not inform me that I needed to immediately hire a probate attorney after the plaintiff's death because the case couldn't proceed until the court appointed me. As you may recall, my attorney previously emailed me, advising me to hire an estate planning attorney, not a probate attorney.

There is a clear difference between the two. He should have told me that I needed to retain one promptly. I had ninety days after the plaintiff's death to submit probate-related documents to the court; otherwise, the case would have been put on hold and would have had to be restarted.

In off-the-record discussions, the probate attorney nearly suggested I find new counsel. He acknowledged it's unusual that I don't have a copy of my contract and the contingency fee agreement. My current attorney, by law, is required to give me signed copies, but my requests for these documents haven't been answered. I'm now waiting for my next appointment with the probate attorney to get an estimate of his fee.

The case is now on hold until the court appoints me as Beth's representative, which could take up to a month for court approval. What really irritates me is that this process could have started the week after Beth's death if my attorney had just taken the time to tell me how important it was to hire a probate attorney.

On September 5, I signed eleven forms required for court submission, establishing myself as Beth's representative. The attorney must file these forms within ninety days of the decedent's death. The probate attorney will oversee this process to ensure the court approves the documents before October 5, which is ninety days after the decedent's death.

When wrongful death occurs, it will be included as a count in the amended complaint. Additionally, it is now necessary to hire a probate attorney to file a Petition for Administration. In paragraph one, the petitioner has an interest in the estate mentioned above as the decedent's surviving spouse and the nominated Personal Representative under the last will, filed with the court.

Paragraph five states that John is qualified under Florida law to serve as a personal representative of the decedent's estate and is entitled to preference for appointment because he was named as personal representative in the decedent's last will. This form, along with four others, will be filed with the court, and the lawsuit can proceed once the court approves me as a personal representative.

After Beth's death, I face a minimum charge of $3,000 plus costs for basic services by the probate attorney to file court documents. I also agreed to pay for additional services billed in six-minute segments at rates ranging from $50 to $400 per hour. I am familiar with the minimum probate service costs, but I am not familiar with the maximum.

My attorney cannot act until I am appointed as the personal representative and become the new plaintiff.

CHAPTER 18

Ring Theft

WHILE WAITING FOR the judge to approve my request to be appointed Personal Representative, I sent Beth's $4700 wedding ring to New York for an appraisal so I could sell it. A few days later, I received a message from the appraiser saying they were not interested in the ring and would be returning it. I couldn't understand why they had no interest in a .76-carat diamond. When they returned the ring, I inspected it and found that it did not match the diamond appraisal description on my purchase document.

The initial problem was that the ring I returned had a four-prong mount, while the ring I purchased had a six-prong mount. I quickly reached out to the appraiser to verify if they had sent the correct ring. They assured me it was the right one, but the diamond was fake. I was stunned. How could it be fake? After careful examination, I determined that the ring was stolen while she was in nursing care.

Beth entered the assisted living facility in May 2018 wearing a $4700 diamond wedding ring. When she died in a hospice in July 2019, the ring I received was a $ 20 fake, indicating she was wearing a counterfeit at that time. It is suspected that her original ring was taken and replaced with a nearly identical imitation during her last rehab stay. While she was in this facility, where she spent 48 days in the memory care unit undergoing physical therapy, the attendants had plenty of time to examine the ring and obtain a fake that closely resembled the original.

While in this rehab, her rings had to be removed and put back on so she could bathe. Given her condition and the fact that the rings looked identical, she couldn't tell whether she received her real ring or a fake. Whoever took the ring could match the fake to the real one, so I suspect this wasn't their first theft of this kind. A lot of thought went into this theft. If they had just taken the ring outright, it would have triggered an investigation by the facility.

However, replacing the ring with a fake diamond would probably go unnoticed, especially since an 82-year-old, sick, and confused resident wouldn't be able to distinguish between the authentic and counterfeit rings. In these cases, the theft might only come to light after the resident's death—possibly years later—when the heir tries to sell what they believe is the genuine diamond ring.

I blame myself for not taking the ring when she was in those facilities, but it's hard to ask your wife, who has worn the ring for sixty years, to give up her wedding ring just because someone providing her healthcare might steal it.

I lack direct evidence to support my conclusions, but circumstantial evidence suggests that my findings are correct. It's hard to imagine a healthcare aide exploiting a sick, confused, and dying patient, but thieves don't consider their victims' condition.

The theft still weighs on my mind, and I keep wondering how they might have gotten away with the ring without trying to replace it with a fake. Neither my wife nor I would have noticed if the ring was missing. When she died and there was no wedding ring, I would have just assumed she lost it and accepted that as the explanation. The idea that it was stolen never would have occurred to me.

On October 9, I called to report a theft to the County Sheriff. A deputy arrived at the house, reviewed the case, and said there wasn't much they could do. He explained that not knowing how long ago the theft occurred would make it harder for them to track down the ring. His second reason for not taking the case was my wife's condition.

Since she is in memory care, there's always a possibility she agreed to swap her real ring for a fake one. He assigned a case number to the complaint, but no actual case exists, and I will have to accept the $4,700 loss.

After reflecting for a few months on the ring theft, I wrote to the rehab center where I suspected the ring was stolen from.

Elizabeth was transferred from the hospital to MCHC on April 24, wearing a $4700 diamond wedding ring. She died on July 8, 2019, while wearing a $20 imitation diamond ring. Her original ring was stolen during that period, but the theft was not discovered until the hospice returned her ring to me.

Reviewing her care from the time she entered MCHC wearing a diamond wedding ring and her stay before moving to hospice, the only time someone would have removed her ring was at MCHC. While there, I know aides often took off her rings to bathe her or for other reasons, then put them back on. For someone to examine the actual ring and find it was fake, it would have to be in a facility where she stayed for an extended period. Neither the hospital nor the hospice fits that description.

The theft of the ring required careful planning. Removing the ring from her finger, substituting it with a replica that looked identical, knowing that an 82-year-old resident in memory care would probably never notice the difference, and counting on the possibility that the resident might live a long time before the theft was discovered. Elizabeth was at MCHC for forty-eight days, during which this scenario could have occurred.

During that stay, a caregiver removed her $ 4,700 diamond wedding ring and replaced it with a fake replica. I am therefore requesting $2318, the current value of the ring as determined by a diamond appraiser. As expected, I am still waiting for a response. This concludes the story of the stolen ring.

CHAPTER 19

Case Resumption

ON OCTOBER 7, the 'Order Admitting Will to Probate and Appointing Personal Representative' was received by the probate attorney and forwarded to me. The signature date was within the ninety-day limit. I informed my attorney that the court had designated me as Elizabeth's representative, and he could now prepare and send his proposed amendment to the complaint. Once again, I requested a copy of the signed contract and contingency agreement.

On November 5, I spoke with my attorney for only the third time in two and a half years. He told me that the amended complaint was being prepared, which would include more specific allegations to counter the June MTD, and that it would be filed soon. I asked to be notified when it was filed and that I would be copied.

Since HPCC is a Medicare facility, I asked whether we could file a lawsuit in federal court instead of civil court to avoid the application of the Sovereign Immunity Statutes regarding damages. The response was no, because no part of section 768.28 of the Sovereign

Immunity Statutes or any other Florida Statutes is intended to waive the state's immunity or that of its agencies from suit in federal court.

The Eleventh Amendment guarantees this immunity. The first part states: "The judicial power of the United States shall not be construed to extend to any suit in law or equity," which grants sovereign immunity to entities from being sued in federal court.

He confirmed that wrongful death cases do not have different damage caps. Florida statutes state that neither the state nor its agencies shall be liable to pay a claim or judgment exceeding $200,000 for pain and suffering. In Florida, if you suffer a catastrophic personal injury, including death, due to a negligent act by a state agency, such as a nursing home, and your medical expenses for treatment surpass $200,000, the maximum recovery allowed is $200,000, according to the statute caps on damages.

The statutes define pain as including both physical pain and suffering, which encompasses the actual physical pain and discomfort the claimant experienced before their death. It also includes mental pain and suffering, which refers to any negative emotions a victim feels due to the physical pain and trauma caused by healthcare negligence.

As outlined, Beth endured physical and mental pain, leading to a $200,000 judgment claim. Loss of consortium damages typically relate to how injuries affect the plaintiff's relationship with their spouse—particularly, the loss of companionship. Beth's account of spending her last year in assisted living, memory care, the hospital, a nursing home, and hospice meets all the criteria for loss of consortium. However, this loss is included in the $200,000 maximum damage award, as specified by the statute.

After receiving the amended complaint, my attorney believed the defendant would likely want to dismiss the case and pursue arbitration. The defendant's next logical move would be to make a settlement offer instead of covering the arbitration costs.

By November 16, I had not heard from my attorney about whether he had filed the amendment. However, I decided to take a different approach to stay informed about the case's progress. On October 15, I submitted a notarized 'Registration Agreement to View Records,' which allowed me to access all the legal documents filed with the court. The case review showed that the attorneys had submitted 25 papers, many of which I was previously unaware had been filed.

I wondered why my attorney didn't tell me about this site right after the case was assigned a court case number. On November 15, court records showed that my attorney filed the amended complaint with the court on November 8. He didn't inform me that it had been filed or send me a copy, as he had promised.

On October 4th, my attorney submitted a letter to the court designating me as Beth's representative, and on October 8th, the court approved the substitution of parties. During a teleconference with the court and opposing counsel on October 1, my attorney informed the court that the plaintiff had passed away. He will file an amended complaint naming a substitute personal representative.

None of the actions mentioned in this paragraph was ever communicated to me by my counsel. I also found out that the court had scheduled a December 9 hearing to discuss why my attorney had not responded to the MTD filed by the defendant. This hearing might have prompted my attorney to submit the amended complaint, which led to the cancellation of the scheduled hearing.

In reviewing the 'Motion for Leave of Court to File Amended Complaint,' the amendment, excluding the cover letter, was 24 pages long and identified the two defendants—the nursing home and the home's administrator. The first paragraph, titled 'Amended

Complaint and Demand for Jury Trial,' states that the plaintiff, John, as personal representative of Elizabeth's estate, deceased, by and through undersigned counsel, now files the Amended Complaint against the defendants, listing the following allegations.

The next 22 pages of the amendment generally follow a standard format, with names and dates added to match the case. It took LGF 120 days to enter the relevant data into the traditional form. His reason for the delay in responding to the MTD was that he included information intended to encourage the defendant to consider reducing the claim and pursuing arbitration after receiving the amended complaint.

Based on my review, the submission was just a standard document, and the only change to the original complaint appeared to be a notice of the plaintiff's death. For example, one section states, "During Elizabeth's residency at HPCC, the employees and agents under the direct control of the defendants were negligent in the following ways." It then lists 23 "Failing-to-dos" covering two and a half pages of the complaint.

These were the same issues outlined in the original complaint. Then, under the heading 'General Allegations Applicable to Defendants,' there are six pages that detail the same allegations found in the General Allegations section but in different language.

The document then outlines Count I: Deprivation or Infringement of Resident's Rights.

The first article states, "The plaintiff incorporates and re-alleges paragraphs one through 28 above as though fully set forth here." It again describes what has already been depicted twice in the previous complaint. Count II NEGLIGENCE.

It states once again, "The Plaintiff incorporates and re-alleges paragraphs one (1) through twenty-eight (28) above as though fully set forth," and then proceeds to describe all the charges previously stated. Count III NEGLIGENCE duplicates Count II and similarly reaffirms the complaints already detailed. In conclusion, after 23 pages of repetitive allegations, the final reason for the amended complaint is stated.

WHEREFORE, Plaintiff JOHN, in his capacity as personal representative of Elizabeth's estate, demands all damages he is entitled to under the Florida Wrongful Death Act, including loss of companionship, care, comfort, society, and mental pain and suffering from the date of Elizabeth's injury onward, along with costs against the Defendant and a trial by jury.

The contingency fee for this lawsuit covers the attorney's expertise in selecting and submitting the correct forms to the court. Concerning the amendment, he didn't need to be creative in detailing the allegations, as the revisions used were the same as I described two years ago in my interrogatories.

It took 24 pages to tell the defendant they screwed up, and we expect them to pay for their negligence. As promised, my attorney still needs to provide me with that information or a copy to notify me when he files the amended complaint. I am not telling him I now have access to all filed court documents and have already obtained a copy of the amended complaint.

On November 12, 2019, I finally received a copy of the contract signed with LGF in August 2017, which states that they were supposed to provide me with a copy at the time of signing. The contract is titled MEDICAL MALPRACTICE/NURSING HOME NEGLIGENCE AUTHORITY TO REPRESENT (Contingent Attorney Fee Agreement).

Under the Attorney Fees section, their fee is 40% of the gross recovery obtained through trial before a judge or arbitration before an arbitration panel.

The paragraph clearly states, "It is further expressly understood and agreed that this employment is upon a contingent fee basis. If no recovery is made by suit, settlement, or otherwise, the client will not owe attorneys any fees."

Provided, however, that if the client discharges the retained attorneys, the attorney will have the right to claim payment from any settlement or suit proceeds, whether secured through the client's efforts or by other attorneys involved later. Nonetheless, they may still be entitled to fees based on the value of their services during their representation (quantum meruit), rather than the percentages specified in this agreement.

In other words, if I decide to fire my current attorney and hire a new one, the former attorney would still be entitled to payment from the settlement equal to the value of their services while representing me. This situation makes it difficult to hire a new attorney because they would find it challenging to determine what contingency fee is owed to the fired attorney.

Under the Costs section, it states, "Client agrees to pay from the net proceeds of any recovery the costs of investigation or other reasonable expenses to prepare and prosecute this action." Under Clients' Rights, the client is entitled to receive an expense summary to date upon request; however, my attorney is reluctant to provide it, claiming that LGF will give it at the end of the lawsuit. According to Clients' Rights, it is illegal to prevent a client from seeing the expenses billed to their case.

Under the section on General Provisions, there is a noteworthy statement: "The undersigned Client at this moment acknowledges that my undersigned attorneys may petition the Court for approval of these fees, which exceed the limitation of Rule 4.4-1.5, and I hereby consent to their representation to the Court that I have been unable to obtain an attorney of my choice because of the limitations outlined in subdivision 4F of the above-referenced rule."

The rule states that the maximum contingency fee for a sovereign immunity lawsuit is 25%. However, since I couldn't find an attorney willing to take the case for that percentage, I have agreed to pay 40%.

Additionally, under this section, "The undersigned Client, before signing this agreement, received and read the Statement of Client's Rights, and understands each of the rights set forth therein. The undersigned client signed the Statement of Client's Rights and received a signed copy to keep and refer to while represented by the undersigned attorney."

I did not sign, nor do I have a copy of it.

Two days later, I received the 'Client's Rights Statement' without any explanation for why it wasn't provided after being signed by LGF two years ago.

CHAPTER 20

Review of Court Cases

I RESEARCHED SOVEREIGN IMMUNITY court cases and found an interesting issue related to Florida's law restricting damages for non-economic damages.

In a hospital lawsuit, the jury awarded the plaintiff $4,700,000 in damages, including $2,000,000 for past pain and suffering. However, the court limited the non-economic damage award to the caps set by Section 766.118, totaling $200,000. It reduced the $4 million verdict, citing the 'limitations on non-economic damages for negligence.'

Although the plaintiff contested it, the court rejected her argument that section 766.118's limits on non-economic damages in medical negligence cases were unconstitutional. The plaintiff then appealed to the district court.

The district court held that statutory limits on non-economic damages in personal injury medical malpractice cases are unconstitutional. Citing a 2014 Florida case, the cap on wrongful death non-economic damages in section 766.118 was deemed to violate the Equal Protection Clause of Florida's Constitution. They instructed the trial court to restore the total damage award as determined by the jury. The defendant appealed to the Supreme Court.

In June 2017, the Supreme Court ruled that these caps 'arbitrarily reduce damage awards for plaintiffs who suffer the most severe injuries.' It eliminated any statutory limits on non-economic damages in medical malpractice lawsuits. The court upheld the district court's decision.

It argued that caps on personal injury and non-economic damages in medical negligence cases, as outlined in Section 766.118, violate the Equal Protection Clause of the Florida Constitution. I will summarize the court's decision, as the reasoning used could also be applied to cases involving sovereign immunity.

The court explained that section 766.118 benefits many by imposing significant costs on a few—namely, those who are most severely injured, those who suffer the most critical harm, and those whose non-economic damages depend on the damages cap. Under the Equal Protection Clause of the Florida Constitution, we determined that reducing damages in this manner is not only arbitrary but also irrational, and we conclude that it "offends the fundamental notion of equal justice under the law."

They also concluded that the cap on non-economic damages "bears no rational relationship to a legitimate state objective, they failing the rational basis test." The Florida legislature's purpose in enacting the statute was to address the crisis in medical malpractice insurance. The legislature claimed that the rise in medical malpractice insurance premiums was harming doctors, causing them to leave, retire, or refuse to perform high-risk procedures, thus reducing the availability of healthcare.

However, the court found that the available data did not support the legislature's claims about a medical malpractice crisis. The opinion stated that even if the legislature's findings were correct, section 766.118 still violates Florida's Equal Protection Clause because the existing evidence shows no rational connection between capping non-economic damages and solving the crisis. There is also no evidence of a direct link between caps and lowering malpractice premiums.

The Florida court cited the Texas Supreme Court's statement: "In the context of persons catastrophically injured by medical negligence, we believed it is unreasonable and arbitrary to limit their recovery in a speculative experiment to determine whether liability insurance rates will decrease."

Additionally, the Florida court opinion states that even if a medical malpractice crisis existed when the law was enacted, "Conditions can change which remove or negate the justification for a law, transforming what may have once been reasonable into arbitrary and irrational legislation."

The court then stated, after reviewing current data, "No rational basis exists to justify the continued application of non-economic damage caps of section 766.118." Caps on non-economic damages serve no purpose but to arbitrarily punish the most grievously injured.

The court also noted that "The only asserted legitimate State interest is the alleviation of rising medical malpractice insurance premiums paid by affected doctors." However, "There is no mechanism to assure the savings are passed on from the insurance companies to the doctors." Therefore, the court concluded there was no evidence of a continuing medical malpractice crisis that would justify the arbitrary application of the statutory cap in a wrongful death case. The court's final opinion upheld the district court's view that 766.118 was unconstitutional.

The Supreme Court stated, "We agree with the district court and hold that the caps in 766.118 violate equal protection under the rational basis test. The caps apply to the plaintiff because the arbitrary reduction of compensation without regard to the severity of the injury does not have a rational relationship to the legislature's stated interest in addressing the medical malpractice crisis."

Therefore, we concluded that caps on non-economic damages for personal injury provided in section 766.118 violate the Equal Protection Clause of the Florida Constitution. However, a dissenting opinion stated.

Most of the court disregards and ignores all the legislature's work and fact-finding. Under our constitutional system, the legislature, not this court, is entitled to make laws as a matter of policy based on the facts it finds. The legislature's task is to decide whether a medical malpractice crisis exists, whether it has abated, and whether the Florida Statutes should be amended accordingly. For this court to determine that a problem no longer exists, if it ever did, so that it can change a statute and policy it dislikes, improperly interferes with the legislative function.

This Statute and the Sovereign Immunity Statute, which limit damages for malpractice, were enacted in the late 1980s and 1990s. The legislature believed that shielding medical providers from increasing malpractice lawsuits and rising liability insurance rates would attract more physicians to practice in the state and help lower healthcare costs by decreasing malpractice insurance premiums.

Opponents, however, argue that neither of those benefits has materialized, and the state has caused more harm than good. Instead of attracting talented doctors, the law has drawn physicians who have faced malpractice suits elsewhere, underscoring the ongoing rise of malpractice insurance and healthcare costs.

Although the Supreme Court ruled that 766.118 was unconstitutional, it remains in the 2019 Florida Statutes. Therefore, attorneys should consider the following before choosing to take on a case.

Lawyers treat entities covered under the Sovereign Immunity statute like physicians who do not have medical malpractice insurance, a practice known as 'going bare.' A USA TODAY study found that 8.3% of Florida's licensed doctors go bare. Many physicians are licensed to practice in Florida despite facing disciplinary actions in other states.

Similar to limits on sovereign immunity, doctors in Florida who do not carry medical malpractice insurance are not required by federal or state laws to obtain such insurance. The state allows these doctors to agree to pay $250,000 if the plaintiff wins the lawsuit. However, federal bankruptcy law creates a loophole. Conversely, the physician can declare bankruptcy instead of paying the damages, and the state medical board cannot discipline them for this action.

By the 1980s, malpractice insurance premiums had become so expensive that some doctors retired early or switched to other fields. The Tort Reform and Insurance Act of 1986 aimed to address this issue by altering insurance regulations. Included in the Act was Chapter 458, which, for the first time, allowed doctors the option not to carry medical malpractice insurance.

The law required doctors to agree to cover any adverse medical malpractice judgment against them up to $250,000. However, lawmakers created another problem by trying to fix one issue while the most problematic doctors in the state had the most substantial incentive to stop carrying medical malpractice insurance. One of the first questions an attorney asks a potential client is whether the doctor has medical malpractice insurance; if not, the attorney typically declines to take on the client's case.

Regarding rising insurance rates, the leading physician-owned medical malpractice insurer in Florida states that a single lawsuit won't necessarily raise premiums, but a history of issues can.

Rates are increased due to a pattern of claim activity showing an individual practitioner has a higher risk profile than the average physician.

Florida lawmakers believed that protecting medical providers from rising malpractice lawsuits and higher liability insurance costs would attract more doctors to the state and lower malpractice premiums. Opponents argue that neither of these benefits has materialized, and malpractice insurance and healthcare costs continue to increase.

The constitutionality of the law has been challenged. However, in 2000, the Florida Supreme Court upheld the exclusion as constitutional, stating, "the statute's disparate treatment of medical malpractice wrongful deaths does bear a rational relationship to the legitimate state interest of ensuring the accessibility of medical care to Florida residents by curtailing the skyrocketing medical malpractice insurance in Florida."

CHAPTER 21

Nursing Home Standards

H PCC WAS GUILTY of medical procedure malpractice, but I wondered how such misconduct could be uncovered before a resident's death. Nursing homes are subject to inspections, but how can medical procedure malpractice be detected if it does not occur during the inspector's visit or after the review has been completed? Inspections are supposed to happen every 15 months, and many non-medical procedures can be performed between inspections.

I was the one who uncovered the wrongdoing through medical research, but how many patients or their representatives are aware of it or have the time to do such research? How many nursing home malpractice lawsuits go unfiled because those affected lack the knowledge to review their medical care thoroughly?

This review examines the nursing home inspection process and the criteria used to evaluate facilities following inspections.

A study by the USA Today Network revealed that since 2013, state inspections have identified 291 violations related to failing to provide adequate and proper care. This broad category can encompass the most serious violations, including those that result in death. Beth received inadequate care, and although she did not experience this outcome at HPCC, it was a contributing factor to her later death.

The study also found 215 cases where nursing homes failed to follow the doctor's orders or disregarded blood test results. This is similar to Beth's situation, where staff did not respond to blood tests or the notification from the patient's representative that the patient was severely dehydrated.

The Florida Agency for Health Care Administration (AHCA) regularly fines nursing homes, with the average fine from June 2012 to 2017 being $4500. Florida law caps the largest AHCA fine for a serious violation at $15,000. This amount is small compared to the millions of dollars homes receive annually from taxpayer-funded Medicare programs.

The AHCA states that "Fines are generally enough to prompt facility improvement," saying, "It is not the amount of the fine; it's a fact of the fine that gets the facility to improve." However, a state senator disagreed, expressing concern that low fines hinder improvement.

He states, "Here is a reality of capitalism."

"If there is no financial disincentive, safety and responsibility tend to become just bottom-line numbers." In other words, fines become an accepted cost of doing business.

FAHA, which licenses and regulates nursing homes, rarely imposes the harshest sanctions. HPCC received a federal fine of $5,850 from 2013 to 2017. They had 33 violations cited during that period, but no state fines were issued.

To quote a FAHA official, "We are required by Florida law to take the least invasive, least intrusive licensure action that we can take under the circumstances. Our action will be reviewed and vetted in every situation, whether a small fine, a moratorium, or a suspension."

Federal government fines are higher, with the average penalty in Florida during that period being $27,000. By law, AHCA is supposed to receive a copy of nursing home lawsuits; however, only some lawyers comply, which prevents prospective residents from reviewing a nursing home's lawsuit history.

How could the violation of medical procedures described in the complaint go unnoticed? The relevant regulations for nursing home inspections include NURSING HOME FEDERAL DEFICIENCY SEVERITY AND SCOPE.

Nursing homes approved to accept Medicare or Medicaid must follow specific federal standards. The Agency for Health Care Administration conducts inspections to determine if federal decertification is needed. When a national deficiency is identified during an inspection, the issue is given a 'scope and severity' rating based on the finding.

Scope refers to the number of people affected by the deficiency. Isolated means that it affects one or a few residents or issues. Pattern refers to more than a few residents or problems and usually involves a group, a unit, or a wing. Widespread covers many residents and may be pervasive or systematic.

Severity indicates the level of harm to health or safety. Immediate Jeopardy refers to harm that is occurring now or potential damage that could happen. An actual injury has already happened. There is no real harm, but the risk of more than minimal harm exists; no actual harm has occurred, and the chance of harm is minimal.

The state and CMS use a grading system to assess the severity of deficiencies identified during inspections. A 'deficiency' is a regulatory requirement that the facility fails to meet.

A nursing home rated as a level 1 on the severity chart indicates that the facility's deficient practice has caused or is likely to cause serious injury, harm, impairment, or death, requiring immediate correction. In this case, the pattern of the facility's practice suggests a reasonable likelihood that similar actions, situations, procedures, or incidents will occur again in the future if not addressed promptly. Level 1 is known as Immediate Jeopardy.

For each deficiency, the survey team first assesses the extent of the problem within the nursing home. It assigns a severity and scope value using the letters A through L and determines whether the deficiency is isolated, patterned, or widespread. J indicates that it is an isolated Immediate Jeopardy and the most severe deficiency, even if it affects the fewest residents.

K poses an immediate pattern jeopardy that affects only a small number of residents, while L is widespread. To establish a finding of Immediate Jeopardy, the inspector must look for the following components:

The first category is harm, which includes two options: actual or potential. The second component is Immediacy, where the investigator evaluates whether the harm or likely harm will happen soon if no immediate action is taken. The third component is Culpability, and the team will ask: Did the facility know about the situation, and if so, when did they become aware? Should the facility have known about the problem? Did the facility thoroughly investigate the circumstances surrounding the incident? Did they implement corrective measures? Has the facility reevaluated the steps to ensure the situation is corrected?

The team evaluates the facility's response to any harm or potential harm that qualifies as Immediate Jeopardy. Just because the facility's staff claims they were unaware of a particular issue or situation does not relieve the facility from the responsibility of identifying and preventing Immediate Jeopardy.

The survey team leverages their experience and knowledge to determine whether the circumstances could have been predicted and if they should have been investigated to uncover any earlier signs or warnings about the dangerous situation. Crises where a facility showed no prior signs or warnings are rare.

Let's review the events related to the current lawsuit. If these events happen during an inspection, would the inspector be aware of them unless a resident or their representative informs them? The inspector could only spot an issue if they saw a resident with an embedded catheter, which would prompt them to ask why it was used and to assess if it posed an Immediate Jeopardy due to its continued use.

Let's begin by defining the scope of the deficiency, which is classified as an 'isolated' issue affecting only one resident. How would the inspector determine whether the practice was limited to a single resident, patterned and involving a few residents, or widespread and systematic?

Whether the discrepancy qualifies as Immediate Jeopardy depends on whether it meets all three components. It falls under the potential Harm category because "the facility's failure to comply with requirements likely to cause severe injury, harm, impairment, or death to an individual." An embedded catheter meets the criteria since catheters are known to cause UTIs, and frequent UTIs can lead to kidney failure and death.

Criterion two is immediacy, which means harm or potential harm is likely to occur soon if no immediate action is taken. In our case, under Medicare mandates, the facility's failure to remove the catheter promptly resulted in the patient continuing to suffer from UTIs. Regarding category three, Culpability, there are questions: Did the facility know about the situation, and when did they become aware of it?

The answer is that the facility was aware of the Medicare mandate against using a catheter as soon as it was embedded. Regarding the question, should the facility have been aware of the situation? If they had read and followed Medicare mandates, they would have known that embedding a catheter violated Medicare directives. Based on the above, the facility would have received a grade of 1 J and faced a significant fine.

How would an inspection team determine if medical malpractice occurs between inspections? How many residents or representatives would recognize that an embedded catheter violates the Medicare mandate and that its continued use could lead to kidney failure and death?

Staffing is another challenge in nursing homes. Beth's catheter was not medically necessary, but it was inserted to reduce the aide's workload in helping her with bathroom needs or changing her diaper. Was this because the facility lacked enough staff and relied on available personnel? The only solution was to decrease the aides' overall workload, three factors that influence staff-to-resident ratios.

Regulation: For assisted living facilities (ALFs), Florida does not establish a minimum staff-to-resident ratio. They only require enough staff to supervise residents and carry out their service plans. However, nursing homes have stricter standards that specify RN and LPN staffing levels; there are no requirements for a specific number of care aides.

Living Up to Standards: Most ALFs meet federal requirements, but many states enforce stricter rules. Studies show that understaffing is common in nursing and ALF facilities, and staffing ratios are rarely met.

Cost: Money plays a crucial role in enabling residents with more funds to access facilities that have better resident-to-staff ratios, since higher costs usually indicate enough employees to provide proper assistance. Studies have shown that nursing homes are often understaffed, and increasing staff levels results in improved care.

Insufficient staffing also leads to high employee turnover and ongoing stress for workers. A resident faces a significant risk of being cared for by someone whose training may be inadequate or by someone exhausted and overworked.

I've noticed frequent turnover among aides caring for my wife in nursing homes, so neither the aide nor the resident truly gets to know each other. The area has 24 ALFs and 15 care facilities, each serving at least 100 residents or patients. Staffing with RNs, LPNs, and aides at these facilities will become more complex and challenging as more facilities open.

A Virginia study found that surveyors couldn't determine if a nursing home or ALF meets federal staffing standards because terms like 'sufficient staff' are vague and the survey process is subjective. The same issue exists in Florida, which requires facilities to have adequate staffing to provide necessary healthcare to residents.

On February 20, 2020, the local newspaper published a front-page article titled 'Nursing homes could get less oversight.' The article discussed the Florida Agency for Health Care Administration (ACHA). It noted that the agency cited three nursing homes with Class 1 violations—the most serious type of violation the agency can impose—over the past three years. Current law requires the agency to inspect these homes every six months for a period of two years. However, two bills being considered in the Florida legislature aim to reduce inspections at problem nursing homes.

Part of the legislation would require the agency to conduct only one additional review after a nursing home has been cited with a

Class 1 or multiple Class 2 violations and lower AHCA inspection fines from $6,000 to $3,000. The AHCA supports legislation that allows the agency to spend less time in well-performing healthcare facilities and more time inspecting those that are problematic. The AHCA states that its resources are increasingly strained as the state's population and healthcare facilities grow.

The agency states, "We want to ensure that we can focus on higher-risk and low-performing providers as we review our workload."

A 2018 investigation by two local newspapers found that many of Florida's worst nursing homes have long histories of failing to meet both state and federal standards, facing little risk of being shut down by regulators. At the time of writing, Florida had 695 nursing homes, with 59 subject to a more rigorous two-year inspection cycle. Of these facilities, 52 received a below-average rating from the federal Centers for Medicare and Medicaid Services, scoring 1.9 out of 5 stars on a five-point scale.

These are the facilities the AHCA plans to prioritize. The bill would allow the agency to extend inspection deadlines for highly rated facilities and focus more on those with poor ratings. Regardless of the proposed legislation, the AHCA still must comply with federal rules requiring all nursing facilities to be inspected every 15 months.

The requirement for AHCA to increase oversight of nursing homes with serious violations became law in 2001, as part of a controversial reform effort that also mandated higher staffing levels to provide the long-term care industry with greater legal protections. However, staffing levels have remained steady over the past six years, with 596 full-time employees in 2019 and only a slight increase to 597 later that year.

During that period, the number of inspections by healthcare providers increased from 18,107 to 19,601, a 7% rise. Incidents in nursing homes increased by 7%, adverse incidents rose by 80%, and regulatory sanctions increased by 108%. Based on these numbers, the consensus is that if the agency's workload expands, lawmakers should increase its budget rather than cut its workload; otherwise, the overall quality of oversight will decline.

CHAPTER 22

Medicare Billing

In November, I received several Medicare Summary Notices. Reviewing one of them revealed billing information that I couldn't believe was true. Beth incurred these charges from January 23 to April 18, 2019. During that time, she was in memory care and was so weak she couldn't turn over in bed, had trouble getting out of her recliner without help, was using a walker or wheelchair to move around, and needed assistance to get dressed.

Is this person a candidate for physical therapy? The answer is no. She is an 82-year-old woman who is ill and will never be able to be mobile without the assistance of a walker or wheelchair. With that in mind, the following services are provided and billed to Medicare.

15 Physical Therapy Sessions	$1980
14 Occupational Therapy Sessions	$2310
1 Speech Therapy Session	$ 165
5 Aid/Home Health Visits	$ 400

5 Skilled Nursing Visits	$ 825
Total Billing	$6075

The period covers the 64 days she was in memory care. The billing shows she received therapy on 30 of those days. Surprisingly, when Medicare stopped paying for physical therapy, the treatment also came to an end. The PT didn't end because her mobility improved, but because Medicare stopped covering the services.

Additionally, Medicare billed $1225 for Home Health and Skilled Nursing, even though she was in a memory care facility. What justifies the home health and skilled nursing visits?

I realize that assisted living facilities are for-profit entities, but collecting payments of this size for questionable services appears to exploit the Medicare reimbursement system.

CHAPTER 23

Death Lawsuit Initiated

O<small>N</small> D<small>ECEMBER</small> 2, since I hadn't heard from my attorney since October 5, a court records check showed he had filed an Amended Complaint on November 8. My attorney had to prepare a new 19-page document that duplicated the original complaint, with the only change being the name swap from Elizabeth to me. The court approved the plaintiff's Motion to Amend the Complaint and gave the defendant twenty days to respond.

Legal documents typed double-spaced with a one-inch, four-sided border often result in multi-page files. Much of the language is standard and used in any lawsuit document, with only names and dates changed.

Section one, GENERAL ALLEGATIONS, has eight one-sentence items.

Item 8 states, "During Elizabeth's residency at HPCC, the employees and agents directly controlled by the Defendants were negligent in the following ways." It then lists 23 negligent actions, each in a single sentence, all beginning with 'Failing to,' such as "Failing to monitor and provide a safe environment."

Section two, GENERAL ALLEGATIONS APPLICABLE TO DEFENDANTS, includes 13 one-sentence statements spanning six pages.

One subsection states, "Elizabeth had the following rights, and the Defendant had a duty to ensure they did not violate any of the 21 one-sentence rights violations." All rights listed are from Florida Statute 400.022 throughout this section and other relevant statutes. My attorney quoted the 21 listed rights violations almost verbatim from the statute.

Next, the counsel lists eight one-sentence statements describing the rights violated under COUNT I, DEPRIVATION OF INFRINGEMENT OF RESIDENTS' RIGHTS. The complaint further expands this section by adding eight one-sentence acts of omission, each starting with "Failure to provide Elizabeth...". Once again, these are omissions taken from FS 400.022.

Next is COUNT II; NEGLIGENCE, which includes 12 one-sentence statements from FS 400.022, and it expands on the count by adding ten more one-sentence nursing home failures using terminology from the section.

COUNT III, NEGLIGENCE, refers to FS 400.022 and includes FS 768, the wrongful death act. This section contains six single-sentence numbered items and seven claims for damages on behalf of Elizabeth's estate. It is the only section that does not adopt descriptions from a statute but instead uses my answers to the interrogatories.

Attorneys often try to impress clients with lengthy documents, like the 19-page complaint filed with the court. They rarely take the time to compile the record thoroughly. At least, in this case, it's clear that all the complaint input either comes from the client or is based on descriptions in the Florida statutes.

The task requires the paralegal to type a document following a standard format typically used in nursing home malpractice cases. The double spacing and large borders indicate volume, as shown by the number of pages, but do not necessarily reflect quality, as my attorney contributes very little original thought.

On Christmas Eve, I had dinner with one of my golf friends and, for the first time, shared what I had been going through over the past two and a half years. He couldn't understand how I could have gone through this experience and was amazed that I kept it all to myself. It finally felt good to open up about my journey.

As I wait for the next step in the lawsuit, I mark the third Christmas since it began and the first without Beth. She loved Christmas. She wanted a tree to decorate the house and to buy me gifts. Her biggest regret was not being able to shop for the grandkids. She loved Christmas shopping and always showed joy in whatever gift I bought her.

After sixty years of sharing holidays with her, facing this one without her is hard. Although she has been in constant pain during the last two Christmases, we still celebrated together. This Christmas will be different. I plan to play golf in the morning, enjoy a deli sandwich, and watch a Netflix movie. The holiday will end, and life will go on.

With the new year, I begin the third year of the lawsuit. On January 3, having not heard from my attorney since October 5, I checked the court records. I found that the defendant's counsel filed a Motion to Dismiss (MTD) on December 31 in response to our amended complaint. My attorney was confident that the amended complaint would cause the defendant to dismiss the case and move directly to arbitration.

The courts discourage MTDs because the standard view is that an MTD only prolongs the litigation process. Did I mention that the defense attorney is on a retainer, so delaying a case increases his legal fees?

The document, titled "MOTION TO DISMISS and MOTION FOR MORE DEFINITE STATEMENT, AND MOTION TO STRIKE," repeats the motion to dismiss made in June 2019.

Come now, defendants (HPCC and LMHS), by and through their undersigned counsel, and pursuant to Rule 1.140 FRCP, move this court to issue an order dismissing the plaintiff's amended complaint, requiring the plaintiff to plead with greater specificity, and striking a portion of the amended complaint. The motion to dismiss lists 23 allegations, which the defendants characterize as vague, ambiguous, and overly broad, making it unreasonable to draft a responsive pleading. The plaintiff should be ordered to plead with more clarity.

I responded to the defendant's objections with more case knowledge than my attorney. I am summarizing the defendant's statements, removing all legal jargon while maintaining the main point of their complaint.

In item 2, the defendant states that HPCC is a licensed nursing home recognized by the state of Florida, owned and operated by the health system, a public healthcare system established through a special act of the Florida legislature. (This act includes the nursing home in the Sovereign Immunity Statute.)

I added this statement to his description: "HPCC is a facility that operates under Medicare guidelines and receives Medicare funding." (This indicates the facility violated the Medicare mandates they are supposed to follow.)

In item 4, in summary, the plaintiff alleged 'statutorily mandated residents' rights were deprived" and listed nine allegations without explaining how and when the rights violations occurred.

My answer is that the rights violations, specifically the placement of a catheter, occurred from May 18, 2017, shortly after the plaintiff's admission to the facility, and continued nonstop through July 29, 2017. During this period, the plaintiff was rushed to the emergency room. The second charged violation, dehydration, lasted from July 1, 2017, until July 29, 2017, when the plaintiff was discharged to the emergency room.

Item 5 states, "The allegations of Count I are so vague, ambiguous, and overbroad that the Defendant, HPCC, cannot reasonably frame a response."

To clarify the vague and ambiguous allegations, the defendant intentionally violated Medicare mandates outlined in CMS 20068. (Previously detailed). The catheter was neither medically necessary nor appropriate, and it was left in place for 72 days.

To clarify the 'vague and ambiguous allegations,' the plaintiff's representative informed the nursing staff, supported by blood tests, that the plaintiff was dehydrated. When the nursing staff agreed with this diagnosis, none of the team members could insert an intravenous line to rehydrate the patient because of vein collapse. This inability to perform a standard medical procedure caused the plaintiff to be rushed to the hospital in a dehydrated state.

Item 8 is lengthy, but in summary, states, "In paragraph 41, the plaintiff alleges the Defendants owed a duty to provide care and treatment within the standard of care, had an obligation to provide custodial care and services consistent with residents' rights in FS 400.022, and held the duty of hiring, retaining, training, supervising, and firing its employees, agents, consultants, and independent contractors." (Here, the defendant refers to items in the Amended Complaint.)

In my response to paragraph 41, as detailed in item 5, it is evident that the defendant did not provide care and treatment that met the standard of care.

Regarding paragraphs 42 and 43, I refer to CMS 20068, which states, "Has the staff involved you in care plan development, including whether interventions reflect preferences and choices, and discussed the risks and benefits of a urinary catheter before insertion."

HPCC did not discuss with the plaintiff or the plaintiff's representative, nor did it address the chances of developing frequent urinary tract infections (UTIs) from the extended presence of an embedded catheter, the resulting kidney failure from serious UTIs, or the possibility of future fatal kidney failure.

Regarding paragraph 46, the defendant failed to properly train nursing staff to insert intravenous lines into the plaintiff to treat the noticeable dehydration. Therefore, the defendant was unable to fulfill its duty of hiring qualified nursing personnel, did not train them in intravenous insertions, and did not verify their ability to perform this procedure.

It is also clear that the nursing staff and supervisors were unprepared to meet Medicare mandates in CMS 20068.

In item 14, the defendant states, "Count III attempts to plead an alternative claim for wrongful death according to FS 768.16; however, it fails to plead the necessary elements to state a cause of action and should be dismissed."

My answer is that wrongful death involves causing a person's death through the intentional or negligent acts of another individual or group.

According to 768.16, Florida Statutes, when a death results from a wrongful act (such as the insertion of an embedded catheter in violation of Medicare mandates), negligence (for example, the nursing staff's failure to perform a proper intravenous procedure), and breach of contract (the resident's right to receive adequate and appropriate health care, protective, and support services, which, as described above, the plaintiff did not receive).

Sixteen states say, "Finally, Plaintiff's Amended Complaint names the facility administrator as a defendant, but the complaint fails to make any allegations against the administrator."

As the facility administrator, the named defendant is responsible for the performance or lack of performance of all supervisors, nursing staff, and other employees.

Item 17 states, "Plaintiff's Complaint is based upon alleged deprivation or infringement of the resident's rights, negligence, and wrongful death under Chapter 400, Florida Statutes, occurring on or about May 18, to July 29, 2017."

I affirm that the Plaintiff's Complaint is based on actual medical records and not on an alleged deprivation or infringement of the resident's rights.

Item 21, the defendant states, "Under Section 768.28(9)(a) FS, the administrator cannot be held personally liable or named as a party defendant in this action and should be dismissed."

Here, the defendant is correct. Employees of state agencies covered under the Sovereign Immunity Statute are immune from being sued. Based on this statute, the administrator should be dismissed and removed as a named defendant. I wonder why the defendant didn't identify this issue in their June 2019 MTD, which would have allowed the plaintiff's counsel to correct it in the amended complaint.

By not doing so in June, the defendant delayed the litigation, causing the plaintiff's counsel to file an amended complaint to remove the administrator.

The defendant did raise an issue that my attorney should have identified. The administrator, named as a defendant in our amended complaint, is an employee of the health system and is therefore protected by the Florida Waiver of Sovereign Immunity Act.

The act states, "No officer, employee, or agent of the state shall be held personally liable in tort as a party defendant in an action for injury or damage suffered as a result of any act, event, or omission within the scope of his employment or duty."

Although the complaint does not accuse the administrator, he is often criticized because the health system employed him. According to Florida Statutes, he cannot be held personally liable or named as a defendant in this case and should be dismissed. Based on the defendant's claim, I emailed my counsel on January 5.

Based on my review of court records, your belief that the defendant would want to dismiss the case and move to arbitration after receiving the amended complaint was mistaken. I chose to respond to the defendant's MTD and will provide you with my answers upon request. Since the administrator cannot be named in the complaint, is answering the MTD a moot issue? Will a new amended complaint need to be filed?

On January 14, I resent the email with the subject line 'Rule Regulating the Florida Bar, Chapter 4', Rule 4-1.4. This rule states the following:

Rule 4-1.4 COMMUNICATION

When informing the client about the status of representation, a lawyer shall: promptly notify the client of any decision or circumstance that requires the client's informed consent; consult with the client on how to achieve their objectives; keep the client reasonably updated on the progress of the matter; and respond promptly to reasonable requests for information.

Duty to Explain Matters to Clients: A lawyer must thoroughly explain a matter to the client so that they can make informed decisions about their representation. Clear communication between the lawyer and the client is vital for effective participation.

A lawyer's regular contact with clients can reduce the chances that a client will need to ask for information about the representation. When a client makes a reasonable request for information, it should be answered promptly. If a quick response isn't possible, the lawyer or a staff member should acknowledge receipt of the request and inform the client of the expected reply time.

Rule 4-1.3 DILIGENCE

A lawyer shall act with reasonable diligence and promptness in representing a client. A lawyer must manage his workload so that he can handle each matter competently.

As shown throughout this story, it's clear that my counsel still needs to meet the requirements of Chapter 4 as previously discussed. However, I need assistance in changing counsel during the course of the case. I even considered representing myself. I hold a law degree from the 1960s, before the invention of the word processor and the internet. After reading a story about Clarence Darrow, the lawyer in the Scopes Monkey Trial, I decided I wanted a law degree—not to practice law, but to say I had one.

Seeing an advertisement for earning a degree through mail-order study, I contacted the school, paid the $400 enrollment fee—a significant amount in the 1960s—and became a student. I received a

36-volume law library to study for written essay tests, which I took after reading each chapter. The answers were typed and sent to the school for grading. I did all my studying at night, and after seven years, I finally earned my law degree in February 1968.

Using my legal knowledge and internet research, I have often annoyed my attorney by asking questions that a typical client wouldn't ask. A prime example is trying to hold him to the Rules Regulating the Florida Bar, as described above. However, since I am not licensed in Florida, the idea of representing myself is irrelevant.

I received an answer, and we finally began some dialogue for the first time in two years.

Attorney: You seem to be one of those 'forests for the trees' kind of people.

Me: Probably an accurate description of me, but humor me. Suppose the Sovereign Immunity Act covers the administrator, making him immune from litigation, as claimed in the defendants' latest MTD. Why wasn't this addressed in their MTD filed in June? Do you need to file an amended complaint to remove him, or can you acknowledge their contention in the MTD response?

Attorney: Thank you for humoring me as well. We can debate whether to include the administrator in the earlier MTD or focus on excluding him; however, I see a potential agreement between the parties to amend again without a hearing, remove the administrator, and get a response to the complaint from opposing counsel.

Me: Thanks; this kind of information helps me see beyond the trees. Continued tree clearing and updated case details will allow me to see the forest.

His response was, "I like this."

CHAPTER 24

2nd Amended Complaint

MUCH OF THE legal information you read here may be repeated because it appears in different documents to answer the defense attorney's questions. In other motions, the defense might ask the same question in various ways, but most of the time, my answer will be the same as in previous responses. These court records are written in detailed legal language to explain why lawsuits can take years to resolve.

On January 18, I received the first bill from the probate attorney. Although the case is still in litigation with no end in sight, I must start paying for the probate filing. I was billed $1,306 for the first part of the $3,000 fee.

On January 27, my counsel drafted a new 20-page SECOND AMENDED COMPLAINT AND DEMAND FOR JURY TRIAL. It essentially repeats the previous document, with two additional items related to the nursing home administrator, as outlined in the 'AMENDED COMPLAINT' filed on December 9, 2019.

The new Complaint explicitly identifies the administrator, stating, "That at all times material hereto, the defendant was licensed by the State of Florida and was serving as the administrator during Elizabeth's residency. According to Florida Statutes, the defendant bears liability arising from his official capacity."

I don't understand this change because the defendant's MTD filed on December 3 stated that "Accordingly, under Section 768.28 Florida Statutes, the administrator cannot be held personally liable or named as a party defendant in this action, and the administrator should be dropped as a named defendant."

I don't see how giving more details about being named in the new motion affects the fact that he is immune. Only a liberal interpretation of the statute might make him a defendant.

In response to MTD's claim, the Amended Complaint contains no allegations against the administrator.

According to Florida Statutes, the MTD states that, based on the statement starting with 'No officer' and ending with his employment or function, the administrator is immune from litigation.

However, the MTD did not include the quoted sentence, "unless such officer, employee, or agent acted in bad faith or with malicious purpose or exhibiting wanton and willful disregard of human rights, safety, or property." The plaintiff might argue that the administrator was responsible for the actions of his nursing supervisor and staff who committed the 'willful disregard of human rights'; however, even with this broad interpretation of 768.28 (9), why is it necessary to include him?

He responded, "I am continuing to discuss the amendment with opposing counsel." I interpret this as indicating he will not submit the Second Amendment Complaint to the court until opposing counsel agrees to include the administrator, even though the defendant stated he is opposed to naming him.

Reviewing court records from the February 10 meeting revealed the following note made by the judge.

The Court decided to proceed after waiting about 10 minutes, and Plaintiff's attorney still did not appear. The motion was granted with leave to amend. Knowing about this scheduled Court meeting for weeks, I felt my attorney insulted the court by not showing up. The court granted the defendant's MTD.

My attorney annoyed me by not showing up, so I contacted the lawyer I had considered firing. He reiterated that it's unlikely to find an attorney willing to take a sovereign immunity case. Suing a state agency protected by sovereign immunity is expensive and time-consuming. The state agencies will deliberately slow down the case because their attorney is on retainer, and since time is money, they will increase the plaintiff's expenses over time.

The Florida legislature and the medical lobby have done a great job of preventing people harmed by malpractice from suing hospitals or nursing homes, which are considered state agencies. As a result, many injured individuals cannot find legal help due to medical malpractice or negligence and have to face the consequences without options. The primary goal of the legislation was to make suing a state agency so difficult that, with the use of caps, the state could effectively block many valid lawsuits. I cannot change lawyers.

After waiting a week for my attorney to explain his no-show reasons, I emailed him, asking: Now that you've pissed off the judge, when do you expect to answer the defendant's MTD? I was surprised to receive a reply and learn I now have a new attorney, my third.

I return to something I read: "Not all so-called law practices practice law and will accept lawsuits with the hope they will be able to figure the case out eventually." Sometimes, I wonder whether I still have one. My first meeting with my new attorney convinced me that I had finally found an attorney.

On February 18, I received a professionally written response to my question addressed to Attorney Two. He explained that a leave to amend means my attorney needs to include more specific facts in the Amended Complaint. A new complaint was filed with the court on February 17, addressing these issues. My attorney stated that the complaint is vague to protect my claim. Before the formal discovery process begins, a complaint is filed so the plaintiff can learn more about the defendant's perspective on the case.

My issue is that the Second Amended Complaint still includes the administrator as a defendant, so I expect opposing counsel to file another MTD. The defense filed another MTD on February 26, with issues that nearly duplicate those in their December 31 MTD.

On January 8, 2020, I celebrated my 87th birthday. My goal is to outlive the lawsuit, and the defendant's attorney plans to extend the case in hopes of stopping me from doing so.

My attorney responded to my question about how he would handle this new MTD. We will make some adjustments to the Complaint, but will oppose the rest. They haven't reached out yet for hearing dates, but you will receive a responsive motion with an amended complaint and an opposition to several points of their action.

"This should be the last round, and I expect a successful hearing." I don't understand what he just wrote, but at least he is responsive to my questions. I responded to all the defendant's complaints and sent them to him.

The plaintiff's response opposing the defendant's Motion to Dismiss the complaint states.

The plaintiff alleges that HPCC violated Medicare-mandated directives (CMS 20068) regarding the use of indwelling catheters. It failed to ensure nurses were qualified to perform the necessary procedures for inserting an intravenous line, as outlined in the alleged violations. The plaintiff has demonstrated that HPCC was negligent in failing to fulfill its legal duty to provide the standard of reasonable care to the plaintiff.

There should be no requirement for a specific time or place for the negligent acts, as they took place from the plaintiff's entry into the facility to her eviction 72 days later. The plaintiff has alleged sufficient facts to give the defendant "fair notice of the nature of the claim and the grounds upon which they rest."

When reviewing an MTD, the Court must accept the facts alleged in the Complaint as accurate. It can dismiss the case only if it determines that the plaintiff cannot prove 'any set of facts supporting their claim.' The plaintiff has met the burden of presenting a 'set of facts.'

Defendant's February 26 MTD raises the same objections as their December 31 MTD, which I previously addressed in detail. The current MTD should be denied.

Despite the defense's rejection of the plaintiff's attempt to name the administrator as a defendant, my attorney seems determined to keep him in the case. In the motion to dismiss (MTD), the defense states that the plaintiff: "Fails to make any allegations against the administrator" and also fails to recognize that, under the Florida Statutes, "No officer shall be named as a party defendant in any action in the scope of their employment function."

Therefore, the administrator should be removed as a named defendant. I, the novice lawyer, agree with the defendant that we should eliminate the administrator. Continuing to include him as a defendant will lead to more defendant MTDs. The only part of the statute that could make the administrator liable states, "Unless such officer acted in bad faith or with malicious purpose or in a manner exhibiting wanton and willful disregard of human rights, safety, or property." The administrator showed none of these behaviors.

My attorney stated that he discussed the issues raised in the MTD with opposing counsel to attempt to resolve them. Rule 3.01 requires the moving party, the defendant, to consult with opposing counsel in good faith to resolve the issues raised by the motion. They did not resolve any of the problems.

His response was to thank me for my MTD response, but the goal was to succeed at the hearing. We need to evaluate their contentions, amend any areas where we might not prevail at the hearing, and then file a response outlining what we are likely to prevail on. Listing the administrator as a defendant is a prime example of an issue we will contest at the hearing. We should avoid another MTD because we plan to address the current one at the hearing, as it is ready to be heard.

When I asked for an interpretation of the 'is ripe' comment, he replied that it means it is ready because the opposing counsel has finally revealed all his cards regarding his legal objections to the Complaint. Now we can address it without worrying about another MTD following it. He again notes that some of the changes will require an amended complaint. He also said he would respond to the entire MTD, and the judge would receive a copy in advance to review at the hearing.

It is the defense's responsibility to schedule oral arguments with the court after an MTD is filed. According to my attorney, they have not filed to be added to the judge's Motion Calendar. There is no specific deadline for when the defense must request a scheduling. I responded that if there is no deadline for filing, what incentive does the defendant have to get on the calendar? He replied that if the defendant believes their MTD will succeed, that would be their motivation. The plaintiff's options are limited until the opposing counsel takes action.

I wrote a newspaper op-ed to bring this case out of the shadows of the justice system and into the public eye. Exposure might be the push the defendant needs to move the case forward. I drafted an op-ed for submission to the local newspaper, sharing my frustration with the public. I plan to write it to vent my feelings, but I will wait to review it with my attorney first.

I asked him if I was subject to any gag order that would prevent me from going public about the lawsuit. He replied that no gag order applied to me, but he advised against it because it could hurt future negotiations. I followed his advice for now.

COVID-19 emerged in March and could indefinitely delay the conclusion of the case. With the courts closed, the lawsuit has reached an uncertain standstill. Even when courts reopen and progress resumes, the defendant might slow down proceedings to a complete halt. As mentioned, since the plaintiff is eighty-seven years old and highly vulnerable to the virus, they might stall the case, hoping he might contract the virus and possibly die.

CHAPTER 25

3rd Amended Complaint

ON APRIL 6, my attorney submitted a 26-page MOTION TO AMEND THE COMPLAINT AND RESPONSE TO MOTION FOR MORE DEFINITE STATEMENT in reply to the defendant's February 26 MTD.

It states, "The motion is in response to the defendant's MTD by filing a Third Amended Complaint following the Fla. R. Civ. P. 1.190 and as good grounds states: Rule 1.190 of the Florida Rules of Civil Procedure provides that a party may amend a pleading with leave of court," and "Leave of court shall be given freely when justice so requires."

Plaintiff has made a sincere effort to engage with the Defendants through a mutually agreeable complaint, but the Defendants have not responded to the plaintiff's multiple requests. The Third Amended Complaint will address the Defendant's Motion for a More Definite Statement.

WHEREFORE, the plaintiff respectfully requests that this Honorable Court issue an order allowing the plaintiff to file the attached Complaint and any other relief the Court deems appropriate.

In the new Complaint, I see that my counsel still names the administrator as a defendant, and the statute is specific. Even though the defendant's counsel raises this issue in their MTD, my counsel continues to insist on naming the administrator as a co-defendant.

The amended Complaint is titled THIRD AMENDED COMPLAINT AND DEMAND FOR JURY TRIAL. It lists 11 items and ends with item 12, which states: Under Sections 768.28 and 400.0233, Florida Statutes, all conditions precedent to filing this action have been satisfied or fulfilled.

Item 13 is titled CERTIFICATE OF COUNSEL, which is the main statement of the Complaint and the lawsuit, and states: Under Florida Statutes, Section 400.0233, the undersigned attorney of record hereby certifies that he has conducted a reasonable investigation into the matters alleged herein and has determined that there are grounds for a good-faith belief that the care and treatment were negligent regarding Elizabeth, and that grounds exist for filing this action against the defendant.

The following general allegations apply to the defendants. They mirror the allegations in the Second Amended Complaint, with many item descriptions expanded and some significant changes. The first is item 19. Let me digress. As you may recall, one of the key acts of misconduct was HPCC's use of an embedded catheter, which ignored Medicare's CMS 20068 mandates regarding catheter use. Items 19 and 20 dispute the defendant's claim that the catheter was medically necessary.

Item 19 states that the urinary catheter is necessary for reasons other than employee convenience because HPCC included Elizabeth's plan of care, which indicated she was diagnosed with obstructive uropathy, a urinary blockage. However, item 20 contradicts this by stating, "Yet there is no mention in any of Elizabeth's other medical records showing a diagnosis of obstructive uropathy." HPCC is attempting to justify its procedures using false information.

Item 22, also new to this amendment, states: Due to the use of this urinary catheter, which was not intended to treat any medical condition but was simply for the convenience of agents and employees of HPCC, Elizabeth developed a series of urinary tract infections that required additional hospitalization because of antibiotic resistance.

Added item 23 states: In addition, while a resident of HPCC, on or about July 12th, 2017, Elizabeth was found on the floor next to her wheelchair, with HPCC agents and employees having allowed her to fall unnoticed, despite being aware that Elizabeth posed a significant fall risk. This item provides another example of HPCC's failure to provide the contracted care as outlined in HPCC's procedure manual.

Two other items addressed the dehydration episode she experienced.

When Plaintiff John asked if Elizabeth's dry condition might require ER admission, agents and employees of HPCC actively discouraged him from seeking emergency room care. Item 27 states: Despite eventually inserting an intravenous tube into Elizabeth to rehydrate her, her condition had worsened to the point that emergency room treatment for dehydration was necessary.

To illustrate the difference in professionalism between my new and old attorneys, I want to share an item description from each that covers the same subject.

Old description: According to Fla. Stat. 400.022, Elizabeth had the following rights: the defendants had a duty to ensure they did not violate them.

New description: According to Section 400.022 of the Florida
Statutes, the rules and regulations adopted and promulgated
under it, as specified in 400.022(1)(I), establish recognized
healthcare standards in the community. Elizabeth possessed
the following rights, and the defendants had a duty to ensure
they did not violate these rights.

The revised version broadens the descriptions of the rights listed
in the Second Amended Complaint.

The significant change from the Second Amended Complaint
is in Count III, titled "Negligence." It now appears in the Third
Amended Complaint as Count III, WRONGFUL DEATH:
The Defendants' negligence in ordering a catheter for nonexis-
tent obstructive uropathy—solely for the convenience of agents
and employees of the defendant—and the defendant's failure to
effectively prevent and treat the urinary tract infections caused by
this unnecessary catheterization directly and proximately led to
Elizabeth's death. Initially, my attorney identified a negligent act by
HPCC as the cause of Elizabeth's death.

On April 13, the MTD hearing was held via telephone conference due to COVID-19 restrictions that prevented in-person contact. The judge granted the defendant's MTD without prejudice (in
part) to address issues related to negligence and wrongful death.
The judge also granted with prejudice as to the administrator individually, and the court gave the plaintiff thirty days to amend the
Complaint.

However, even though the court has removed the administrator
from the complaint, my attorney insists on keeping him in. His
decision to do so sparked a series of emails that followed.

Question: Why is the administrator still listed as a co-defendant when agency employees are immune from being named defendants in a lawsuit?

Answer: Under the Sovereign Immunity Statute, he can be named as a defendant in a lawsuit in his official capacity. As noted in the minutes, this issue has been challenged. He can be named under Fla. Stat. 768.28(9)(a), which states, "The exclusive remedy for injury or damage suffered as a result of an act, event, or omission of an officer, employee, or agent of the state or any of its subdivisions or constitutional officers shall be action against the head of such entity in her or his official capacity..."

Question: The rest of that sentence states, "Unless such act or omission was committed in bad faith or with malicious purpose or in a manner showing wanton and willful disregard of human rights, safety, or property." It would take a broad interpretation to suggest that the administrator's actions or inactions meet those conditions. Since the administrator wouldn't be liable for damages, what is the benefit of naming him as a co-defendant?

Answer: The exception you mention permits the official to be sued in their official capacity if they act maliciously, since that exceeds their authority.

Question: How would you define malicious?

Answer: Malicious relates to malice, a mindset marked by intentionally doing a wrongful act without justification or excuse.

Humor me. A sovereign can only be sued in court for prospective injunctions to prevent further violations, and the administrator does not meet this requirement. Regarding malicious conduct, just last year, the court defined 'Malicious purpose' as conduct done with spite, ill will, and hate—an extremely high standard to satisfy. Why wouldn't a defense attorney use either of these objections in a Motion to Dismiss challenging the naming of the administrator?

Answer: Good question. I'm still trying to understand what the defense attorney is thinking. Drafting the changes requested by the judge will take little time, but I learned before the hearing that the defense attorney has some issues with the new Complaint. I've already prepared a response to anticipated problems. What will take time is coordinating with him. I want to move this case forward.

Question: I value working with you, mainly the open exchange of information. Please don't take it the wrong way when I play devil's advocate. I have a good relationship with my new counsel, but I need help convincing him to reconsider naming the administrator as a co-defendant.

Curious, I looked up the legal definition of a motion granted 'with and without prejudice.' A motion granted 'with prejudice' means it is permanently dismissed. In contrast, a motion dismissed 'without prejudice' allows the plaintiff to try again and address the issues the defendant identified in the MTD. The court permits the plaintiff to fix the defects and refile the Complaint on its merits.

The judge has also, with prejudice, dismissed the administrator as a co-defendant from the Complaint.

Let me update you on our current status in the lawsuit. The court must approve the Third Amendment before it can be issued. Additionally, a new complaint has been filed, with the administrator removed as a named defendant. The defendant will have ten days to respond and may file another MTD, which could revert us to the situation we had in June 2018.

My email exchange with my attorney regarding the inclusion of the administrator in the Complaint was pointless. The judge resolved that by saying, "Motion is granted 'with prejudice' as to the administrator individually." He removed the administrator from being named as a co-defendant in the lawsuit, which I had raised since my attorney filed the first complaint in April 2019.

A novice with a law degree obtained in 1968 should not be advising my attorney, who will receive 40% of any settlement. The Florida Sovereign Immunity Statutes make an officer of a sovereign immunity agency immune from being named as a defendant in a lawsuit. It took a judge to tell my attorney the same facts I had been explaining for over a year. The episode that frustrates me is that we had just spent days exchanging emails where I told him the administrator is immune.

He kept telling me how he would find exceptions, allowing him to include the issue in a new complaint, even though he knew the judge had made it moot. We are now back to where we were in April 2019. My attorney has 30 days to file a new Amended Complaint, and the defendant will have 20 days to respond. Think of all the unnecessary motions and amendments filed over the naming of the administrator as a defendant. After re-reading, I sent the following email to my attorney.

Reading the minutes of the April 13 hearing prompted me to look up the legal meaning of 'with and without prejudice.' Based on those interpretations, our email chain over the past week has been pointless. Correct me if I am wrong, but I see the statement 'Motion granted with prejudice' as meaning the administrator has been permanently removed from the Complaint as a co-defendant.

You already knew this, so why did we spend last week trying to figure out how to include him in the suit? I told LGF in 2019 that the administrator didn't meet the criteria to be named a defendant in the lawsuit and should be removed. It took a judge to confirm the same facts I had been sharing with you for over a year. I am still waiting for a response to my email.

The judge issued the following order on April 17 in response to the meeting held on April 13. This matter came before the court on April 13, 2020, for a hearing on Defendant's Motion to Dismiss, Motion to Strike, and Motion for a More Definite Statement. The court, fully advised on the matter, orders as follows:

The Defendant's Motion to Dismiss Counts I, II, and III of the Plaintiff's Second Amended Complaint is hereby granted without prejudice. Paragraphs 41, 42, 44–49, and 51 are now stricken; the defendant (the administrator's name) is dismissed as a party with prejudice. The plaintiff has thirty (30) days from the date of this order to file a Third Amended Complaint.

On April 28, my attorney filed a 26-page THIRD AMENDED COMPLAINT with the court, updating the Complaint submitted on April 9. The Complaint was sent for review, but has not yet been formally filed for action. This new Complaint is only 12 pages long compared to the previous 26, and it removes the administrator from the suit.

The most significant and professionally described change is in the section titled GENERAL ALLEGATIONS APPLICABLE TO DEFENDANTS, which lists 27 allegations of malicious conduct. Removing the administrator has shortened the Complaint by four pages.

The following change appears in the section titled COUNT I, DEPRIVATION OR INFRINGEMENT OF RESIDENT'S RIGHTS.

Item 34 of this section states: "The acts and omissions of the Defendant which deprived Elizabeth of her resident rights include, but are not limited to." The revision from April 9 listed 24 acts and omissions. The newly amended Complaint has reduced this number to 7 by focusing only on the most relevant acts, thereby minimizing the defendant's attorney's nitpicking and trimming five pages from the Amended Complaint. You wonder how my new attorney can present the same facts in 5 fewer pages. It again makes me believe that my previous attorneys operated under the theory that quantity, namely the number of pages, equals quality.

The section COUNT II NEGLIGENCE now states BREACH OF STANDARD CARE. The paragraphs the judge ordered to be removed have been eliminated, reducing the Complaint by six pages. The section still addresses the same breach of standard care but is more concise.

The new Complaint, titled COUNT III: NEGLIGENT HIRING, added a section. The first four items in this section describe the defendants' duty to hire, train, and supervise employees to ensure they provide care and services to residents safely and effectively. Item 47 states that the defendants breached their duties to Elizabeth by failing to hire, train, and supervise employees properly, thereby preventing them from delivering the services outlined above.

The count summarized item 48 as: "As a direct and proximate cause of the Defendant's acts and omissions in breaching their duties, Elizabeth suffered bodily injury and resulting pain and suffering, disability, disfigurement, mental anguish, loss of capacity for the enjoyment of life, expense of hospitalization, medical and nursing care, and treatment, and aggravation of a previously existing condition," a standard sentence included in every medical malpractice suit with only the name of the plaintiff changed.

The final section is COUNT IV - WRONGFUL DEATH. It again reviews the acts and omissions of the defendant. It concludes with the statement: "WHEREFORE, the plaintiff, as personal representative of the estate of Elizabeth, demands all damages to which he is entitled under the Florida Wrongful Death Act, including loss of future support, income, companionship, care, comfort, society, and mental pain and suffering from the date of injury to Elizabeth and into the future, with costs against Defendant HPCC, and a trial by jury."

On May 5, the defendant submitted a 9-page response to the Third Amended Complaint. In summary, they agreed that Elizabeth was a resident of HPCC. HPCC was legally required to provide her with nursing home residents' rights under FS 400.022. However, the defendant denied all other claims made in the 12-page amended Complaint. They listed each allegation number and rejected them individually. The defendant did not admit responsibility for any of the 54 allegations.

Furthermore, the defendant added three pages to the ANSWER TO PLAINTIFF'S THIRD AMENDED COMPLAINT, including what they call SEVENTEEN AFFIRMATIVE DEFENSES. I won't list all seventeen defenses, but understanding the complexity and legal jargon of this document requires reading it. I have only responded to the defenses that are relevant to the case. The defense will list every possible reason they can think of, knowing many might not be used, but it's better to list them all now than to need them later and find they were omitted.

Defendants have explicitly responded to each paragraph of the Third Amended Complaint, now asserting various affirmative defenses.

THIRD AFFIRMATIVE DEFENSE: The defendants contend that the incident or damages claimed by the plaintiffs were caused by the condition and independent intervening acts beyond the defendants' control. Therefore, the plaintiffs are precluded from recovering damages.

I find it hard to understand how the defense can claim this as a valid argument. The reason is that arguing the insertion of an indwelling catheter, which clearly violates Medicare mandates, and the nursing staff's failure to insert an intravenous feeding line were beyond the defendant's control. If not, then who was responsible?

FOURTH AFFIRMATIVE DEFENSE: Defendants are entitled to the protections and provisions outlined in Florida Statutes 766.102, 766.104, 768.13, 768.28, 768.76, and 768.78.

This defense required me to research all the referenced statutes online and find a relevant one that might apply.

766.102 "Medical negligence, standards of recovery; expert witness." It states: (1) In any action to recover damages for death or personal injury, where it is claimed that such death or injury resulted from the negligence of a healthcare provider, the claimant must prove by a preponderance of the evidence that the healthcare provider's action breached the prevailing professional standard of care.

The general professional standard of care for a healthcare provider is the level of care, skill, and treatment that, considering all relevant circumstances, is recognized as acceptable and appropriate by reasonably prudent healthcare providers in similar situations. Failing to follow Medicare mandates regarding the use of a catheter constitutes a breach of the prevailing professional standard of care, which constitutes medical negligence.

FOURTEENTH AFFIRMATIVE DEFENSE: That any injury the plaintiff may have suffered was solely due to the natural, unavoidable process of human disease and the known risks linked to medical treatment. I included this to demonstrate how far the defendant will go to deny responsibility.

FIFTEENTH AFFIRMATIVE DEFENSE: The medical intervention was performed with the patient's informed consent, in accordance with Fla. Stat. 766.103.

766.103 Florida Medical Consent Law states that "Obtaining the patient's consent or another person authorized to permit the patient" follows an acceptable standard of medical practice. The person giving consent would generally understand the procedure, the medically acceptable alternative methods or treatments, and the inherent risks and hazards involved in the proposed treatment or process. Written approval meets the requirements; the plaintiff did not provide any such consent.

I have summarized some of the 99 documents submitted to the court to facilitate the progression of the lawsuit through the legal process. As you will see, it is not straightforward, and it's like traveling from Boston to New York via Chicago, to use an analogy. The frustrating part of this lawsuit is that all this documentation is required to bring a case to trial when both the defendant and plaintiff's attorneys know the case will never actually go before a courtroom.

The case could have been resolved more quickly if the two parties had pursued mediation and reached a mutually agreed-upon agreement. Some aspects of this lawsuit delay a quick resolution.

The defendant, who has substantial financial resources, has hired outside counsel to handle the case at an estimated rate of $50 to $250 per billable hour. Settling this case without the defense passing through Chicago would undermine the lucrative opportunity for the defendant's counsel. Additionally, the trip through Chicago requires the plaintiff's attorney, who is paid a 40% contingency fee of the settlement, to travel the same route.

This journey also prompts the plaintiff's counsel to reconsider pursuing a lawsuit against the doctrine of sovereign immunity. The plaintiff's counsel may spend the same amount of time on a two-hundred-million-dollar case with a 40% fee as on a two-hundred-thousand-dollar lawsuit with a 40% contingency fee. So, why should the defense counsel settle a case in three months when they can take three years to achieve the same results?

After months of complaints, amended complaints, second complaints, motions to dismiss, and numerous other documents, my attorney finally submitted the third amended complaint to the court.

CHAPTER 26

Discovery

THE LEGAL DEFINITION of 'discovery' is a procedural tool used by a party in a civil case before trial, which requires the opposing party to provide information essential for preparing the requesting party's case that the other party possesses.

The term 'civil law' mainly involves one party failing to act or avoiding action that causes harm to another person. In civil lawsuits, the plaintiff has the burden of proof, known as "preponderance of the evidence," which refers to the strength of the evidence, not its quantity.

A plaintiff does not need to prove a wrongful death civil case beyond a reasonable doubt; they must persuade a judge that the nursing home's misconduct caused the plaintiff's death. Civil damages, such as those awarded in this case, are monetary compensation provided when a person experiences a loss due to another party's wrongful or negligent actions.

Although the defendant has denied all the allegations made in the Third Amended Complaint as detailed above, they have now issued a NOTICE OF SERVING INTERROGATORIES, stating: The defendant propounds interrogatories to the plaintiff, to be responded to within the time and manner prescribed by Florida Rules of Civil Procedure. Attached to this are DEFENDANT'S INTERROGATORIES TO PLAINTIFF. The questions in this section are directed to me to answer.

Interrogatories are written questions sent by the defendant that the plaintiff must answer. The defendant can submit up to 25 questions, each requiring a detailed response of at least one sentence. The law states that both the plaintiff and defendant should exchange information about the facts of the underlying incident, the plaintiff's allegations, and the defendant's responses.

I recognize that discovery is part of the legal system, but I question whether it is just another process that delays settling a case. Support for this idea is shown in some of the 15 questions the defense asks me to answer. I doubt the relevance of these questions to the defendant's counsel, knowing that answering them would require weeks of research. Most of these questions have already been answered in my interrogatories.

Q: Provide a detailed account, including inclusive dates, of each injury and illness the decedent experienced over the past ten (10) years before their death.

Q: The name and address of each physician consulted by the decedent regarding their health, including the purpose of each consultation.

Q: What are the names and addresses of each hospital where the decedent was a patient before their death, including the specific dates of hospitalization?

Q: Itemize all medical and hospital expenses incurred or paid because of the death of your decedent, including the date each fee was incurred, the name and address of the person or entity to whom each payment was made or from whom the costs were incurred, and the dates of all fees.

The last four questions on the interrogatories were the relevant ones.

Q: If you claim that your decedent experienced conscious physical pain or mental anguish, please provide the following details: the exact time on the day of the accident when it occurred; the same time afterward when they died; the specific period during which they were consciously alive after the accident; and the actual duration between the time of the accident and their death during which they suffered conscious physical pain and mental anguish.

A: The events leading to Elizabeth's death began shortly after her admission to HPCC on May 18, 2017, and continued to worsen until she left HPCC on July 29, 2017. Due to medical misconduct at HPCC, she kept suffering from severe urinary tract infections, many of which resulted in trips to the emergency room and hospital stays. She experienced increasingly painful and severe urinary tract infections along with depression from May 18, 2017, until her death on July 8, 2019, in hospice, caused by kidney failure due to prolonged urinary tract infections.

Q: List the name and address of each person known or believed by you, your attorney, or other representatives to be an eyewitness to the event described in the Complaint, and specify their location at that time; also include those who are not eyewitnesses but may know the facts underlying the allegations of negligence.

A: The witnesses to the wrongdoing were the plaintiff and the defendant's agents and employees. They were aware of it, but lacked the necessary staff experience to address the visible decline in Elizabeth's condition. The most detailed witness is the plaintiff, who observed all the acts of omission described.

Q: Describe each act or failure to act by the defendant that you believe was negligent and contributed to the legal cause of the incident.

A: The case involves both acts of omission and acts of commission. HPCC, a Medicare facility that is directly violating Medicare mandates, inserted a urinary catheter without any known medical necessity, fully aware that it would cause Elizabeth to suffer a lifetime of urinary tract infections. Regarding an act or omission, the facility admitting Elizabeth, who was severely dehydrated, did not have a staff nurse capable of inserting an intravenous line.

As stated, the defendant and the plaintiff may ask each other questions using interrogatories. Based on that right, my attorney filed a PLAINTIFF'S NOTICE OF SERVING THE FIRST SET OF NURSING HOME INTERROGATORIES with the court and the defendant for a response.

On May 20, I had a 75-minute phone call with my attorney, which was informative and helpful for both of us to talk and get to know each other. My primary concern was that I wasn't notified when the defendant answered the Third Amended Complaint, and I only found out about the defendant's response by checking the court records myself.

I told him that the Third Amended Complaint was a well-prepared, professional document that clearly summarized our allegations, reducing the Complaint from 26 to 12 pages. I was especially upset about not knowing the defendant's affirmative defenses. He told me that the dismissal of all allegations in the Complaint was expected and that the listed affirmative defenses are included in every defendant's answer. He also said he would send me future copies of the court-submitted document.

We then discussed the affirmative defenses. After reviewing the statutes the defense referenced, I questioned why he included some of them. He explained they had no intention of using all of them, but the defense wanted a variety of referred-to statutes so he could choose from them, not necessarily use all of them.

Here's what I learned. I believed that a nursing home covered by sovereign immunity couldn't be held liable in court, but damages might be awarded through arbitration. Let me review the events leading up to the pre-suit mediation. After the unsuccessful conciliation in March 2019, I asked Attorney Number Two if the next step was to go to trial. He informed me that the nursing home contract stipulated that all disputes with the nursing home would be resolved through arbitration.

Based on the information he provided, I prepared the detailed arbitration presentation I had previously outlined. When I told my current attorney that, in my understanding, the nursing home had to go to arbitration instead of trial—per the attorney's advice—he assured me that my belief was incorrect. He said HPCC could go to trial but would avoid it because of the negative publicity it might cause. Now I understand why Attorney Number Two never responded to my emails asking when he would initiate arbitration. A review of the nursing home contract revealed no such arbitration agreement.

The contract states, "The parties expressly consent to and agree to the venue for any legal action as being solely the Twentieth Judicial Circuit, regardless of any laws affecting venue." After my conference, I am confident, as I mentioned before, that my two previous attorneys were not qualified to handle a case involving sovereign immunity. The firm took the case with the idea that they could learn as they went. My current counsel, who has been with the firm only a short time, was assigned my case based on their experience with similar issues. My research on arbitration, especially my presentation, will remain valuable for a jury trial.

After our discussion, the conference went well, and I now have a higher opinion of my counsel's ability. He has agreed to keep me updated as the case progresses, and I can schedule a conference call whenever I need to speak with him. I told him I have a law degree and might ask him questions that 99% of his clients would not ask, so please humor me when I do.

Should you tell your attorney that you also have a law degree? It's like telling your doctor you have a WebMD degree and plan to ask him medical questions from the internet. Overall, the conference clarified things, and I trust my attorney's ability to handle this case.

The defendant has had their opportunity to answer their interrogatories; now it's our turn. My attorney has submitted a document titled PLAINTIFF'S FIRST REQUEST TO PRODUCE TO DEFENDANT to the court and the defendant. A request for the production of documents, which is part of the discovery process, is a request made by a party in civil litigation asking the opposing party to submit certain documents, in this case, to the plaintiff for inspection. The 'discovery' rules determine what evidence the plaintiff can examine.

Any non-privileged matter relevant to either party's claim or defense can be discovered through a request to produce documents. The party receiving the request may approve or deny the inspection of the identified records. A request for production helps each party gather and organize its evidence for trial. During discovery, anything not protected by privilege related to the case is generally discoverable. A request to produce documents will specifically identify the records requested. The document reads:

Under Rule 1.350 of the Florida Rules of Civil Procedure, the request requires the Defendants to produce or duplicate documents for inspection. The section titled 'Definitions' clarifies the term 'documents' through a three-paragraph explanation of what the plaintiff considers to be documents, followed by legal language, before reaching the central part of the request. The defendant has 45 days to respond to the production request.

The defendant shall produce the items and matters listed below. This section includes 65 detailed questions or document requests, such as facility policies. All 65 requests are valid; however, it may take the defendant up to 45 days to provide the requested information. I will not list the items in the 12-page document but will wait for the defendant's response.

My attorney filed a document with the court titled PLAINTIFF'S NOTICE OF SERVING FIRST SET OF NURSING HOME INTERROGATORIES. The document responded to the defendant's service of the earlier detailed interrogatories that I had submitted.

Here, the plaintiff has submitted 22 questions to the defendant, which the nursing home and administrator are required to answer within 30 days of receipt. The questions were more detailed, asking for specific responses that would give the plaintiff a clear understanding of the HPCC's defense. Two relevant questions were:

Do you claim that any healthcare provider, including but not limited to physicians treating the plaintiff, failed to meet an accepted standard of care in their treatment?

Do you assert that any physician who treated the plaintiff while they were a patient at HPCC issued an inappropriate, incorrect, or substandard order for medication or other treatment?

You can see why it's so hard to find an attorney willing to take on a sovereign immunity case, given the contingency fee cap. So far, the plaintiff's and defendant's attorneys have submitted 53 documents to the court totaling 271 pages, and the case might settle months or even years from now.

For each paper the defense submits, the plaintiff's attorney must prepare a response for a hypothetical trial, showing why lawsuits often take a long time and why courts become crowded. The defense's delaying tactics discourage attorneys from pursuing cases involving sovereign immunity.

The defendant's actions make clear that this case is far from over.

The defendant's interrogatories requested the names of all doctors Beth had seen in the past five years, and I listed six. Defense counsel then issued each of them a SUBPOENA DUCES TECUM WITHOUT DEPOSITION. YOU ARE now ORDERED to appear at the defendant's law offices during regular business hours within 15 days of service of this subpoena, and to bring the following concerning Elizabeth with you at that time and place.

A COMPLETE COPY OF YOUR FILE OR CHART, including but not limited to office notes, written reports, consultation notes or reports, telephone messages, correspondence, signed informed consent forms, sign-in sheets, and patient information forms.

All x-ray films, images, scans, diagnostic studies, and their reports for the patient named above are in your possession and control.

Copies of all documents related to MEDICAL BILLS for expenses incurred and payments received for services provided to the patient named above, including but not limited to itemized statements, office ledger cards, spreadsheet printouts, invoices, bills, claim forms, paid receipts, and bank deposit slips.

This subpoena requires you to provide copies of your entire file, even if you believe some documents are irrelevant or unimportant. If you do not: (a) appear as directed; (b) submit the records instead of appearing as required; or (c) object to this subpoena, you may be held in contempt of court. You are subpoenaed by the attorney listed on this subpoena. Unless excused by the attorney or the court, you must respond as instructed.

How would you, as a doctor, feel about receiving a subpoena for a patient's medical records when you haven't seen them in years? It needs to be clarified how the requested information relates to the lawsuit. However, the attorney requesting these records is on retainer with LMHS, and reviewing them becomes billable hours.

On June 30, the defendant submitted their response to the Plaintiff's Request to Produce—a request for the opposing party to provide documents for review. The plaintiff provided the defendant with a list of 65 papers.

The defendant willingly provided requests for policies, proce-dures, mission statements, and other documents because they were publicly accessible. However, when asked for records of significance related to the case, their response was "Object to the question as being overbroad, vague, ambiguous, immaterial, irrelevant and not calculated to lead to the discovery of admissible evidence," which was attached to 26 of the 65 documents.

A request for the production of documents is a stage in the litigation process where each party gathers and organizes its evidence in preparation for trial. The burden is on the defendant to provide copies of all requested documents or to refuse to do so based on privilege.

The receiving party may allow or refuse the requesting party the right to examine the specified records. If they have that right, why would they provide documents that could be incriminating? This Request to Produce added 19 pages to the court record but offered only limited useful information.

Some examples of documents the defendant considered irrelevant, and my explanation of why the plaintiff thought they were relevant.

Requested document:

Written staff education plans were in place during the plaintiff's residence. The reason for this request is that the document is relevant to determining whether the staff were aware of federal Medicare operating mandates and trained to provide medical assistance when needed. Is the nursing staff periodically reviewed to ensure they can perform intravenous insertions and are familiar with the Medicare directive CMS 20068?

Document requested:

All resident family council minutes or documents that record the council's discussions, plans, or decisions during the plaintiff's residency. Reason for request: This document is relevant because these minutes would show whether HPCC notified the plaintiff or her representative of the health risks associated with an embedded catheter.

Document requested:

> All reports or written summaries of data regarding the resident's status or condition. Reason for request: Condition status reports are essential because they would show if the plaintiff exhibited signs of severe dehydration that ultimately led to her being hospitalized in a non-responsive state.

Document requests:

> According to Florida Statutes, copies of all reports must include staff-to-resident ratios and compliance records related to staffing requirements. Reason for request: This information is essential because the staff-to-resident ratio in May 2017 was low, which led to the decision to insert a catheter to reduce the workload on an understaffed aide population, thereby preventing aides from needing to assist residents with toileting.

Once again, what value does a request for documents hold if both the defendant and the plaintiff can decide that the requested records are irrelevant?

On June 30, the defendant responded to the 22 interrogatory questions sent by the plaintiff on May 13. The simpler questions, such as names of officers or other publicly available information, were answered. However, the key questions were not answered, including an example of a specific question and the response provided to 15 of the 22 questions.

Question: Do you claim that any healthcare provider, including but not limited to physicians who treated the plaintiff, failed to meet accepted standards of care in their treatment? Answer: Currently unknown, and discovery is ongoing.

Consider this answer: The defendant was served with an NOI in April 2018, and as of June 2020, they are still in the discovery phase to determine if any medical provider's care was below the accepted standard. Once again, if the defendant can choose to answer only irrelevant questions for the plaintiff, the discovery process becomes pointless.

As part of the discovery process, I was deposed by the defendant's attorney for two hours via Zoom in May.

The deposition wasn't meant to gather information, as the defense's question asked, "Give me the names of some of the people you play golf with." The real goal was to see what kind of witness I would be if the case went to trial. Depositions are costly, covering expenses for a recorder and transcripts. Did the defense attorney succeed in his aim by deposing me?

Let me shift gears here. I started watching a Netflix series about Lenox Hill Hospital in New York. The series captures all aspects of life in a busy hospital. What stood out to me was the delicate surgeries performed in the operating room, along with the careful attention from the doctors and nurses.

Seeing this, Beth immediately came to mind. She loved working as an operating room nurse—a role not often afforded to nurses due to the specialized skills required to work smoothly with surgeons and anticipate their needs. Beth valued this responsibility highly and was one of the few nurses in the hospital whom surgeons specifically requested to help in the operating room.

The series also covered childbirth, including some difficult deliveries, and reminded me of my son's tough birth. A child she struggled to have for eighteen years, suffering three miscarriages, not knowing if the baby she just delivered would survive.

Everything turned out well, and we had a healthy, bright child. She was devoted to him and served as his primary caregiver, reading children's books to him from a young age, helping with his homework, supporting him through his challenges, and being the unseen force behind his current success. He learned baseball and golf from me, but his knowledge of the game came from his mother.

Seeing husbands and wives sitting with a sick or recovering spouse brought back many days I spent by her bedside in the hospital. Her constant pain and the feeling of needing to pee all the time with no urine to pass were heartbreaking.

Only a woman who has gone through this can understand the pain of a urinary tract infection. It's a condition she might face once or twice in her life, so only she can imagine what it's like to have twenty-five UTIs in two years.

The series depicted the doctor speaking with the patient's parents or spouses and providing updates on the patient's condition. During her last hospital visit, I never had a doctor sit down with me and say that the end was near. Nurses were the ones who kept me informed, along with my ability to see and interpret her lab results. I looked at her GFR, which shows her kidney function is declining to stage five kidney failure, and I realized she was dying.

A hospice representative agreed with my diagnosis and decided she was a good candidate to be moved to the hospice house, the same hospice where she had volunteered for years. She sat with dying patients to give their caregivers some free time. I then became the sitter. It would have been helpful to have a doctor confirm or agree with my assessment of her dying, but the outcome would have been the same regardless of who made the decision.

CHAPTER 27

Request to Produce

MY ATTORNEY SENT me 270 pages of the defendant's request to Produce, which included 260 pages of trivial information, such as organizational charts, mission statements, licenses, and surveys.

There was a key piece of information—the Census Reports. The Census Daily Detail shows the highest facility occupancy as 107 residents and the highest Medicare bed occupancy as 49 residents. On the day Beth was rushed to the hospital, July 29th, the facility had a total population of 96 residents, which was 90% of its maximum capacity. Only 34 of the 38 Medicare beds were occupied by residents, representing an 89% occupancy rate.

HPCC's statement on August 2 that Beth couldn't return to the facility due to no available beds was false. HPCC did not want Beth back because she required too much care and attention.

The records also showed that the facility billed Medicare $9,725 for 60 days of questionable physical and occupational therapy. I understand why HPCC wanted her out of the facility so they could admit a paying therapy resident.

The 270 pages revealed nothing new but increased the hourly rate the opposing counsel could bill the defendant and postponed the lawsuit by another month. I started an email chain with my attorney.

The latest interrogatories reveal nothing. What does their response to our questions about the standard of care, being 'discovery is ongoing,' actually mean? Does the defendant suspect that a healthcare provider may have fallen below the accepted standard of care? You would think that the three years the defendant had to know about our intention to sue would have been enough time to complete discovery.

Discovery has been pointless because neither party is willing to reveal anything the other doesn't already know. Since discovery hasn't found any material issues, why not move for 'summary judgment' or a 'jury trial'?

He responds: Defense attorneys often object to our requests and can force us to fight for the records. Before proceeding with depositions and challenging the records, I would like to engage a nursing home expert to review the pre-suit documents and our own discovery. This will add value to the case and help guide how we request information and whom we depose.

My response: We have strong documentation to support our case, and I don't believe an expert can significantly strengthen our position. Our primary document is CMS 20068. The dehydration issue is a solid backup, but HPCC cannot contest the charge that, as a federal Medicare facility obligated to follow the Medicare guidelines outlined in CMS 20068, it knowingly disregarded that mandate. Further discovery should focus on just one question.

Were the facilities management, doctors, and nursing staff familiar with CMS 20068, and did they knowingly ignore the catheter mandates?

Attorney's answer: To succeed or go to trial in a nursing home case, we will need an expert. I am happy to answer your questions and keep you involved and informed as much as you want, but we will not follow your instructions on how to handle the litigation or case strategy. A phone conference might be appropriate to discuss the matter further and involve an expert.

In the scheduled June 17 conference call, I will object to bringing in a nursing home expert. We have CMS20068, the smoking gun, and records showing the defendant violated that Medicare mandate, which contributed to the Plaintiff's death. LGF has managed this case for three years, so why are you now calling in an expert?

The defendant's nursing home violated another federal standard in its research. The Omnibus Budget Reconciliation Act (OBRA), also known as the Nursing Home Reform Act of 1987, sets national standards for the care of nursing home residents. One of the improvements in the act is to reduce the inappropriate use of indwelling urinary catheters.

Nursing homes are required to follow federal rules to participate in Medicare programs. They must also meet the OBRA quality of care standards when caring for residents to ensure they provide the level of care and skill residents expect.

Nursing care requirements under OBRA include showing proper respect to individuals with urinary problems, including the use of urinary catheters only when appropriate, as outlined in the regulations to prevent adverse consequences related to such use. These regulations further support my argument that we already have the 'smoking gun'—the Medicare and OBRA regulations—and HPCC has violated both.

These regulation violations are described as 'negligence per se,' meaning an illegal act that is 'in itself' or inherently unlawful. The action is considered serious and does not require additional proof of criminal intent. In a civil case, proving someone guilty of an illegal act 'per se' only involves showing that HPCC violated a statute and that violation caused the Plaintiff's damages. HPCC has no defense because records show they broke both regulations.

OBRA also states, "Provide each resident with sufficient fluid intake to prevent dehydration." Rushing the plaintiff to the emergency room in a non-responsive state due to dehydration was another allegation in our case. Dehydration risk factors include coma, altered mental status, tachycardia, lethargy, lightheadedness, reduced skin turgor, and abnormal lab values.

Plaintiff exhibited all of these symptoms. Severe dehydration can cause orthostatic hypotension, which can lead to shock. If rehydration is not quickly achieved, it can result in painful conditions such as renal failure, heart attack, and stroke. HPCC breached the contract by allowing the Plaintiff to become so dehydrated that she had to be rushed to the hospital. By taking on a resident's care, HPCC implicitly warrants that it has the necessary skills to treat the resident and will exercise ordinary skill and care.

Nursing homes must deliver adequate and proper quality care, which involves doing the right thing at the right time and in the right way for the right person. The facility failed to respond promptly to a medical emergency and did not exercise the standard care and skill expected. The consensus of all medical opinions is that there is no excuse for dehydration.

The main goal of our June 17 call was for him to justify why a nursing home expert is needed. I told him that HPCC's violation of Medicare and OBRA rules on catheters and dehydration should already support our case. That is a simple case brief for a novice, but not for the Court.

Although HPCC's medical records suggest they violated both statutes, we cannot make that claim. A medically trained expert must provide the statement. My attorney needs to prepare the case, assuming it will go to a jury trial, so an expert is essential. I agreed to the $1,500 expense.

CHAPTER 28

Medicare Complaint

INDEPENDENT OF THE lawsuit, I needed to find a way to get HPCC sanctioned by Medicare for its misconduct. My solution was to file a formal complaint with Medicare. After many phone calls, I was connected to the organization contracted with Medicare to review all written complaints from beneficiaries about the quality of services that do not meet professionally recognized healthcare standards.

However, I encountered one issue: a three-year statute of limitations for filing a Medicare 'Quality of Care Complaint.' Since HPCC performed the unauthorized use of an embedded catheter in May 2017, it falls outside this three-year window. However, because I am filing this complaint on July 17, 2020, I consider July 29, 2017, the date my wife was hospitalized in a dehydrated state, as the start date, which places me within the three-year limit.

On July 17, I submitted three formal Quality of Care Complaints to K, the vendor contracted by Medicare, to investigate these issues—the first involved misconduct related to dehydration at the nursing home. The second concerned the catheter embedding, which remained in place for 52 days at the time of transfer from HPCC to the hospital on July 29. Medicare mandates that embedded catheters be removed as soon as possible to prevent future urinary tract infections. Its 52-day retention does not comply with Medicare's requirement for prompt removal.

I did not file a complaint about the nursing home eviction because this does not qualify as a quality-of-care issue.

I chose the Medicare complaint route because, like what's happening now, a lawsuit to hold the nursing home accountable for medical malpractice can take years to resolve. A Medicare complaint is expected to take up to 60 days, and I hope the Medicare report will support my claim of medical malpractice by HPCC. The following are the formal complaints filed with K.

Charge: Elizabeth was rushed by ambulance from HPCC to the hospital emergency room on July 29th, 2017, in a non-responsive state. She was severely dehydrated and suffering from a urinary tract infection and pneumonia. The emergency room doctor started aggressive intravenous rehydration, eventually restoring her to a responsive state. She had been non-responsive for two hours.

For background information, I sent K the same dehydration scenario I prepared for arbitration, as described in Chapter 15. The events leading up to the dehydration and the outcomes have been detailed through this story and do not need to be repeated.

Claim: HPCC did not follow standard operating procedures to prevent resident dehydration, failed to respond to the res-

ident's representative that she was dehydrated, and when they finally acknowledged she was severely dehydrated and needed an IV procedure, there was no nurse on staff qualified to insert an IV.

Charge: On July 29th, 2017, Elizabeth was rushed to the hospital in a non-responsive, dehydrated state from HPCC with an embedded urinary catheter. Despite CMS 20068, the catheter should not still have been embedded. Medicare states that a catheter is only implanted if the resident's clinical condition warrants it.

Once again, I described the charge using the description I prepared for arbitration in Chapter 15.

Although the catheter was inserted before the three-year statute, it was still embedded on July 29th, within the three-year limit, violating Medicare guidelines. HPCC should have removed it before her departure.

To justify the use of the urinary catheter for reasons other than the convenience of agents and employees, HPCC documented in Elizabeth's care plan that she had been diagnosed with obstructive uropathy, a urinary blockage. However, there is no record in Elizabeth's other medical files indicating that she was ever diagnosed with obstructive uropathy.

Over a span of more than two years, Elizabeth experienced 25 UTIs, with 12 of those requiring hospitalization. Eventually, the infections worsened to the point where they caused her kidney failure, which led to her untimely death on July 8th, 2019.

Claim: HPCC violated Medicare guidelines by transferring Elizabeth to the hospital on July 29, 2017, with a cathe-

ter that should have been removed and by providing false medical information to justify that the catheter was still in place. One of OBRA's regulations aims to reduce the inappropriate use of indwelling urinary catheters. Nursing homes must follow federal requirements to participate in Medicare programs.

The failure of a nursing home to comply with OBRA quality of care mandates, particularly in this case, the failure to remove an improperly inserted catheter when transferring a resident from the facility, constitutes a failure to exercise the reasonable care and skill a resident should expect. I argue that the July 29th, 2017, failure to remove the catheter falls within the three-year statute of limitations, and that the violation should be reviewed by K.

A call to the organization I contacted informed me that the complaint was entered into the system on July 22nd, and a review, which will take at least sixty days, has begun. I argued that the facts I provided to K met the criteria to file a 'Quality of Care Complaint,' and I believed they would agree with my findings after K's investigation.

At this point, my attorney provided me with the expert's name—a doctor specializing in internal medicine who 'will officially author any opinions.' Still unsure about the necessity of a nursing home expert, I decided to act as a lawyer once again. I believe this is a cause-and-effect lawsuit. We identify the 'cause'—embedding a catheter in violation of Medicare guidelines, as documented in Elizabeth's health records—so why do we need a $1500 opinion from a nursing home expert to confirm what we already know?

If an expert is needed, shouldn't it be a urologist who can explain the 'effect' of embedding a catheter and leaving it in for an extended period? Only a urologist can detail the resulting urinary tract infections, kidney failure caused by ongoing UTIs, and the ultimate death due to kidney failure. I do not believe an internal medicine doctor can make this same diagnosis. My attorney told me that the case was still a 'nursing home complaint,' not a 'wrongful death suit.' Therefore, a nursing home medical expert would prepare a statement; a urologist doesn't need to schedule one.

On August 14, I emailed him to ask whether he had received the expected opinion from the nursing home expert doctor and, if not, to wait before requesting it. I told him I was expecting a Medicare report that would support our case and be much more valuable than an opinion from a nursing home expert. I was confident K would suggest Medicare sanctions.

CHAPTER 29

Case Update

To PURSUE THIS lawsuit, LMHS has hired an outside attorney. Since LMHS is a public health care system, they are paying outside counsel tens of thousands of dollars of my money to fight against me. Therefore, I should know how much has been paid to this attorney. On August 3rd, I sent a Freedom of Information Act request to their Compliance Department asking for an accounting of all compensation paid to the outside counsel so far.

On August 14, I received a response. LMHS stated that the documents I requested are exempt because they are part of ongoing litigation. Focusing on the 'exempt at this time' notation, I will submit a new FOIA request, asking the same questions after the pending litigation.

In March, I prepared an article for the newspaper, but my attorney advised me not to publish it because it could jeopardize the case. It's clear that not publishing it didn't help the case either.

The public needs to understand the challenges of filing a wrongful death lawsuit against a 'deep pockets' defendant. On September

22, I submitted a 600-word op-ed to the newspaper about the Florida Sovereign Immunity Statutes. Although it wasn't published, I plan to try again after the case is over. The op-ed will be published later in this story.

On September 11, I received an email from my attorney: "I wanted to update you that I have received the full verbal report from our nursing home expert and expect to get a written report soon. It was much more than I expected, and he uncovered some things we hadn't considered. Once I receive the report, I plan to list the expert and use the opinion, which requires an email from me."

Me: Haven't we just added a knife to a smoking gun we already have in this fight?

Him: I believe we now have someone qualified under the evidence code to testify that the gun went off and who pulled the trigger. He also identified several issues that we had not previously considered, which HPCC could have addressed to prevent the incident from happening.

Me: Who sets the order setting the case for trial?

Him: The judge generally issues a standard order when scheduling a case for trial. Either side can request a trial date once they believe the necessary discovery has been sufficiently completed for the judge to grant a trial. The judge will review the docket and consider objections and arguments against setting the trial. The judge can approve or deny the request to schedule a trial. Typically, the judge will order the case to proceed to mediation or non-binding arbitration before trial. We need more information to request a trial date from the Court.

I received the expert's opinion, and it was just as I expected—confirming what we already knew. The points he added did nothing to strengthen an already documented case. His report states, 'I have reviewed the records provided to me regarding Elizabeth.' The care at the nursing home was negligent in keeping the indwelling catheter in despite recurring UTIs. (We already knew this)

The nursing home was negligent in continuing multiple Central Nervous System-active medications for Elizabeth despite her increased risk of falling. It violated the patient's rights by convincing her husband not to transfer her to the ER and by not discussing alternative treatment options with him. It also breached the standard of care due to inconsistencies in the medication list among providers.

Did not supervise providers. The patient was seen weekly, mainly before 9 AM, which raises questions about her mental status examination. (Not relevant)

I will be billed $1500 for this useless expert opinion.

On October 7, I received an order scheduling a case management conference via Zoom from my attorney. It was sent to both attorneys and scheduled for November 24. During the meeting, the attorneys must be prepared to discuss, and here is a list of twelve items that are too detailed for me to include. Also included is an Agreed Case Management Plan and Order, which each attorney must complete and agree to, along with deadlines for completion.

CHAPTER 30

Complaint Response

DURING A PHONE call on September 30 with K, the organization investigating my Medicare complaints, I was informed that they had ruled in favor of HPCC. I had three days to request Reconsideration, and I immediately told the clinical reviewer that I did want Reconsideration and would submit my reasons in writing. On October 2, I received their written report and will summarize their findings and my response to it in my Reconsideration request.

Quality Concern No. 1: You were worried about whether your wife received proper treatment because she had an indwelling catheter and developed a urinary tract infection without a supporting diagnosis.

Analysis and Findings: HPCC placed a Foley catheter to drain urine from her bladder before discharge due to her condition, including her non-weight-bearing status. She had an obstruction, which caused urine retention. HPCC

attempted to discontinue the catheter, but her bladder would not empty all the urine. A urologist was consulted and recommended she keep the Foley catheter in place because of her failed voiding trials and urinary retention.

Based on your wife's record, the peer reviewer indicated it was appropriate to place a catheter due to her condition, including a diagnosis of urinary tract obstruction. Our peer reviewer professionally considers that the services provided meet all recognized healthcare standards.

My response was that the above finding was incorrect, as follows:

Charge 1: Medically unsubstantiated placement of a catheter. Elizabeth was transferred from GCMC to HPCC on May 18, 2018, with a fractured tibia and fibula. Records indicated she was suffering from a urinary tract infection, and the hospital had removed her catheter. Shortly after arriving at HPCC, a new catheter was inserted. There was no medical justification for this placement, nor are there records showing that a bladder scan was performed to detect urine retention.

My first question is, why would a catheter be inserted in a resident with a UTI or someone who is just recovering from one? If it were deemed necessary to insert the catheter, the hospital transfer records would have suggested it.

The catheter was inserted, as per HPCC, because she had a urinary retention problem, but there is no record of HPCC performing a bladder scan to confirm urine retention. I scheduled an appointment with her urologist.

When she arrived at the office on July 29th, she said, "I have to pee." The nurse immediately checked her bladder and confirmed it had been properly emptied.

The doctor's first question was, "Why is she on a catheter?" I told him I had no idea why HPCC had put her on one.

His answer was, "I know why; it was for the convenience of the staff not to have to take her to the bathroom or change diapers." There is no reason she should be on a catheter, and the longer it stays, the more likely she is to develop frequent and severe UTIs.

I have enclosed two pages relevant to a 24-page visit report (Exhibit A). His prediction of future UTIs was accurate. When I returned, I informed the floor nurse at HPCC about the urologist's concerns regarding the catheter and his recommendation for removal. HPCC took no action.

She remained on the catheter for the fifty-two (52) days she stayed at HPCC. Even though the catheter was inserted, she still experienced a constant urge to urinate. As someone who is not a doctor, I believe the logical step for HPCC would be to perform a bladder scan to see if she was retaining urine.

She did not have a urinary problem, as indicated by an empty bladder, which confirms the urologist's diagnosis. Since bladder scanning showed the bladder was emptied, the logical conclusion is that the catheter was not relieving her urge to urinate. Leaving it in place could be harmful to her future health.

The catheter stayed in place when she was rushed to the emergency room in a non-responsive state. At the ER, she was also diagnosed with pneumonia and a UTI, and the doctor questioned why she had a catheter. The catheter was removed when she moved to another nursing home after being implanted for 72 days.

As her urologist predicted, during the last two years of her life, she experienced twenty-seven (27) suspected UTIs, leading to fifteen (15) hospital admissions due to their severity (Exhibit B). One was so severe that the hospital was unable to identify the bacterial growth and sent it to the CDC for analysis. She was placed on a PICC line for ten days of antibiotics to treat the CDC-identified sepsis.

Throughout her hospital stays, she was consistently placed on an external suction catheter instead of an embedded catheter because the hospital concluded that an implanted catheter was a significant factor in causing UTIs. With each admission, her GFR kidney function declined from 60.0 in June 2017 to 13.9 in June 2019 (Exhibit C). Ultimately, suffering from kidney failure, she passed away in July 2019, with the extended embedded catheter being a contributing cause of death.

During her twenty-seven visits to the hospital, they scanned her bladder at least thirty times because of her feeling like she needed to pee, and each time the scan showed the bladder was emptying properly. If HPCC had scanned her in June 2018, the scan would have shown that the bladder was not retaining urine, and catheterization would not have been necessary.

I refer to CMS 20068 (Exhibit D), Urinary Catheter or Urinary Tract Infection Critical Element Pathway, which I described earlier. HPCC was in direct violation of Medicare rules regarding the use of an embedded catheter. If HPCC had performed the proper medical procedure of scanning the bladder to check for a urinary tract issue and found no retained urine, it should have removed the catheter.

HPCC did not follow the mandate of "removal of the catheter as soon as possible unless the resident's clinical condition shows that catheterization is necessary." HPCC was therefore guilty of medical misconduct by not complying with CMS 20068.

Now, regarding her suspected diagnosis: Although there are no medical tests to confirm the alleged diagnosis, Elizabeth's 'I have to pee' mantra aligns with symptoms found in SSD. In SSD, the person feels the need to pee even when there is no urine in the bladder and no known medical reason for the urge.

There is no cure, but muscle relaxers, physiotherapy, and regular exercise may help alleviate symptoms. Her doctor and the hospital's bladder scans indicate that no medical condition requires HPCC to insert a catheter. The final piece of information comes from a lawsuit complaint.

To verify that the urinary catheter was necessary for reasons other than the convenience of HPCC's agents and employees, it was included in the Plaintiff's care plan, which stated she had been diagnosed with obstructive uropathy, meaning a urinary blockage. However, none of the Plaintiff's medical records show a diagnosis of obstructive uropathy.

HPCC's independent contract doctors, none of whom are urologists, made the initial diagnosis of obstructive uropathy. The test for urinary retention involves a cystoscopy or other urinary tract imaging tests, such as ultrasound, VCUG, MRI, or CT scans, to identify other conditions that could cause urinary retention. There is no evidence that HPCC provided the standard of care listed.

Additionally, the Analysis and Finding states, "A Foley catheter was placed to drain urine from her bladder due to her non-weight-bearing status." Non-weight bearing does not meet the CMS 20068 definition of a clinical condition that requires catheterization. She was able to use a walker and the toilet with the help of an aide.

The findings also state, "She was also found to have an obstruction, causing urine retention." However, none of the earlier listed tests were performed to locate the site of the obstruction, assuming such an obstruction existed. I have records of her last four visits to her urologist, and none indicate she had any voiding problems. Her HPCC records show no evidence that any of these tests were carried out. The diagnosis of uropathy was based solely on the resident's 'I have to pee' statements. There was no clinical indication that catheterization was needed, and thus, no reason for it to remain in place for seventy-two days. HPCC was in direct violation of Medicare CMS 200068 regarding the use of catheters.

Concern No. 2: You are worried that your wife was not properly evaluated and treated. Specifically, you mention her skin turgor was slow to bounce back, and she was dehydrated, a condition that was not assessed or addressed by HPCC, which led to her being sent to the hospital.

Analysis and Findings: Your wife was hospitalized for an extended period, during which multiple UTIs worsened her condition. HPCC monitored her lab values weekly and, as needed, to watch for dehydration. As she ate less frequently, they administered intravenous fluids. She received IV fluids before her transfer to the hospital because her kidney function results were slightly elevated.

Her electrolyte levels showed she was mildly volume-depleted but not dehydrated. The peer reviewer noted that dehydration typically presents as a high sodium level. She was sent to the hospital due to a UTI and pneumonia. According to her records, the peer review confirmed that HPCC correctly identified dehydration, which was not indicated by the lab tests.

The peer reviewer concluded that your wife received a thorough evaluation and appropriate treatment. In our peer reviewer's professional opinion, the services provided met all recognized standards of quality healthcare.

Whose records were they reviewing? Because they certainly did not match my wife's. When K states that HPCC sent my wife to the hospital due to a UTI and pneumonia, it is clearly incorrect. She was admitted in a non-responsive state caused by severe dehydration, and it was the hospital that diagnosed the UTI and pneumonia. My written response was.

Charge 2: HPCC allowed the resident to become severely dehydrated, despite her husband informing staff of her condition. She was then taken to the emergency room in a non-responsive state due to dehydration. Elizabeth's husband told the nursing staff that his wife was severely dehydrated, supported by his performing a turgor test and her increasing CMP BUN readings, which peaked at 25 with the high range being 17 (Exhibit E).

When it became clear that increasing fluid intake wouldn't resolve her condition, it was decided that she needed an IV to be rehydrated intravenously. The next day, when I found her without an IV, I was told the nurses had tried to insert an IV line, but her veins kept collapsing. HPCC chose not to act and instead attempted to rehydrate her by encouraging her to drink more. If they believed she needed IV fluids to rehydrate, then drinking more wouldn't have corrected her condition.

As her condition worsened, I asked for her to be taken to the emergency room for rehydration, but I was told it wasn't necessary and that someone would find a nurse to insert an IV. By the time they started the IV, her condition had declined too much, and she was rushed to the ER in a non-responsive state shortly afterward.

She received aggressive rehydration in the ER to help her regain consciousness.

Referring to the Analysis and Findings, it states that multiple UTIs complicated her stay. Regarding Charge 1, why would a resident with numerous UTIs remain on an indwelling catheter?

Regarding the statement, "Her laboratory values were monitored weekly and as needed to check for dehydration," I was responsible for reviewing those values and informing the nursing staff if she was dehydrated. To verify this, I refer to her CMP BUN readings (Exhibit E) from June 26, 2017, to July 29, 2017, which ranged from 21 to 25 mg/dL. On the day she was sent to the hospital in a non-responsive state, her BUN reading was 25, with the top of the normal range being 17.

Immediately after hospital rehydration, the GFR dropped to 8. Regarding the statement, "She was provided intravenous fluids," HPCC administered her IV fluids a few days before she was rushed to the emergency room. I documented this false statement when I quoted the nurses, "We could not get an IV line in because her veins kept collapsing."

The information, "She was admitted to the hospital for a UTI and pneumonia," was the condition found after admission. She was admitted for severe dehydration and being in a non-responsive state. Aggressive rehydration began immediately upon her admittance to the emergency room.

It is unclear why K did not fault HPCC for not having trained staff capable of inserting an IV line and for neglecting the resident's condition until she was found unresponsive. HPCC did not deliver the standard nursing care required for the resident. Based on the attached records and discussions with her urologist, I have documented that an embedded catheter was unnecessary, and proper testing would have confirmed this. The statements regarding Quality

Concern No. 2 are incorrect and need reevaluation based on the enclosed records.

I sent my narration and the exhibits to K on October 3. I received a reply on October 5. They rejected my reconsideration, and I couldn't believe their reasoning. The following is an expert's analysis and findings.

Your Quality Concern 1: The use of an embedded Foley catheter. A review of medical records indicates that your wife had a history of recurrent urinary tract infections. Due to urinary retention, she was admitted to a skilled nursing facility with an indwelling catheter. (False) She could not void independently, so she medically needed to keep the indwelling catheter in place.

A Foley catheter does not prevent UTIs caused by urinary retention. (False) In this case, keeping the Foley catheter in place was medically necessary and appropriate. Our peer reviewer's professional opinion was that the services provided met all applicable recognized standards of healthcare.

Quality Concern 2 Dehydration: A review of medical records showed that the nursing staff closely monitored your wife while she was at HPCC. She received intermittent intravenous (IV) fluid therapy, and there was no evidence of significant dehydration or kidney impairment during her care. On the day of discharge to an acute care hospital, she experienced a low blood pressure episode in the context of worsening mental status.

At that time, her needs required a higher level of care. She was transported to the hospital appropriately. (False) In the professional opinion of the peer reviewer, the services that were the subject of this concern met all applicable, professionally recognized standards of healthcare. This is the final decision, and no further appeal rights are available.

I decided I couldn't ignore the information in the letter, so I responded. The first thing I did was check if there was a higher level of appeal, despite what the letter said. I sent the following letter to K in reply to their letter dated October 5.

You stated this is the final decision and that no further appeal rights are available. Despite this, I will seek another agency to appeal this decision. In your letter dated September 28, you mentioned for Reconsideration, "You can give us more information and documents, including medical information, that will help with your request." I submitted four pages of narration and five charts, which you received on October 5. I responded to them the same day.

You claimed to have completed a thorough review of the quality-of-care concerns I raised. Your initial evaluation took sixty days, and your review of the additional information only took a couple of hours, as you responded the same day you received it. A one-hour review does not meet your 'fully comprehensive review' criteria.

Before I proceed, I would like to quote the disclaimer from your referenced UpToDate website.

The content on the Up-To-Date website is not meant to replace medical advice, diagnosis, or treatment. Always talk to your doctor or a qualified healthcare professional for any medical questions or concerns.

Elizabeth followed Up-To-Date's recommendations and consulted her urologist, Exhibit A, who stated, "Asked to see patient for the necessity of an indwelling Foley." Plan: REMOVE FOLEY

CATHETER. She did everything your Up-To-Date website recommended, but the nursing home ignored the urologist's advice.

Again, quoting your Up-To-Date website, "The clinical presentation of a urinary tract obstruction depends on the site of the obstruction, the degree of obstruction (partial or complete), and the rapidity with which the obstruction develops."

There is no evidence that medical tests were performed to assess the size, severity, or progression rate of the obstruction. According to his opinion, the doctor at the nursing home decided to insert the catheter without any supporting medical tests.

Let me do the same since you rely on websites for your information. I could refer you to many sites that detail the complications associated with an embedded catheter, but I will quote only one.

According to the Centers for Disease Control and Prevention (CDC) website, "The most important risk factor for developing a catheter-associated UTI (CAUTI) is prolonged urinary catheter use. Therefore, catheters should only be used for appropriate indications and removed as soon as possible."

HPCC did not adhere to either of these recommendations. They failed to establish 'appropriate indications' through medical documentation, and they kept the catheter in place for fifty-two (52) days. FMCC, the nursing home she moved to after being denied readmission by HPCC, removed the catheter.

After being in place for seventy-two days, the nurse decided that the catheter was doing more harm than good and removed it. There were no adverse effects on the resident, and she was able to void, although with some difficulty due to the extended time the catheter had been in place. She was able to do so for the rest of her stay at FMCC.

Next, there is a false statement under Analysis and Findings for Concern 1. She was not admitted to the skilled nursing facility with an indwelling catheter. The nursing facility inserted the catheter, a fact HPCC never denied. In the same analysis, you stated, "She medically needed to keep the indwelling catheter in place." Still, no evidence was found through urology medical exams to support that statement. Her urologist recommended that the catheter be removed, and the nurse at FMCC followed through on this recommendation. As a result, she was able to void and wear diapers.

It is difficult to understand how your reviewer completely disagrees with the medical community, including doctors, urologists, hospitals, and your client's CMS 20068 Medicare mandates, which strongly advise that catheters only be used when medically necessary. If they are used, they should be removed promptly. His statement, "keeping the Foley catheter in place was medically needed and appropriate," was made without any medical evidence to support that it was indeed necessary or appropriate.

Number 2 concern is her dehydration; your entire analysis and findings need to be corrected.

You say, "Documentation shows the nursing staff closely monitored your wife." If HPCC was so closely monitoring her, then what explains the BUN readings shown in Exhibit E?

What does the first paragraph in the Findings section of your letter have to do with the dehydration issue? I have documented that she did not receive IV fluid therapy because her veins kept collapsing, and they could not insert a feeding line. If the records indicate that she received such fluid treatment in the days leading up to her emergency transfer to the hospital, those records are likely false. They should undergo a proper review by the relevant agency.

A false statement claims: "On the day of discharge to an acute care hospital, she had an episode of low blood pressure in the context of worsening mental status. At that time, her needs required a higher level of care, and she was appropriately taken to the hospital."

Now, let me tell you the true story, which I detailed in my Reconsideration document. It seems that the reviewer did not read the document but relied on a false account of events from a nursing home. On the morning of May 29, 2017, HPCC called to inform me that my wife was found in a non-responsive state, and they were waiting for instructions from the doctor.

HPCC, instead of taking immediate action, did nothing until hearing from the doctor. My next call revealed that HPCC was rushing my wife by ambulance to the emergency room in a non-responsive state. The hospital diagnosed her with severe dehydration, and the doctors performed aggressive rehydration procedures. She was also diagnosed with a UTI and pneumonia. Does this sound like a resident who was 'closely monitored by the nurses?

The statement, "At the time, when transferred to the hospital, her needs required a higher level of care," is true. She did because she was nearly dead, which is why she needed the higher level of care. When she was discharged from the hospital, HPCC refused to take her back, claiming they had no beds, despite records showing that many Medicare beds were available. I found another nursing home on short notice, a facility that fell short of the capabilities of HPCC. So much for the 'need for a higher level of care.'

CHAPTER 31

Newspaper Op-Ed

D ESPITE MY ATTORNEY'S advice not to send the op-ed, I wrote it in March. My duty was to inform the county's citizens about the Sovereign Immunity Statutes and how they affect them if they face medical malpractice. I submitted the op-ed to the paper in October, adhering to the 600-word limit.

HOW FLORIDA'S SOVEREIGN IMMUNITY STATUTES PROTECT NEGLIGENT HEALTH PROVIDERS.

I am in the third year of a wrongful death lawsuit against a nursing home. In direct violation of Medicare mandates, the facility began a procedure that ultimately caused the premature death of my wife of sixty years. However, under Florida Sovereign Immunity Statutes (FSIS), my ability to seek proper compensation is limited due to caps on the damages I can recover.

Sovereign immunity means that the king, who creates the laws, cannot be wrong, according to old English law. Therefore, by being protected under sovereign immunity, the defendant cannot be held liable or sued. However, the parent organization has waived immunity for medical malpractice or wrongful death lawsuits.

By waiving their immunity, one might assume the defendant would face substantial damages if found negligent at trial. However, this is a false assumption because the waiver restricts the damages in a winning lawsuit to a maximum of $200,000, making it difficult for an attorney to find a client willing to sue an FSIS defendant. The waiver also limits the attorney's contingency fee to 25%.

Now, let's consider a hypothetical situation. You go into surgery to have your right kidney removed, but due to hospital negligence, the surgeon removes your left kidney instead. Because of their negligence, you face huge medical bills or even death. As a result of either or both incidents, the FSIS defendant is liable for a maximum damages award of $200,000.

Let me digress and quote a December *article from The Wall Street Journal.*

This summer, the St. Louis County Police Department paid $750,000 in a wrongful death settlement for a PIT BULL shot years ago during a SWAT raid, even though police claim the dog had acted aggressively. Something is wrong when a dog's life is valued at $750,000, but the Florida legislature considers a human life worth only $200,000.

Based on the described medical misconduct, the victim or their heirs would not have trouble finding an attorney to represent them — this is a false assumption. Pursuing a medical malpractice lawsuit can be both time-consuming and costly. Assuming a maximum settlement, your attorney, which is unlikely due to court-ordered mediation, would only collect $50,000 for years of litigation.

FSIS has fulfilled the Florida legislature's aim of reducing medical malpractice lawsuits by limiting damages and attorney contingency fees. Under FSIS, even in a hypothetical case involving kidney removal, the victim would likely have difficulty finding legal representation to sue an FSIS agency. Many legitimate malpractice cases are not litigated because statutory caps bar attorneys from taking them.

The issue with low caps is that they discourage lawsuits against covered agencies. They make the agency less responsible for its actions, less likely to address litigated medical malpractice, and less accountable to taxpayers who pay the bill. Lawsuits are intended to compensate victims, correct negligent practices, and prevent similar negligence from harming others in the future. FSIS caps do nothing to ensure these corrections are made.

After waiting weeks without seeing it published, I emailed the paper to ask if the article met all the criteria for an op-ed. No response. I thought it wasn't published because I included an actual lawsuit reference, so I rewrote the first paragraph, making it a generic example instead of a personal one.

If someone living in Florida suffers a serious injury or death due to medical malpractice, and the responsible party is an agency or agent covered by applicable law, you may file a lawsuit against them. This revision removed my personal viewpoint from the op-ed and replaced it with a generic plaintiff. Not expecting it to be published, I sent it to some of my golfing friends.

I submitted the attached 600-word op-ed to the newspaper to inform the county's citizens about the Florida Sovereign Immunity Statutes. In this case, the defendant is LMHS, a public health care system established by a special act of the Florida legislature. LMHS is classified as an independent special district under Florida law and is therefore exempt from sovereign immunity under the Florida Waiver of Sovereign Immunity Act, the focus of my op-ed.

The newspaper refused to publish the op-ed without giving a reason. I suspect it's either because it involves ongoing litigation or due to the sensitive nature of the subject and the defendant. LMHS doesn't want the county's citizens to find out what the statute might reveal.

With Covid-19 spreading through Florida like wildfire, I, an 87-year-old, am vulnerable. The wealthy defendant seeks to extend the lawsuit beyond the Plaintiff. You may share the attachment with any acquaintances who live or spend winters in the county, informing them that they are subject to the statute if they are treated at the LMHS.

I was eager to publish the op-ed, so I reached out to the top official at the newspaper and explained my case. I sent her the following letter.

An op-ed explaining Florida's Sovereign Immunity Statutes to county residents was sent to the newspaper weeks ago, but was not published. This op-ed acts as a public service announcement for anyone treated at LMHS, including those in doctors' offices, nursing homes, or hospitals.

Since the op-ed wasn't published, I shared it with many friends who mostly had the same reaction. Like about 99% of the county, they were unaware of the statutes and couldn't understand why the paper chose not to publish the article to inform the public.

The LMHS would prefer that the citizens of the county not become aware of the statute, as the sensitivity of the topic might influence the publication of the article. Using the words from my recent notice of a price increase, "Credible journalism is more critical than ever, and the paper is committed to producing in-depth stories." Not publishing a public service op-ed does not align with the paper's mission statement.

The Florida legislature has accomplished its objective with the passage of the Sovereign Immunity Statutes. It has decreased medical malpractice lawsuits, not because the claims lack validity, but because caps on damages and attorney fees make even legitimate cases too expensive and time-consuming for lawyers to pursue—the public needs to know this.

On October 30, I received an email requesting a tagline for the op-ed and a corresponding image. I used the tagline 'Plaintiff in a wrongful death lawsuit' and sent a photo in response. The editor informed me that the op-ed would be published. So, my persistence paid off, and I am now eager to see what response I get from the publication.

I kept waiting for the op-ed to be published, but nothing happened. The op-ed is either too controversial or involves a legal issue. It is an active lawsuit, which might be why the paper didn't publish it. It's a shame because an extremely informative op-ed would benefit not only the citizens of this county but also all Florida residents whose medical system is covered by the statute. As a result, they will remain unaware of Florida's Sovereign Immunity.

Not seeing the op-ed published, I tried a different approach and wrote a letter to the paper's mailbag, where individual opinions are shared in 200 words or fewer. On November 23, I submitted this letter with the headline 'Information Suppression':

In September, I submitted an op-ed titled 'How Florida's Sovereign Immunity Statutes Protect Negligent Health Providers' to the newspaper. The article explained how the statutes apply to every resident of the county who uses LMHS's doctors, nursing homes, or hospitals. The law outlines the maximum damages a harmed individual can recover from a medical malpractice injury or death, as well as your attorney's top cap of a 25% contingency fee.

Lawsuits seek to compensate victims for their losses, address negligent practices, and prevent similar harm in the future. Statute caps should support these goals. They reduce the liability of negligent health providers, making them less likely to face medical malpractice claims and decreasing their accountability to taxpayers who cover the costs. The paper declined to publish my Letter to the Editor because of the issue's sensitivity.

It has been over a month, and neither my op-ed nor my mailbag letter has been published. Two reasons might explain why they haven't appeared. The first reason is that the subject matter is too sensitive or controversial, because it involves the local hospital, which causes the newspaper to hesitate before publishing the documents.

The second reason could be the tagline. A tagline is a brief statement in italics at the end of an op-ed that mentions the writer, such as if a garden topic has a tagline like 'the writer is the president of the city garden club,' which indicates they are knowledgeable about growing tulips. Taglines are often associated with titles like CEO, president, chairperson, etc. My tagline, a concerned citizen or a plaintiff in a wrongful death lawsuit, doesn't convey the writer's authority through a title, even though they have experienced the effects.

CHAPTER 32

K's Ruling Appeal

A FTER BEING REJECTED when I appealed K's decision regarding my quality-of-care complaint, I searched various Medicare websites for alternative options. That's when I learned about Medicare Fraud. The Medicare definition of fraud states, "Fraud means an intentional deception or misrepresentation made by a health care provider with the knowledge that the deception could result in some unauthorized benefit to the health care provider."

HPCC's medical report from July 29th, 2017, states, "On the day of discharge to an acute care hospital, she had an episode of low blood pressure in the context of worsening mental status. At that time, her needs required a higher level of care, and she was appropriately taken to the hospital."

The actual events of that day should have stated, "Resident was found non-responsive and severely dehydrated and transferred to the hospital emergency room." HPCC's fraudulent submission to K, the quality-of-care investigator, was the basis for their decision that HPCC 'did meet all applicable recognized standards of care.' HPCC's intentional deception or misrepresentation of facts led to their actions being considered as meeting the standard of care when an accurate account of the incident might have resulted in them being cited for not meeting the 'applicable recognized standards of care.' How do I report Medicare fraud?

My complaint is that HPCC committed healthcare fraud by submitting false medical incident reports to a Medicare contractor investigating quality-of-care complaints. HPCC knew that when they submitted these reports, they falsely described the medical events, and they received a favorable decision from K stating that the services provided, based on these false incident reports, met recognized healthcare standards.

HPCC, a defendant in a wrongful death lawsuit, allegedly devised a scheme to falsify medical reports to secure a favorable K report, thereby strengthening its pending case.

My next step was to start a Medicare investigation into fraud and misconduct related to HPCC's programs. Their false reporting to a quasi-governmental agency, K, the investigation agency, prevents Medicare from imposing program exclusions and civil monetary penalties because their quality of care does not meet recognized healthcare standards, which amounts to fraud.

On November 15, I began calling every Medicare number I found online. After many people told me, "You called the wrong office; you need to call this office," I eventually reached a representative. I explained that I wanted to file a charge. Most Medicare fraud charges involve financial transactions, and Medicare cannot tolerate fraudulent medical statements. K must depend on medical statements provided to them by HPCC, and I believe that their descriptions of the July 29th incident were dishonest.

A Medicare representative said that this kind of case was not on his list of recognized frauds, so he referred me to a higher authority for review. After hearing my story, they advised me to submit my complaint to the Office of the Inspector General. On December 13, I filed a Medicare fraud complaint with the OIG using their form. It states, "Your description of events cannot exceed 1500 words." I described HPCC's alleged fraudulent actions.

HPCC provided misrepresented event summaries to K, the agency contracted by Medicare, to investigate the quality-of-care complaints. Actual hospital medical reports show HPCC's description of events was fraudulent. Medicare guidelines state that K must accept the medical reports provided by HP as fact and cannot decide on the quality-of-care description furnished by the complainant. K cannot determine whether the information supplied by HPCC was accurate.

HPCC's account of the events weakens the credibility of the medical documents in the complaint. Therefore, K, who is supposed to be an impartial fact-finder, is limited to making decisions only based on the statements submitted by HPCC. Medicare fraud involves intentional deception or misrepresentation by a healthcare provider, knowing that such actions could result in unauthorized benefits for the provider.

This is an example of a single event. When she was found unresponsive, my wife was taken to a hospital emergency room, where she was diagnosed with severe dehydration, a UTI, and pneumonia. This information comes from 83 pages of hospital medical reports documenting her five-day stay.

HPCC's description of the event provided to K: "On the day of discharge to an acute hospital, she experienced an episode of low blood pressure along with worsening mental status. At that point, her needs required a higher level of care. She was properly taken to the hospital."

HPCC met the definition of Medicare fraud. Based on HPCC's report, K determined that HPCC provided the accepted standard of healthcare and thus dismissed the quality-of-care complaint. The benefit of the fraudulent reporting was that HPCC avoided program exclusion and civil monetary penalties.

The OIG is very secretive, not acknowledging receipt of complaints or indicating whether a complaint is under investigation. The only benefit I might have gained is discovering that a Medicare fraud complaint has been filed against HPCC.

I obtained my information from the K report and would like to review HPCC's official account of the events. I emailed my attorney.

During discovery, can you obtain the response from HPCC regarding the quality-of-care complaint sent to K, the investigating agency, in 2020? I have documented two complaints with hospital and medical reports; however, my accounts cannot be used by K because their investigation guidelines rely solely on medical records provided by the provider.

Medicare guidelines state, "They must take the medical records submitted by the provider as factual." A review of some records submitted by HPCC to K shows they are not accurate. The benefit gained from HPCC's fraudulent statements, rather than a precise description of the questioned quality of care, could prevent Medicare from potentially imposing program exclusions and civil monetary penalties. I filed an OIG fraud report and will need HPCC's response for backup.

The second piece of information of interest.

AOL News highlighted a news story a few weeks ago: "TR's cause of death revealed as her partner speaks out." The highlights of the report read as follows: "The That '70s Show star died at age

65 from a urinary tract infection. Robert's cause of death was from a urinary tract infection, which spread to her kidney, gallbladder, liver, and then bloodstream." Does this incident support our claim that UTIs cause kidney failure and death?

He replied that he could not use discovery to obtain HPCC's response to my quality-of-care complaint, which was sent to K. Florida statutes consider such information privileged and therefore exempt from public records. I was determined not to be discouraged from trying to get HPCC's response, so I tried another approach. While researching K's letter, which denied my claim of poor quality of care from HPCC, I found a possible way to obtain HPCC's response. On January 15, 2022, I sent the following letter to K.

Your quality-of-care review process states that K's decisions are based on medical records sent by the provider, and information sent by the complainant will not be the main factor in your decision. Medicare guidelines stipulate that medical records provided by the provider must be accepted as accurate and factual representations of the patient's condition. It must then be assumed that the Analysis and Findings detailed in your letter of 5 October 2020 were based on the nursing home's medical records supplied by the provider.

Based on the review of hospital records related to the quality-of-care complaint events, the statements indicate that the words in the Analysis and Findings, as described by the providers, constitute intentional deception or misrepresentation. These actions by the nursing home meet the criteria for Medicare fraud. Therefore, I must receive copies of all medical records sent by HPCC that were used to make your decision. The requested documents do not meet the confidentiality definitions outlined in 42 CFR Part 480(b) (1–4), as the provider's identity is already known.

A formal complaint of Medicare fraud against HPCC has been filed with the Office of the Inspector General, following a recommendation from the Centers for Medicare & Medicaid Services (CMS), not the Medicare program. According to the information provided by HPCC, K's final decision forms the basis for the complaint. Section 480.103 (b) states that data must remain confidential and not be disclosed except where 'necessary to assist federal agencies responsible for identifying fraud cases.' The requested record will serve as significant evidence, along with the medical evidence I have provided, to assist the OIG in any investigation they may conduct.

As expected, I am still waiting for a response to my request. Not letting this issue rest, I decided that if I couldn't get HPCC's answers to K from K, I would go to HPCC to get their responses. Based on this, I filed a Freedom of Information Request with HPCC, which is covered under sovereign immunity and considered a government entity, making it subject to FOIR. On January 26, a FOIR was sent to HPCC's risk manager, requesting all medical records and nurses' notes sent to K in 2020 in response to the quality-of-care complaint related to Elizabeth's care while she was a resident at HPCC.

Still frustrated by my inability to find an agency to file a complaint about the investigative procedures used by K, as directed by Medicare, I started searching online. I contacted and spoke with many, but they were unable to address my concern.

Not giving up, I decided to contact K's home office and emailed the Communications Director, asking him, "Should I file a complaint against K's quality of care investigation procedures with K or with the Health and Human Services (HHS), the federal agency to whom K reports?"

Without wasting any time, I immediately sent the following email. Per K's recommendation, I am raising concerns about the validity of K's evaluation of quality-of-care complaints I filed. The attached details show that Medicare's guidelines state the medical records submitted by the provider must be accepted as fact, and that medical documentation provided by the complainant is not a factor in K's decision.

The provider's statements to K were found to be false based on hospital records related to one of the quality-of-care complaints.

My concern is, "How can K be an unbiased investigator of quality-of-care complaints when only the provider's records are used, and records provided by the complainant are disregarded?" The following narration accompanied the email referencing a K-QIO investigation.

A quality-of-care complaint involving multiple incidents, along with supporting hospital records, doctors' statements, and lab reports, was submitted to K on August 6, 2020. HPCC Nursing Home responded to my complaints that contradicted my documented account of events. I want to highlight one of the quality-of-care complaints: on July 29, my wife was found unresponsive and was rushed to the hospital emergency room by ambulance.

Here are some notes from her hospital records: The patient is a poor historian and is not answering questions at this time because she is tired and cannot be awakened. Unable to perform RO: mucous membranes are dry. She appears lethargic with poor skin turgor. BU is reading 25. CBC with Diff, Comprehensive Metabolic Panel, and RT ABG are abnormal. She was found very dry in the ER, and the doctor initiated a borderline hypotensive protocol.

She received antibiotics and aggressive IV fluid therapy. She is currently afebrile. Differential diagnosis includes sepsis, bacteremia, UTI, dehydration, intracranial bleed, and CVA. Chest X-ray shows left lung infiltration and effusion. Her mental status improved with hydration. The patient has a urinary tract infection and left lower lobe infiltrates, consistent with pneumonia. She needs to be admitted for IV antibiotics, hydration, and further testing. My wife spent five days in the hospital, and her medical records from her stay took eighty-four (84) pages to document. When admitted, she had an embedded catheter.

Here is the documentation the nursing home submitted to K regarding the same incident on July 29th.

On the day she was discharged to an acute hospital, she experienced an episode of low blood pressure along with worsening mental status. At that time, her condition required a higher level of care. She was transported to the hospital properly. According to HPCC's statement of events, ignoring my submitted documentation and K's professional opinion as our peer reviewer, the services provided met all relevant and recognized healthcare standards.

Here is an explanation of K's reason for their decision. Our decisions are based on the medical records provided by the provider. The complainant may submit additional information to help us better understand your concern, but it will not be the primary factor in our decision. Medicare guidelines state that medical records from HPCC must be accepted as fact, and K cannot determine if the records contain false information.

According to K's guidelines, only statements from the provider, regardless of their accuracy, are to be considered. The complainant's detailed complaints about the quality of care, supported by pages of medical charts, hospital records, and doctors' notes, are dismissed, and the complainant's documentation is ignored. Given these evaluation guidelines, how can K serve as an unbiased judge of the facts?

There is no connection between HPCC's account of events and the hospital's documented version of the same circumstances. Medicare fraud involves intentional deception or misrepresentation by a healthcare provider, knowing that such actions could lead to unauthorized benefits for the provider.

In this case, the benefits gained are not affected by Medicare's potential to impose program exclusions or monetary penalties. Another advantage HPCC secured is having a K that determines whether the provider, based on the provider's false statement of fact, met the recognized standard of healthcare. HPCC, the defendant in a wrongful death lawsuit, can use as an exhibit at trial that K concluded HPCC met the standard of care.

My wife had an embedded Foley catheter when she was admitted to the hospital. The catheter was inserted shortly after she arrived at the HPCC on May 18. She was in an immobilizer brace, which required assistance to use the bathroom.

The lawsuit claims that the catheter was not placed for medical reasons but for the convenience of the aides, so they wouldn't need to attend to her bathroom needs. When she was admitted to the ER, the catheter had been in place for 52 days. The following excerpts from the doctor's notes taken during my wife's ER visit discuss the UTI and the catheter.

Final Diagnosis: Urinary tract infection without hematuria, site unspecified, dehydration, and lung infiltration were also relevant to this visit. We will treat sepsis empirically; however, we believe this is likely severe dehydration. The patient had baseline dementia, but gradually worsened and became dehydrated. In the ER, she was febrile but hypotensive, requiring IV fluids. Her hypotension was corrected with hydration. The UTI seems to be related to colonization of the Foley catheter.

The initial urine culture from the Foley catheter showed growth of enterococcus and yeast. After replacing the catheter, the urine culture revealed normal genital flora. Consult a urologist to determine why the patient needs an indwelling Foley catheter. Does she need a long-term Foley? She moved to a new nursing home after hospital discharge, which raised questions about the necessity of the catheter. After being in place for 72 days, the catheter was removed, and she was diapered.

Another quality-of-care complaint sent to K involved HPCC's complete disregard of CMS 20068, Urinary Catheter or Urinary Tract Infection Critical Element Pathway, and I outlined the directive's requirements. Once again, based on HPCC's false reporting of the incident in question to K, K concluded that the services related to this concern met recognized standards in healthcare.

However, her regular urologist, not the house doctor, determined through his examination that there was no medical reason for her to have a Foley catheter, and he recommended that HPCC remove it. He said my wife would be subject to UTIs for the rest of her life because of the time the catheter was in place. He was right. Two years after leaving HPCC, she suffered many UTIs, which became more severe, eventually shutting down her kidneys and leading to her premature death.

Another incident involved HPCC's nursing staff being unable to insert an IV feeding tube to hydrate my wife because her veins collapsed, leading them to stop the procedure. This event resulted in my wife being rushed to the ER in a non-responsive state due to severe dehydration. According to misleading information from HPCC, K stated that they met the criteria for providing standard healthcare.

I concluded that submitting false medical documentation to K, a vendor hired by Medicare to investigate quality-of-care complaints, counts as Medicare fraud. I filed a formal Medicare fraud report with the Office of the Inspector General based on the recommendation of the Medicare supervisor.

K's value dedication statement says, "We are driven by a customer (Medicare) first approach and work tirelessly to improve our customer relationships. How can K make an unbiased decision based only on the provider's information with that value statement? Isn't the complainant also a customer?"

Based on the provider's fraudulent statements, K determined that the provider did meet all applicable professionally recognized standards of healthcare. My quality-of-care complaints should be reevaluated using the complainant's medical information. Medicare has a copy of the court order appointing me as my wife's representative, authorizing me to discuss events concerning her.

After sending the letter, I received an email from the site listing different contacts I could reach regarding my complaint. It once again showed that I was failing to get someone to address my issue. I started calling various agencies as suggested in the email, listened to the 'our menus have changed' message for an hour, and pressed 1 or 2 to connect to the department I thought could handle my complaint.

My usual response was, "We don't handle complaints like this; why don't you try so and so?" So and so couldn't answer my complaint; why not try so and so? The one with the authority to investigate my complaint was CMS at HHS, and their email led me on a wild goose chase to other agencies. At this point, I decided to stop my search for someone to listen to me. But then I was surprised.

I received an email from the Contracting Officer's Representative, Division of Beneficiary Reviews & Care Management, within the Quality Improvement & Innovation Group at the Centers for Medicare & Medicaid Services—Kansas City. It began with acknowledging the receipt of my message sent to the CMS QIO.

His role involves overseeing K and reviewing their handling of complaints and quality of care reviews.

He expressed sympathy for the death of my wife, and I respect your efforts to ensure that the care provided to your wife was appropriate. Please provide me with K's quality-of-care reviews of your complaint. Now that I am at the top of the food chain at the Department of Health and Human Services, if I cannot get answers here, my search for justice will come to an end.

On February 9, I received a letter from CMS and will share some key points. They praised me for exercising my right to request a quality-of-care review and expressed frustration with K's final decision that HPCC's care met all professionally recognized healthcare standards. K has an agreement with Medicare to evaluate quality-of-care complaints from Medicare beneficiaries.

When K's independent physician reviewers identify an episode of care that does not meet the standards of care, K will assist a provider in improving the area where the care was inadequate, preventing the same issue from affecting future patients. I will determine whether K followed the proper processes and procedures in addressing your concerns about the quality of care.

My assessment of K's completed quality of care review is to evaluate the methods used in responding to your complaint, including the information you submitted, the use of medical records, the selection of an appropriate peer reviewer, the timeliness of the response, as well as the clarity and completeness of the reply. K's physician review considered your concern while examining the medical records.

CMS does not have the authority to alter a K finding. If you believe there is incorrect information in your records at HPCC, you may request the provider to amend the record. You raised concerns about Medicare fraud, and filing a complaint with the Office of the

Inspector General was the appropriate course of action. I regret that your experience with K did not meet your expectations; however, K followed the review process required by my examination.

Based on what you know about me, I couldn't let this letter go without replying. I put a lot of effort into responding to CMN's final line of the letter. My response follows.

Let's begin with K's letter dated October 5, which outlines HPCC's response to my accusation that HPCC sent my wife to the hospital unresponsive.

"On the day of discharge to an acute care hospital, she experienced an episode of low blood pressure in the context of worsening mental status. At that time, her needs required a higher level of care. She was properly transported to the hospital." In my letter to you dated February 5, 2018, I documented, through hospital records, that the above statement was false and that there was no correlation between the described events and what actually occurred on July 29, 2017.

Following your suggestion, I began preparing a Medicare fraud complaint against HPCC to submit to the Office of the HIPAA. I wanted to document my complaint with evidence showing that HPCC made the statement above. To gather this documentation, I asked K to send me copies of HPCC's response regarding the July 29 incident, but K refused, citing confidentiality. My only option was to file a Freedom of Information Act request with HPCC for the documents they sent to K in response to my quality-of-care complaint.

On February 13, I received two five-pound FedEx boxes from HPCC. The boxes contained 1600 pages of my wife's medical records from her stay at HPCC. I spent five hours reading every page to find the statement mentioned earlier, and the only reference to the incident was the statement "DC-based on census discharge event."

Finding no evidence that HPCC provided the information above, I conclude that the report attributing the information to HPCC was a fabrication by K. If my assumption is correct, I was mistaken in filing an OIG Medicare fraud complaint against HPCC when K, not HPCC, authored the statement. It is now K's responsibility to provide documentation supporting HPCC's information. I understand this is a serious allegation, but the decision now rests with you.

Based on my review of those 1600 pages, I find it difficult—assuming K used the same documents—to understand how they reached their conclusions on my other quality-of-care complaints.

Let me provide another example of a questionable investigation. On 5/18/17, HPCC inserted a catheter into my wife. By 5/25/17, they diagnosed her with a urinary tract infection. I find it hard to understand how a knowledgeable investigator would allow a catheter, known in medicine as a leading cause of UTIs, to remain in place for 65 days.

Meanwhile, the nursing home tried to treat her UTI, and she still had a UTI when she was rushed to the hospital on 7/29/17. A peer reviewer decided it was appropriate to place a catheter, but never addressed removing it when my wife was diagnosed with a UTI.

The peer reviewer found that the nursing home met all established healthcare standards. I may only have WebMD, but I know that catheters and urinary tract infections are incompatible. I could cite other questionable opinions, but that would be a pointless effort.

On February 16 at 6:00 PM, I received a call from Tom (not his real name), the contracting officer at CMS mentioned above. We had a productive 20-minute phone call. I reiterated my dissatisfaction with K's investigation and updated him on my ongoing lawsuit. I appreciated the call and explained that I had spent many months trying to contact him through various agencies. Since he is Medicare's representative, there was one topic on which I needed to share my opinion.

By overlooking the faults of HPCC, as detailed in my letter, Medicare is accepting its practices as a standard of acceptable medical care. As a result, Medicare remains unaware of how many residents of HPCC are using convenience-embedded catheters, which directly violate Medicare's directives regarding catheter restrictions. Additionally, Medicare will not know how many residents could end up in a non-responsive state due to HP not having enough nursing staff to insert an IV feeding tube.

How many residents will be rushed to the hospital in a non-responsive state that HPCC will classify as caused by high blood pressure? I told him the only action HPCC would fear more than a wrongful death settlement would be Medicare sanctions and potential fines. These could force Medicare to require HPCC to change its healthcare practices and conduct inspections to make sure these changes are implemented.

Tom said he didn't think he could provide what I was looking for to resolve my dissatisfaction with K's findings. He said he understood my frustration and my need for my late wife's medical records and accurate treatment. While K conducts Medicare quality-of-care reviews, it's not its job to find fraud or verify the accuracy of medical records.

On February 18, I received an email from Tom informing me that the statement about my wife's transfer to the hospital for 'low blood pressure' was not based on the provider's medical records but on the physician reviewer's assessment of her condition before her trip to the hospital.

While I understand you disagree with K's review decision, two independent physician reviewers conducted a peer review of the medical records, using their clinical judgment to reach their conclusions. I recognize this may not yet meet your expectations; however, I appreciate you bringing your quality concerns to K for review. As mentioned during our conversation, if you wish to speak with K's Medical Director about your quality review, I would be happy to arrange that meeting.

I responded by saying I wanted to talk to the Director, and if he gave me his email address, I would send him my questions in advance. Tom replied by forwarding my questions to him, and he would pass them on to the Medical Director. On February 19, I sent the following letter to Tom to forward to the Director. I'm sure it's not what he expected.

Following Tom's suggestion at HHS, I am sending you questions regarding the investigation of quality-of-care complaints filed with K. These questions are based on my review of 1,600 pages of documentation related to my wife's stay at HPCC and 84 pages of hospital reports about her emergency room visit on July 29, 2017. I must assume that K used the same documentation to determine that HPCC met all relevant professional standards of healthcare. Let me start with the use of a Foley catheter.

As a contracted Medicare vendor, I am confident that K is aware of CMS 20068, "Urinary Catheter or Urinary Tract Infection Critical Element Pathway." If not, I would like to mention three elements of Medicare's mandated care plan.

1. Make sure that a resident who enters the facility without an indwelling catheter is not catheterized unless the resident's clinical condition shows that it is necessary.

2. Ensure that a resident who enters the facility with an indwelling catheter or receives one later is promptly assessed for removal, unless their clinical condition necessitates continued catheterization.

3. Ensure a resident gets appropriate treatment and services to prevent urinary tract infections.

Using CMS 20068 as my guide, I want to present the following facts and relevant questions.

Fact: Due to the patient's condition, the hospital removed a urine catheter on 5/17 before transferring my wife to HPCC. It is recommended that HPCC perform a void study if necessary. On May 18, HPCC reinserted a Foley catheter despite no clinical evidence indicating it was required, such as a bladder scan.

The first record of a bladder scan was on June 6, when a straight catheter was used if PVR exceeded 300. The Foley catheter was removed and replaced with a straight catheter. No documentation shows the results of bladder scans to justify catheter placement on June 18.

Question: Considering CMS 20068, why did K decide to insert a catheter without the resident's demonstrated clinical need for one, to meet all applicable recognized standards of health care? Why didn't K criticize HPCC for intentionally violating Medicare regulations related to embedded catheters?

Fact: The resident's ongoing need to urinate despite the Foley was the reason HPCC removed it. On May 30, a bladder

scan showed an empty bladder, yet she still felt the urge to urinate, which indicated that the Foley wasn't effective. The Foley was removed on June 23, but she continued to feel the urge to urinate. It was reinserted on June 26, even though her urologist said her urination needs persisted with the catheter in place.

Although her bladder was empty, she still felt the need to urinate. In other words, she is experiencing SSD rather than urine retention. He also expressed the opinion that the catheter insertion by HPCC was for convenience and not medically necessary.

Question: Given the urologist's diagnosis that the urge to urinate is psychological and not caused by urine retention, why did K approve the continued use of the Foley?

Fact: On 5/18/17, HPCC inserted a catheter in my wife. On 5/25/17, they discovered she had a urinary tract infection. I find it incomprehensible that a competent investigator would allow a catheter, known by the medical profession as a major cause of UTIs, to remain in place for 65 days. Meanwhile, the nursing home attempted to treat her UTI, which she still had when she was rushed to the hospital on 7/29/17.

Question: How could a peer reviewer determine that it was appropriate to place a catheter but not address its removal once my wife was diagnosed with a UTI? Why was it not questioned why it remained inserted for 65 days? Meanwhile, HPCC attempted to treat a drug-resistant urinary tract infection.

Let's address the dehydration concern. K states that a review of medical records shows the nursing staff monitored your wife closely throughout **this** episode of care. Your wife received intermittent intravenous (IV) fluid therapy, and there was no evidence of significant dehydration or renal/kidney impairment during this episode.

Fact: In early August, I told the nursing supervisor that my wife was severely dehydrated and suggested she consider IV rehydration. She agreed, and they planned to start the IV. The next day, I returned to find no IV line in my wife. When I asked why, the nurse said, "We tried to put in an IV line, but her veins kept collapsing, so we discontinued trying."

On 7/10, I informed the nurse supervisor that my wife's BUN reading was 25, indicating dehydration. On 7/11, the Palliative Care Visit notes include: 'Per husband, when do we feel it is critical to treat pt.'s dehydration, discussed at length with husband?' I also discussed with the husband whether the patient should be taken to the ER for an IV, given that there have been multiple unsuccessful attempts at IV insertion, which supports my previous statement.

On 7/12, the nursing notes state, "Level of consciousness lethargic, response slowly to verbal stimuli, obtunded, very drowsy, responds to tactile stimuli." The doctor's notes from his 7/21 visit indicate that the husband is overly concerned about his wife's dehydration. Her mucous membranes were dry, along with dark urine in her Foley. Doctor note from 7/2: Dehydrated—will get IV fluids with normal saline. The husband requests to return to the ER if we cannot administer fluids through the IV lines.

Question: HPCC was aware of a hydration issue in early August, but only successfully inserted an IVF line on August 23. How can K claim that my wife was closely monitored for hydration by the nursing staff?

Fact: On August 29, the nursing notes state, "Special instruction: indication of lethargy, STAT immediately. Urinalysis, STAT immediately, indicates lethargy. Monitor lethargy every shift until the condition improves. Monitor vital signs every shift until the change of state is resolved. Significant changes in condition—decline in condition."

At 9:00 AM, I received a call from HPCC informing me they had found my wife unresponsive and were waiting for the doctor's orders. At 10:00 AM, a follow-up call told me my wife had been rushed to the emergency room, still unresponsive. The doctor's notes from 7/29 state: In the morning, she had hypotension and was given IV fluids. She recovered, but her mentation was sluggish, and she was sent to the hospital at her husband's request.

Is the doctor saying I requested that she be sent to the ER, not his? The Nursing Home Discharge Document—Item J1550 Problem Conditions—Dehydration. K's description of the events reads as follows: On the day of discharge to an acute care hospital, she experienced an episode of low blood pressure amid worsening mental status.

At that time, her needs required a higher level of care, and she was properly taken to the hospital.

Question: If K's reviewer had access to the same HPCC documents that HPCC provided me, how could they make the false statement?

Fact: The following are excerpts from the doctor's notes recorded during my wife's emergency room visit on July 29, 2017. The patient was tired and not answering questions as usual. She appears lethargic, has dry mucous membranes, poor skin turgor, and is drowsy but arousable. CBC with Diff, Comprehensive Metabolic Panel, Proteome INR, and RT ABG are abnormal. BUN reads 25—Diff rental—diagnoses: sepsis, bacteremia, UTI, dehydration, intracranial bleed, CVA. CXR shows infiltrate and effusion in the left lung.

In the ER, she was found to be severely dehydrated; a borderline hypotensive protocol was initiated. She received antibiotics and aggressive IV fluid therapy. The patient, who had baseline dementia, experienced worsening mental status and was extremely dehydrated. In the ER, she was in A-fib but hypotensive, requiring IV fluids. Her hypotension was corrected with hydration, and her mental status improved. Her BUN at discharge was 11.

K failed to conduct a thorough investigation by not obtaining the hospital ER reports from the day my wife was in a non-responsive state. K only relied on HPCC documents tracking her stay at the nursing home, but stopped the investigation without understanding her condition, effects, or diagnosis upon arriving at the ER.

Question: Does the ER summary above seem consistent with the person K investigators mentioned was sent to the ER due to an episode of low blood pressure? HPCC violated Medicare mandates, as outlined in CMS 20068, on July 18, 2017, when they embedded a catheter without medical justification. HPCC should have been promptly cited by K.

The above documentation confirms that K cannot serve as an unbiased investigator if the investigation depends on medical records provided by the doctor, hospital, or lab. I recorded my initial complaints in those records, but these efforts were unsuccessful. K claims that Medicare guidelines specify that medical records must be regarded as factual.

As shown above, those facts should be reviewed to determine what the nursing home did wrong and what it did right. The reason I'm so insistent on the use of the catheter is that, two years after leaving HPCC, my wife suffered 25 UTIs, 12 of which required hospitalization. The UTIs eventually became so severe that they shut down her kidneys, leading to her premature death.

On February 22, I received a call from K's Medical Director's office, inquiring about my availability to participate in a video conference with the Director, a peer case reviewer, and Tom. I offered some options and scheduled a virtual meeting for February 25. K asked if I had any objections to the recorded meeting being used as a training tool for future reviews, and I expressed no disapproval of the recorded session. I then prepared the following preamble to explain to K why I am so firmly committed to this case.

Why am I so determined that K finds HPCC did not meet all recognized healthcare standards? HPCC is a Medicare-certified facility that receives millions of dollars in Medicare reimbursements each year. Any judgment against them would be viewed as a cost of doing business and a minor error in their financial statements. Monetary settlements do not motivate HPCC to cease the practices for which they are being sued.

HPCC can write off any judgment as a business expense. However, the facility cannot ignore the one action they fear most: a Medicare sanction and potential monetary penalty. To pursue those sanctions, I turned to K. I submitted documentation on two quality-of-care complaints I believed did not meet professionally recognized standards of healthcare. My submission included pages of narration and medical records to support my allegations. I then waited months for K's investigation results.

I could not believe K's final opinion, which, in theory, stated that all my quality-of-care complaints were invalid and that HPCC had met all applicable, professionally recognized healthcare standards. These standards included HPCC's embedding a Foley catheter without medical justification, a direct violation of CMS 20068, which prohibits the use of a catheter. It also included HPCC, allowing a resident to become so dehydrated that she was rushed to the hospital in a non-responsive state because the facility did not have a staff nurse who could insert an IV line.

The statement initially contributed to HPCC was later found to be authored by K. It described the resident being transferred to the emergency room due to low blood pressure. Still, the ER notes showed the resident was severely dehydrated and unresponsive. K's claim that the resident was sent to the ER because of low blood pressure aligns with Medicare's definition of fraud. What I saw as medical malpractice, K considered to be established standards of health care.

My original submission regarding concerns about the quality of care was for K to review the documentation. If my allegations proved true after an investigation, it would show that Medicare HPCC did not meet Medicare's accepted healthcare standards. However, K, after reviewing, decided there was no reason to support my claims, which is a significant decision in my case. I am involved in wrongful death litigation where HPCC is the defendant.

If the case goes to trial, K's opinion that HPCC met all recognized professional standards of care could be admitted as an exhibit by the defendant. The defendant might argue that an investigation by a Medicare representative also found the defendant met all recognized professional standards of care and, therefore, should not be held liable for the plaintiff's death.

Ninety-nine percent of plaintiffs in a sovereign immunity lawsuit eventually get tired of the delays, settle out of court for much less than they would be entitled to, and move on. However, the defendant was unlucky in this case because I am part of the 1%.

I could not believe K found no validity in my complaints about the quality of care, and I strongly expressed my disbelief in letters. In my recent review of the 1600 HPCC medical records and the 84 pages of hospital records related to the 'low blood pressure' transfer to the emergency room, I am even more concerned that I was examining a different set of documents than those provided to K by HPCC.

It also became clear that K did not follow up on the hospital records documenting the residents' transfer to the emergency room. My frustration is expressed in these questions.

In summary, K cannot be an unbiased investigator of care concerns if their decisions are based solely on the provider's medical records without considering those of the complainant. I agree that medical records from the provider should form the basis for a decision.

Still, those records must be thoroughly examined to ensure that both the valid procedures and the incorrect ones documented by the provider are given equal consideration in the decision. K states that their review aims to help providers deliver higher-quality healthcare. They will never achieve that goal by praising a provider for safe care and not recognizing inadequate care.

On February 25, I took part in a two-and-a-half-hour video conference with the Medical Director, the Project Director from K,

Tom, my HHS representative, and two nurses. The purpose was to review the latest questions I sent to the Director.

As K's Medical Director and a doctor, her duty was to persuade me that K had completed the case investigation they were hired to perform. She paid little heed to my points, as most of the discussion was dominated by K's Chief Medical Officer. I wanted to bring up the issue of prolonged Foley catheter use and dehydration to get her perspective on it.

She argued that the catheter was necessary due to her urine retention. She detailed her medication and noted that her pain medication could cause urine retention. The UTI was treated with the catheter still in place because urine retention presented a greater risk of infection than the removal of the catheter.

Beth's urologist, who said the catheter was placed for nursing home convenience and wasn't necessary, should have removed it. I argued that HPCC had installed the catheter, not him, and it wasn't his responsibility to remove it. She counters that she was his patient during the office visit, and he could have removed it. She felt she had justified the extended use of the catheter.

I challenged her explanation. I started by telling her that the hospital had removed the catheter before transferring my wife on 5/17 to HPCC, with the instruction for HPCC to perform voiding studies. On May 18, HPCC reinserted the catheter, citing urine retention as the reason. However, there is no record showing that HPCC conducted a bladder scan to confirm urine retention. The director agreed with me and said HPCC was negligent in not demonstrating that they performed voiding tests.

I quoted Medicare's directive: "Ensure a resident who enters the facility without an indwelling catheter is not catheterized unless the resident's clinical condition demonstrates catheterization was necessary."

Ensure that a resident who later receives one is promptly considered for catheter removal, unless their clinical condition indicates that catheterization is necessary for their continued care. HPCC inserted the catheter, citing urine retention as the clinical reason.

There is no record in HPCC's files showing that a voiding study was conducted to support their claim. Although the hospital recommended that HPCC perform voiding studies, the first mention of a bladder scan in HPCC's reports is not until 6/6, which was 18 days after the catheter was inserted. The Foley catheter remained in place for the 52 days my wife was at the facility, and there is no record of any bladder scan results in HPCC's documentation.

I argue that my wife's constant crying out, "I have to pee," was the reason the catheter remained in place, even though her sensation of needing to pee was considered psychological rather than physical. The only bladder scan recorded in the nursing notes showed an empty bladder, yet the resident still felt the urge to pee, supporting the idea that her desire to pee was psychological. This incident alone should have led to the removal of the catheter.

Regarding the treatment of her urinary tract infection, the Director stated the catheter was left in due to urine retention, but there is no documentation to support this retention. No evidence in the HPCC records indicates that bladder scanning studies confirmed their diagnosis of urine retention. We concluded that the discussion with the Director agreed that HPCC was negligent in failing to record the results of their bladder scans, if such scans were performed.

The Director also quoted the emergency room urologist saying that, since she had urine retention, the catheter should be left in place. I countered this by stating that there is no documentation showing his statement was based on a bladder scan, not just HPCC's medical records transferred with the patient.

Next, we discussed the dehydration issue on 7/29 when my wife was rushed to the emergency room. The doctor said they properly hydrated her at HPCC, and a 25 BUN reading was not high, even though the top reading on the lab reports was 17. When asked about K's statement that the transfer was due to low blood pressure, she said that was one of the reasons for her being lethargic.

The doctor spent a lot of time explaining my wife's medications and the exhausting conditions they could cause. I couldn't get her to admit that my wife was transferred to the emergency room because of dehydration, and she kept emphasizing that a 25 BUN was not a sign of severe dehydration. My response was that the ER doctor's notes stated, "She appears lethargic, mucous membranes are dry, poor skin turgor, drowsy but arousable. She received antibiotics and aggressive IV fluid therapy."

Although the Director did not think she was severely dehydrated, the ER doctor believed she was. I once again explained the incident when the nursing staff couldn't insert an IV feeding line and how the doctor's notes indicated the husband was very worried about the resident's dehydration. I pointed out that her BUN was 25 upon entering the ER and 11 when she was discharged.

I cannot explain what happened during the two-and-a-half-hour meeting because the Director spent a considerable amount of time discussing medications, reviewing medical records, and providing medical reasons for some of HPCC's actions. K had never had anyone question their actions like I did, and the meeting attendees didn't realize I had enough knowledge from WebMD not to accept all of K's claims that HPCC's actions were within standard health-care practice.

I researched the hazards of long-term embedded catheter use as I promised her I would. The consensus is that Foley catheters are strongly discouraged for extended periods. Research also indicated that urine retention should be investigated to see if an obstruction is present, allowing the doctor to take corrective action and avoid the need for long-term catheter use.

HPCC never recommended that I schedule an appointment with her urologist to examine her and check for a blockage causing urine retention. Every website highlights that long-term use of a urethral catheter carries serious health risks and is a significant cause of UTIs affecting the urethra, bladder, and kidneys, usually linked to extended indwelling catheter use.

The decision to insert a catheter depends on whether the patient experiences frequent infections and UTIs, which my wife developed five days after the catheter was placed. CAUTIs are considered the most complicated UTIs and the most common complication of long-term catheter use. I researched and stand by my claim that HPCC's use of a long-term catheter violated accepted healthcare standards.

It was an excellent discussion, and the doctor effectively justified her belief that HPCC did not violate standard healthcare practices. She was responsible for explaining K's investigation procedures, and she did so. I managed to get her to admit that HPCC was negligent in not showing bladder scan results, provided they performed any. My counterarguments to her approval of HPCC's actions were just as valid, but she has an MD. My main goal in filing the quality-of-care complaint with K was to have them acknowledge the negligence in care and thereby strengthen my wrongful death case.

I failed to get K to admit that the supervision of HPCCs needed improvement, but I gathered enough information to suggest that some of their practices might need revision. This meeting marked the end of my contact with K. At the end of the session, one of the nurses joined the call. She said she had never seen a husband show such interest in his wife's healthcare in her twenty years of career. She wanted to compliment me.

K had never encountered anyone who challenged their findings, nor did they think a layperson could go head-to-head with a Medical Director for two and a half hours. The Medical Director's goal was to prove that K had thoroughly investigated my complaints using medical jargon and hypothetical cases. In her mind, she succeeded; in mine, she never justified K's findings in response to my complaints.

I thought my attorney might be interested in my conference, so I emailed him. Last week, at their request, I participated in a video conference with the Chief Medical Officer and Project Manager of K, the vendor contracted by Medicare, to investigate 'quality-of-care comments,' along with two very experienced nurses and a representative of HHS. K requested the meeting to respond to the three-page letter I sent to HHS, which K reports to, documenting and questioning their response to my complaints.

Since this was a first, K asked if I objected to recording the conference so it could be used as a training aid for other complaint investigations; I didn't. What happened next was something none of the other attendees expected.

For two and a half hours, my WebMD argued with their MD, K's Chief Medical Officer. I documented HPCC's failure to meet what K called "meeting all applicable professionally recognized standards of health care." I can't record all the topics discussed in the meeting, so I will focus on the one issue affecting our lawsuit: embedding a Foley catheter.

The MD justified the catheter placement due to the patient's urine retention. She explained that the catheter was left in while treating the patient for a drug-resistant UTI because urine retention posed a greater infection risk than removing the catheter. The MD agreed that a bladder scan was the standard medical procedure for documenting urine retention. HPCC nurses' records show they performed only one scan, well after the catheter was inserted.

That scan stated, "bladder scan indicates empty bladder." Based on the patient's urge to urinate, the catheter remained in place. HPCC ignored the urologist's statement; he believed the catheter was placed for convenience, the patient's urge to urinate was psychological rather than physical, and the catheter should be removed. On June 6, the first order was issued for a bladder scan to be performed every six hours; however, no records indicate the results of these scans.

The order ended on June 12, and there have been no further orders for a bladder scan since then. I informed the MD that the hospital removed the patient's catheter on May 17 before transferring her to HPCC, suggesting that the nursing home perform bladder scans. On May 18, HPCC embedded the catheter, which violated Medicare CMS 20068 guidelines. Since HPCC did not perform a bladder scan on May 18, they also did not document a clinical condition requiring the catheter to be embedded.

Not performing bladder scans during the period of the embedded catheter did not indicate that catheterization was necessary. After my dissertation, the MD agreed that HPCC was negligent in not recording the results of bladder scans, assuming they had been performed. The MD reluctantly acknowledged that there was no documented clinical reason for the catheter to remain in place for the 52 days the patient was at HPCC.

Quoting 'Medscape,' using a Foley catheter for a prolonged period is strongly discouraged because these catheters pose significant health risks. Catheters are a leading cause of UTIs, and untreated symptomatic UTIs can result in urosepsis and death.

I hoped that submitting my complaint to K would lead K to impose Medicare sanctions and potentially financial penalties against HPCC for apparent violations of Medicare rules. The one action HPCC would fear more than a legal judgment. Such sanctions would generate publicity and result in increased Medicare inspections to ensure they address the issues raised. I was hopeful that K would request these sanctions from Medicare, but my effort was unsuccessful.

After two and a half hours of challenging the Chief Medical Officer's defense of HPCC, going to trial would be straightforward. By overlooking HPCC's faults, as I explained, Medicare considers their actions acceptable medical practice. In doing so, Medicare remains unaware of how many HPCC residents are using convenience-embedded catheters that violate Medicare's catheter use restrictions.

CHAPTER 33

Reminiscence

One of my clients mentioned selling his father's car, who was declining in health, which reminded me of the most painful task I ever had to do. Beth was always an independent woman. When we bought our first home in Florida in 2002, she decided we couldn't be a one-car family and needed her own wheels. So, we went car shopping during a trip back to New York. The trip didn't take long. She saw the car she wanted at the first dealership we visited—it was a silver Pontiac with a sunroof.

We made the deal, and she had her wheels. That fall, she drove it back to Florida, following me. A scary incident happened during the trip when an eighteen-wheeler ran me off the road onto the shoulder, causing dirt and dust to fly as I recovered without damage. We had to exit at the following interchange so she could calm down. We didn't have a radio or cell phone so that she couldn't contact me after the incident.

Now that we were residents of Florida, she was happy to get her car and the independence that came with it. She could share our one car there since she only spent four months a year in Buffalo. We arranged for her to fly to Buffalo in June and return in October, while I drove both ways.

In 2017, after her fall and declining health, it became clear she would never drive again. I decided to sell her twenty-year-old car, which looked brand new, just as it did when it left the showroom, and had only 16,000 miles on it. I showed it to a golfing friend, and he bought it right away. When I sold the car, it broke Beth's heart. If the vehicle was in the garage, even though she knew she'd never drive it again, it was still there.

Her independence still felt just outside the door. When the garage was empty, she realized her freedom had also disappeared. She would now have to rely on others for tasks she once managed herself. Her hours of shopping alone, eating lunch out, and usually buying something for me that I didn't need.

They were gone. Like I'm sure many others have felt, her life as she knew it was over. I can never forget her silent weeping as the car left the garage and began to move down the street. Her life had ended, and she would never forgive me for selling her car.

CHAPTER 34

Case Management Plan

H ERE IS AN example of a document submitted to the court that is necessary to move a lawsuit forward to trial. It explains why navigating the halls of justice is not a straight path, but rather a twisting one.

In October 2020, the court issued an 'Agreed Case Management Plan, and Order' listing deadlines for the plaintiff and defendant to submit agreed-upon events to the court. The following is an example of the first event, including dates and responses, as well as the schedule of events extending into October 2021. The first event is the Disclosure of Fact Witnesses.

My attorney named eight individuals, including any witnesses identified in depositions and discovery responses, and added to that list the following:

Plaintiff reserves the right to call all witnesses, including expert witnesses, listed by any party to this lawsuit, including, but not limited to, those identified in Defendant's Expert Witness List.

Plaintiff reserves the right to call impeachment and rebuttal witnesses who have been deposed in this case.

Plaintiff reserves the right to object to any witnesses listed by the Defendant and to amend this witness list if witnesses are identified through discovery after the service date here or at trial.

Plaintiff reserves the right to call treating physicians and other healthcare providers listed on this Witness List for treatment after the service date to testify at trial.

All treating physicians, nurses, rehabilitation therapists, occupational therapists, and other individuals involved in providing the Plaintiff with medical care.

Plaintiff reserves the right to add additional witnesses to this Exhibit List before trial.

All witnesses listed on Defendant's witness list.

All persons listed on any other party's Witness and Exhibit Lists, whether still a party at trial.

Records of all supervisors and custodians from the Defendant's employer.

My counsel must list everyone he might call because the defense could object to their being called if he contacts a witness not listed above.

In addition to the Witness list, there is an Exhibit List.

- All records of the healthcare providers listed above.
- All applicable Florida Statutes and County Ordinances.
- Those exhibits are necessary for impeachment purposes.
- All exhibits listed on any other party's Witness and Exhibit Lists.
- Plaintiff's medical records.
- Hospital records of Plaintiff.

- X-rays, MRI films, CT scans, and other Plaintiff diagnostic tests.
- Collateral source policies and records about the Plaintiff.
- Income tax returns and insurance records about the Plaintiff.
- Clinical Practice Guidelines and Associated Publication of the US Public Health Service about the Plaintiff's condition.
- All depositions that were taken in this matter.
- Any Answers to Interrogatories.
- Any Responses to Requests for Production.
- Any records identified by Defendant.
- Any pleadings contained in the court file.
- Any documents created by Defendants, including those kept as part of Plaintiff's normal business activities and medical records.
- All exhibits listed on Defendant's Exhibit List.
- All anatomic charts, diagrams, drawings, and models created by Defendant for Plaintiff.
- All photographs and literature used by Defendant's Experts and Defendant.
- Burial records of Plaintiff.
- Records of the US Social Security Administration.
- Plaintiff reserves the right to supplement this Exhibit List later.
- The defendant must also file a 'Plaintiff's Witness and Exhibit List.'

One last example of a document request: On February 25, the Plaintiff issued a 'Plaintiff's Northup Request to Produce,' which requests that Defendant, within 30 days, provide copies of all affidavits and transcripts of testimony from any experts identified by the Defendant, whom the Defendant plans or has indicated they plan to call as witnesses at trial. It also seeks other documents intended solely for witness impeachment that are in the possession of the Defendant and that the Defendant reasonably expects or wants to use at trial to impeach the Plaintiff's experts. This is the actual lengthy sentence from the document.

I could continue describing the document, but I've already provided an overview of the paperwork required to pursue a lawsuit, especially one that is unlikely to ever go to court. The defense attorney plans to use trial preparations to delay this case, which we know will eventually be settled through court-ordered mediation. By doing so, the defense attorney increases his retainer fee while also adding to the Plaintiff's attorney's expenses for preparing the same documents, now under a fixed contingency fee.

As of now, eighty-two documents have been submitted to the court, and they are still deciding which additional documents will be submitted.

Until August's mediation, the only activity will be attorneys exchanging document requests through the court. Due to COVID-19, the mediation scheduled for June has been moved to August 3.

On May 10, my attorney informed me that he wanted to add a urologist to his list of experts, which I had suggested when he hired the $1,500 geriatric specialist. Choosing a urology specialist will be costly.

On February 19, my probate attorney submitted a new document to the court, informing the court that the petitioner cannot file a Final Accounting and Petition for Discharge within the deadline set by Florida Probate Rule 5.400 because a wrongful death lawsuit is currently ongoing.

The petitioner estimates that a Final Accounting and a Petition for Discharge can be filed on or before March 1, 2022. It seems my probate attorney sees no end to the lawsuit anytime soon.

CHAPTER 35

Medicare Recovery Right

O N April 16, 2021, I received a letter from the Medicare Benefits Coordination and Recovery Center (BCRC) informing me of Medicare's right of recovery, as outlined under the Medicare Secondary Payer provision. It states that conditional Medicare payments related to your case for the incident on May 18, 2017, have been made. These conditional payments are subject to reimbursement to Medicare from any proceeds you may receive through a settlement, judgment, award, or other compensation.

Based on the available information, Medicare has identified $55,562.43 in conditional payments that we believe are related to your case. Enclosed is a list of claims that make up this total.

Please review this listing carefully and let us know if it needs updating as soon as possible. (For reader information, on the 26 pages, there are 200 incidents listed with 715 DX codes, which are used to identify procedures so Medicare can pay the doctor for his service. I can determine whether the charge applies to Medicare's conditional payments by defining each DX code.)

Attached is a Payment Summary with 26 pages of medical charges BCRC deemed relevant to our case. The list includes medical bills from May 18, 2017, to April 19, 2019.

If you believe the attached list of conditional payments is incomplete, incorrect, or that you are not responsible for reimbursing Medicare for these payments, please submit written documentation along with an explanation to support your dispute or rebuttal.

This letter confirms my responsibility for paying Medicare $55,562.34, which will be deducted from any settlement I receive from the lawsuit. Please note that the conditional payments Medicare requested from me were not paid directly to me but to the hospital. My understanding is that the hospital retains its conditional costs, but I need to reimburse Medicare for the conditional payments they disbursed to the hospital. Is there an issue with this arrangement? To comply with BCRC's request and make the payments, my only option would be to sue the hospital to recover the conditional costs.

On April 19, I called BCRC to ask about their letter. After completing the initial steps, I finally spoke to a representative from the Recovery Department. After providing her with all the required identification, she asked how she could assist me. I told her I had questions about some statements in the letter.

She told me she couldn't provide the information, even though the letter was addressed to me, because I wasn't authorized to have her disclose the case details. The only way I could get the info was to fax them a death certificate showing I was the beneficiary's spouse. So, for the third time, I faxed a copy.

Later, after giving them time to obtain the death certificate, I called again. Instead of detailing my experience, I will share a copy of the letter I sent to BCRC on April 23, which summarizes the findings of my investigation.

To fulfill your request, "I will review the listing carefully and let you know as soon as possible if the listing is incorrect." To facilitate an expedited review, I need clarification on the topics covered in the letter from BCRC.

Based on your statement, "If you have any questions concerning this matter, please contact the Benefits Coordination & Recovery Center." When I called BCRC on April 19, I was told they could not provide any information until the center received a copy of the death certificate. I faxed the certificate on April 19. A return call to BCRC informed me that it took 48 hours for the fax to reach the center.

In a call made 48 hours after I faxed the certificate, I was informed that it would take up to 45 days to review, and they could only provide information once the process was complete. When I asked to speak to a supervisor, the representative hung up on me. So, I decided to respond to their letter without BCRC's help.

It is clear to me, based on the medical charges you mention, "We believe are related to your case," that BCRC has misunderstood the meaning of 'Date of Incident.' I can correct your report by describing your incident date, which I was attempting to obtain in my abruptly ended information request. I will provide the accurate version of the incident, without relying on your understanding of it.

The resident arrived at HP Care Center (HPCC) from the hospital with a displaced comminuted fracture of the left fibula. HPCC placed her leg in a brace to immobilize it, which made it difficult for her to urinate without assistance. Because helping her to the bathroom each time she urinated could be inconvenient, HPCC violated Medicare guidelines regarding the restricted use of an embedded catheter and, on 18 May 2017, inserted a catheter.

Once again, in violation of Medicare guidelines, the catheter was left in place for 72 days. After discharge, because HPCC used the catheter without a medical reason, the resident developed more urinary tract infections, which eventually became resistant to antibiotics. The frequent UTIs gradually impaired her kidney function, leading to complete kidney failure and her eventual death. Although the incident started on May 18, 2017, the medical consequences didn't become clear until many months later, resulting in significant medical costs.

The Notice of Intent was not filed with the courts, naming HPCC as Defendant, until April 13, 2018. All conditional payments made before that date should not be included and, therefore, should not be considered under Medicare Secondary Payer provisions. The new Date of the Incident should be April 13, 2018, to reflect claims that Medicare has paid conditionally. A review of the Payment Summary shows that $43,382 of those charges were for the rehab facility, rehab doctors, physical therapy, and pain management to treat the fractured tibia and should not be charged to the corrected incident report.

After reviewing the Payment Summary, I found only $9,966 in charges that may be related to the correct incident. I need to know the DX codes associated with these charges to confirm they are for treating urinary tract infections. Asking for a copy of the DX codes is one of the questions I still need to raise. Therefore, the Payment Summary of conditional payments shows $45,596 in costs that I am not responsible for reimbursing to Medicare.

An explanation supporting my dispute will require BCRC to provide me with the medical documentation used to justify the charges listed on the Payment Summary. I will also need a list of all the DX codes on the Payment Summary to help me review the documents provided. Since the beneficiary passed away in August 2019, I question why Medicare is still investigating this case file to recover any remaining Medicare conditional payments.

With a lawsuit scheduled to resume in June, BCRC must provide me with a final accounting by May 31. If I do not receive such documentation, I will accept the $9,966 as BCRC's final account.

Since my attorney was not copied on the Medicare information, I emailed him to ask whether he had submitted a Proof of Representation with BCRC. In a reply email, he sent me a letter stating they had sent it to Medicare on September 5, 2017.

Upon seeing the letter, I understood how BCRC arrived at the $55,000 conditional payment figure. The letter states, "Please be advised this firm represents Beth for injuries sustained in a Florida accident on 18 May 2017." The letter referenced the fractured tibia as the accident, but as I mentioned in the letter sent to BCRC, the broken leg was not the incident being litigated.

I told my current lawyer that I had notified my second lawyer on 4/4/17 that Medicare was using the wrong incident date, specifically for a broken leg. Medicare requested that the incident date be corrected so that they wouldn't continue processing charges unrelated to the case. Not surprisingly, the second lawyer did not inform Medicare of the updated incident details, so they continued to collect $55,000 in condition payments from the broken leg incident that occurred on May 18, 2017.

The letter mentioned above states, "Accordingly, this letter is to request under Florida Statute 768.76(6), that Medicare review their records to determine if benefits paid on Beth's behalf resulted from the injuries she sustained on the date mentioned above."

By law, Medicare must send this information within thirty days of receiving this certified mail, explicitly stating, "The provider of collateral sources will waive any right to subrogation or reimbursement unless it provides the claimant or claimant's lawyer with a statement asserting that payment of benefits or the right of subrogation or reimbursement is within 30 days after the claimant's notification to the collateral sources." This is a typical autocratic explanation of why Medicare is sending me all the charges.

I noticed my counsel was not copied on the information from Medicare, so I emailed him the following. Not being copied on BCRC's April 14, 2021, letter means you are not recognized as my attorney, who may receive information from BCRC. If the 9/5/17 letter is the only notice given to Medicare, it has expired. The Consent Form is only valid for a limited period.

Medicare will not release information from a beneficiary's records without proper authorization. You need to submit a new Consent Form to discuss matters with BCRC, along with a Proof of Representation Document. Additionally, you must update the accident date and description in any recent filing. His response is to wait until we see the result of your letter to BCRC before proceeding.

On May 6, I received a response from Medicare to my letter. They agreed with some of my reasoning and reduced the condition payments from $55,562 to $23,135. However, I disagreed with the medical expenses on their updated listing, so I decided to refile my objections to the listed items. On May 14, I finally contacted BCRC by phone and spent 41 minutes discussing their Beneficiary Conditional Payment Letter.

The outcome of the discussion was that, to challenge conditional payments, I would need to review each of the 715 charges listed on the Payment Summary and explain why these charges are not part of the lawsuit and should therefore not be applied. Following these instructions, I conducted my investigation and sent a summary of my findings to BCRC on May 11th.

The first task was to inform BCRC that they used the wrong incident date, 18 May 2017, and description. I explained that this was the date Elizabeth was transferred from the hospital to HPCC with a fractured tibia and fibula for rehabilitation. The fractures resulted from a fall at home and are not the basis for the lawsuit. It was also the day the litigated catheter insertion occurred, but the effects of that procedure and the condition payments would not become evident for many months.

I told them that the litigation involves a wrongful death claim caused by kidney failure. The incident date should be June 11, 2019, when hospital doctors diagnosed the kidney failure and began treatment. I based this on Medicare guidelines, which state, "When an incident is not evident over some time, the date the incident became evident is the date it was identified."

I then began investigating the $55,562.34 in conditional payments that BCRC believes are connected to your case. Each payment entry includes the provider's name, the DX code, the dates, and the payment amount. To review everything thoroughly, I needed the DX code description, and when I asked BCRC for it, I was told to look it up myself.

A DX code is the number a doctor or hospital uses to identify the condition a patient is being treated for, and it is the number submitted to Medicare for payment. I went online and found a website called Code Comprehensive Search. By entering the DX code, I could get a definition of the diagnosis the code represents.

For example, I482 was the main code for atrial fabrication. In some cases, such as hospital visits, the main code may be followed by multiple subcodes. For instance, one charge had twenty-one subcodes. Instead of investigating each subcode, I told BCR that my investigation focused on the primary code used.

Based on the primary DX code, my letter explained whether the charge applied to the case. Instead of detailing my findings, I will go straight to my conclusion. In reviewing the 200 primary DX codes listed as condition payments on the Payment Summary Sheet, I find that NONE of the $55,562.34 BCRC mentioned as conditional charges applies to the incident.

On May 3, I received a response from BCRC confirming that they had accepted my revised incident date of June 11, 2019, and had removed $55,562.34 from the related conditional payments. They then provided me with a new Payment Summary that included two pages of conditional payment charges related to the updated incident date, totaling $6,578.89.

I am sure BCRC has never had anyone question their conditional payments summary as I have. Still, my efforts led to a $48,984 reduction in the conditional costs I would need to reimburse to Medicare. Riding this wave, I decided to push my luck further and, on June 3, sent the following letter to BCRC.

Plaintiff—Elizabeth, Defendant—LMHS. The DX code N179, kidney failure, confirms my position that June 11 should be the incident date. I now want to explain Florida's Sovereign Immunity Statutes. BCRC has sent the Plaintiff a Beneficiary Conditional Payment Letter stating that Medicare has the primary right to recover conditional payments for Medicare Part A paid to the Defendant, which can be retrieved from the Plaintiff. In a typical lawsuit, the Plaintiff would include these conditional payments in the final settlement. Those funds would then be paid to BCRC by the Plaintiff to fulfill their obligation. However, this case is not a typical lawsuit.

Florida's Sovereign Immunity Statutes apply to this lawsuit, and the Defendant is identified as a sovereign immunity entity. The Defendant's maximum liability for pain and suffering is $200,000. According to the Statute, the Defendant is protected from any additional claims, including conditional Medicare payments. To fulfill BCRC's priority recovery claim, the Plaintiff must deduct that amount from their pain and suffering settlement.

In summary, the Plaintiff must reimburse Medicare for the conditional payments made to the Defendant, who is allowed to retain those payments. While BCRC may be protecting Medicare's interests, it overlooks the Plaintiff's claim, as they contribute to the Medicare system. In this case, the Defendant wins, Medicare wins, and the Plaintiff—whose wife died due to the Defendant's misconduct—remains the primary loser.

The proper way to recover Medicare conditional payments in a Florida Sovereign Immunity Statutes case is for BCRC to bill the Defendant for costs covered by Medicare's priority right of recovery. The Sovereign Immunity Statutes would block the plaintiff's attempt to recover those payments from the Defendant. Therefore, the Plaintiff requests a waiver of recovery.

On May 17, I received a letter from an organization called O, which is part of UnitedHealth. They are trying to recover the medical benefits paid out for the injury in question. In other words, like Medicare, they aim to recover 20% of the medical benefits that AARP paid on behalf of your dependent for injury treatment. The attached letter is a two-page, 82-line summary of every payment made by AARP from May 2017 through April 2019, with amounts ranging from $2.36 to $4,606.00. My task was to review the 82 charges and identify those with which I disagreed. The total amount O is seeking to recover is $9,644.69. The following is my response to that letter.

Let me start by correcting your incorrect Date of Injury. This case involves a wrongful death lawsuit caused by kidney failure. Medicare states that if an event is not immediately apparent, the incident date is when it first becomes detectable. Therefore, the incident date is June 11, 2019, when doctors diagnosed kidney failure and initiated treatment.

All medical payments listed on the Summary for AARP are not relevant to this case. Medicare's BCRC, adjusting to the new incident date of June 11, 2019, should remove all conditional payments from the Beneficiary Condition Payment Letter before that date. I request a corrected copy of the letter showing the removal of all mentioned charges.

On June 18, I received a BCRC letter stating that I am ineligible to file a request for a Medicare waiver of conditional payments. A waiver cannot be considered until I receive a formal letter requesting the recovery of Medicare's payment. Medicare will not issue a formal letter until it is informed of a case settlement.

At the same time, I received another copy of a Payment Summary Form indicating that BCRC has designated $6,578.89 as the total conditioned payment I owe to Medicare based on the June 11 date. I was hoping my request for a waiver would prevent me from analyzing the payment summary. Still, I now have to review all the charges again and identify those I don't consider applicable. I reviewed every DX code shown on the overview and submitted the following letter to BCRC on June 22.

Subject: Dispute of Conditional Payments Listed on 6/16 Payment Summary Form. My request for a waiver of payment exempts me from analyzing your attached Payment Summary Form. Until I receive a formal letter requesting recovery, I must correct your identified conditional payments. The following summary shows that your total reimbursement of $6,578.89 is incorrect, which BCRC believes pertains to my case, and I dispute it as detailed below.

The wrongful death lawsuit involves kidney failure believed to be caused by medical malpractice at a nursing home. Therefore, Medicare conditional payments should cover hospital and doctor bills related to treating the kidney failure. According to ICD-10Data.com, codes N17 through N19 are specific ICD-10-CM codes used to identify renal failure for billing.

N18.9 specifies Chronic Kidney Disease, Unspecified, while N19 indicates Unspecified Kidney Failure. TOS 60 for GCMC lists 20 different DX codes, of which only two use the codes N179 and N184, and a code I129 may also apply. I'll provide examples of some of the other 17 codes listed: F0281 Dementia, F411 Generalized Anxiety Disorder, R630 Anorexia, Z932 Ileostomy status, and Z66 DNR. Conditional payments made to these codes do not apply to the date of the incident.

Since I am not aware of the dollar amount assigned by the hospital for each code, I can only estimate code values by dividing $5,833.96 by the 20 codes, which results in approximately $291.70 per DX code. Since I found only three codes related to renal failure, the $5,833.96 hospital conditional payment for the incident should be reduced to $875.10. Regarding the individual doctors' conditional payments: For EG, he lists four DX codes, but only N179, kidney failure, is applicable. The other codes—I10 Hypertension, I4891 A-fib, and N390 UTI non-specified—are not appropriate. His billing drops from $177.71 to $44.43. For Dr. RK, only one of his two codes, N179, is applicable, resulting in a reduction of $12.13.

For example, the other code used is unspecified N390 degenerative nervous system disease. The other doctors have identified their codes as N179 and N184, which are associated with acute kidney failure, and their billing of $542.87 could meet the criteria for conditional payments. The corrections above reduce the $6,578.89 condition payments shown on the June 16, 2021, Payment Summary Form to $1,474.54. I am available to discuss my billing logic upon request.

After sending the above letters disputing BCRC's conditional payments, I finally reached my goal.

On July 12, I received a letter from BCRC stating: "After reviewing the claims in question, we agree with the dispute, and the case has been adjusted accordingly." In other words, the case has been closed, and the original $55,562 conditional payments, which I owed to Medicare, have been reduced to zero.

It is unprecedented for BCRC to waive conditional charges before a case settlement and to issue a formal letter requesting the recovery of Medicare's costs. I am convinced that my knowledge of the DX codes, which allowed me to dispute charges, was the key factor in Medicare's decision to drop all charges. Showing that any charges would be paid by the Plaintiff rather than the Defendant, in accordance with Sovereign Immunity Statutes, may also have helped close the case.

Additionally, I submitted a letter with O, the agency retained by AARP, to recover $9,644 of their portion from the original $55,562 owed to BCRC. According to the attached CMS letter, BCRC has determined that the estate of Elizabeth owes no conditional payments, and their case has been adjusted accordingly. As a result, O no longer needs to pursue recovery of medical benefits paid on Elizabeth's behalf, and your case should be closed. Please request that O issue a formal notice of closure to me.

It was hard to believe that three months ago, I was facing a $55,562 charge from BCRC and a $9,644 bill from O. My efforts to dispute these charges and present my case resulted in a reduction of $65,206 from my lawsuit.

My review of all the DX codes billed to Medicare by the medical profession shows that many DX codes do not apply to the condition. CMS has never questioned their 'conditional payments,' as I have, and I am one of the few who have had CMS waive payments without a final lawsuit being completed.

CHAPTER 36

Mediation Preparation

O N AUGUST 2, my attorney and I discussed tomorrow's mediation. He told me he couldn't find an expert medical witness to support our position based on HPCC's records. The expert depends on HPCC's medical records, which we argue are incomplete and lack the necessary tests to justify their reason for leaving the embedded catheter, which we claim contributed to her death. He stated that without an expert witness, there's no chance of proceeding with a wrongful death case. I asked the expert doctor to send me the medical records he is using to form his opinion.

The expert bases his opinion on a single sentence in the July 29 hospital report: 'Patient has failed voiding tests in the past.' This statement, according to HPCC's records sent to the hospital, seems to be a cover-your-ass remark meant to justify the need for a catheter. After reviewing the doctor's notes for his opinion, I sent the following email to my attorney.

The expert bases his opinion on the statement, "Pt has failed voiding trials in the past." This statement was made on August 1, 76 days after the catheter was inserted on May 18, 2017. Records will show that the catheter was implanted without supporting evidence that the resident failed a bladder scan. My review of hundreds of documents shows no notation of the resident failing a voiding test.

The statement "It has failed voiding trials in the past" is based on information provided to the hospital by HPCC, as there is no record of the hospital conducting voiding tests. I reiterate that the only voiding trials performed by HPCC indicate no need for a catheter. The expert's opinion is based on incorrect information. If this is the only statement the expert relies on for his argument, he still needs to do his homework to understand the basis of those failed voiding trials.

Regarding the language about leaving the catheter in, she arrived at the hospital with an embedded catheter, and Dr. B relied solely on the word of HPCC. The expert needs to review Dr. B's report, where he questions the necessity of the catheter and his plan for its removal. I recommend sending him the completed Mediation Summary that provides the whole story and instructs him to expand his investigation beyond the hospital statement on which he is basing his opinion.

It is crucial to find an expert witness who agrees with our stance that she did not need the catheter. He must be ready to challenge the defendant's two expert witnesses, who argue that the catheter was justified. Our case hinges on the lack of bladder scanning trials supporting the catheter, so we need to locate a physician who supports our argument. The estimated cost for consulting a doctor who aligns with our position ranges from $3,000 to $5,000. Finding a doctor to oppose another at this stage is nearly impossible.

The deep pockets defense can easily find two expert witnesses to testify that the catheter was justified. Besides the two experts HPCC can call, they can also cite the findings of K, the Medicare Quality of Care vendor I filed my Medicare complaint with. As previously explained, despite my documented summary that HPCC violated Medicare mandates on using an embedded catheter, K ruled that HPCC followed standard medical practice.

I am now willing to consider any reasonable settlement offer. My attorney advised me to prepare talking points outlining our case for the mediator, but I got caught up in the details, and the talking points grew to four pages. Much of what follows has already been stated earlier in the story, but this will be the first time the mediator hears it. My talking points offer the most detailed description of our case.

HPCC is a Medicare facility that receives millions of dollars in Medicare reimbursements and operates in accordance with Medicare's quality of care guidelines. I want to reference the Medicare order, CMS-20068. Ensure that a resident who enters the facility without an indwelling catheter is not catheterized unless their condition requires it.

HPCC knowingly violated that directive by inserting a Foley catheter without performing a voiding test to check for urine retention. Without testing to determine if catheterization was necessary, the catheter was placed for HPCC's convenience to lessen the workload of the understaffed and overburdened aides.

The second directive on CMS 20068 states: Ensure that a resident who enters the facility with an indwelling catheter or receives one later is assessed for removal promptly, unless the resident's clinical condition indicates that catheterization is necessary. The catheter, inserted on May 18, remained in place on July 29, 72 days later, when the resident was sent to the hospital in a non-responsive state.

In my review of 184 pages of records from HPCC, there is no mention of the resident failing a voiding test, which would be the only reason to leave the catheter in place. In fact, on June 4, 2017, the nurse's notes state, "bladder scan with no urine in the bladder." During her stay at HPCC, her urologist recommended removing the catheter. His records show no medical evidence that she needed a catheter, and he believes HPCC left it in for the convenience of the nursing home staff.

Despite having a Foley catheter in place, he believed her need to urinate was neurologic and psychiatric in origin, a view shared by the urologist at HPCC, who also stated that her urge to urinate—which was the reason for the catheter—was not physical but psychiatric. Two doctors, including a urologist, questioned the necessity of a chronic catheter and recommended its removal in the hospital.

The third directive states that residents receive appropriate treatment services to prevent urinary tract infections whenever possible. My wife had a UTI on May 26 and still had it when she was hospitalized on July 29. She was treated with various drugs during that time, which caused the facility to declare that the UTI was drug-resistant.

When she arrived at the hospital, the doctor noticed the catheter was dirty and suspected it might have caused her UTI. The initial evidence suggests that the embedded catheter may have played a role in her recurring UTIs. Her new healthcare facility agreed with her urologist that the catheter was unnecessary, removed it, and successfully treated her UTI.

My final comment on the risk related to catheterization for HPCC. HPCC's Patient Care Plan states that the problem began on May 18, 2017, with an alteration in urinary elimination and risk for infection related to an indwelling catheter. HPCC was aware of the risks associated with an embedded catheter—residents' rights under Chapter 400.022 of the Florida Statutes are outlined.

Residents have the right to be adequately informed about their medical condition and proposed treatment, unless they are deemed unable to give informed consent under the laws of the state of Florida. They also have the right to be fully informed of any non-emergency changes in care or treatment that could impact their well-being. Additionally, residents have the right to participate in planning their medical treatment, including the right to refuse medication and therapy, unless their physicians direct otherwise. They should be aware of the consequences of their choices.

My wife, a registered nurse with 40 years of experience, including 15 years in nursing facilities, is well aware of the risks associated with using an indwelling catheter. With that knowledge, she would never have agreed to have a catheter inserted unless medical evidence, such as a bladder scan, indicated it was necessary. She never had the chance to give consent to her treatment. Therefore, HP was in direct violation of Chapter 400.022.

Any violation of the residence specified in this section constitutes grounds for action by the agency under 400.102. Section 400.102 states that the agency may take action against the licensee for: "An intentional or negligent act materially affecting the health or safety of residents of the facility."

Medscape states: "Using a Foley catheter for a prolonged period is strongly discouraged. Indwelling urethral catheters are a major cause of UTIs, and not treating them may lead to urosepsis and death. The death rate among nursing home residents with urethral catheters is three times higher than among those without."

The Omnibus Budget Reconciliation Act (OBRA), also known as the Nursing Home Reform Act of 1987, is a piece of legislation that has significantly improved the quality of care in nursing homes.

One of the main improvements was reducing the improper use of indwelling catheters. Nursing homes must meet the federal requirements to participate in Medicare and Medicaid programs.

A nursing home's failure to meet OBRA quality of care standards when caring for a resident shows a lapse in providing the reasonable care and skill they are expected to deliver. This includes only using urinary catheters when appropriate, as specified in regulations, to prevent adverse outcomes. HPCC has violated Medicare and OBRA requirements related to the use of catheters.

Medical review states, "Too many unnecessary catheters are done, and some recipients have died from complications caused by urinary catheters." Foley catheters are an inappropriate treatment for my wife's incontinence. Every patient should be informed about the risks of urinary catheters and be offered alternative, less invasive procedures.

For example, a bladder scan can easily measure bladder volume. My wife had a catheter inserted immediately upon arriving at HPCC without being informed of the risks of urinary catheters or shown a justification, such as a bladder scan, for inserting the catheter.

The article states: "It is quite common for patients to get UTIs from catheters, and some infections can be deadly. A nursing home-acquired UTI is often not a simple infection to treat because the bacteria are more likely to be drug-resistant," as determined by HPCC's doctors.

Health Line states: "A catheter-associated CAUTI is one of the most common infections a person can get; bacteria or fungi can enter your urinary tract through the catheter, multiply, and cause an infection. Catheters should not stay in place longer than necessary, as prolonged use raises the risk of infection. Prompt treatment of a CAUTI is essential because an untreated UTI can develop into a more serious kidney infection."

I could also mention other reputable health organizations, such as the CDC and Mayo Clinic. However, I have observed that embedding a catheter is not a typical medical procedure because of the current and future medical risks involved. After reviewing the details, I find it hard to understand how a urologist could justify an indefinite-duration embedded catheter. Two years after leaving HPCC, my wife had 25 UTIs, with 12 requiring hospitalization for treatment.

Women typically experience a UTI only 2 to 3 times in their lives. With each infection, her kidney function declined until her kidneys eventually failed. I sat with her in hospice for two weeks, during which she kept asking, "When can I go home?" and "God, please make me better."

The catheter embedding, which violated Medicare and OBRA guidelines on the restricted use of embedded catheters, along with poor management, contributed to my wife's death. Knowing that a catheter is a significant source of UTIs, HPCC continued to treat a drug-resistant UTI while leaving the catheter in place. According to WebMD, it is recommended to remove the catheter if a UTI cannot be cured with an implanted catheter.

Now, I would like to address the issue of dehydration. In August 2017, I informed the nursing superintendent that my wife was dehydrated. I supported my observations with elevated BUN lab readings, which are a standard medical indicator of dehydration, and a torque test. Ultimately, the staff agreed that my wife needed intravenous rehydration and planned to begin the procedure that night.

Not finding my wife on an IV the next day, I asked why. When nurses tried to insert an IV, I was told her veins kept collapsing, so they stopped trying. They planned to rehydrate her by encouraging her to drink more. When her condition did not improve, I requested that she be rehydrated in the hospital emergency room. Instead of sending her to the hospital, they said they would find someone to place an IV.

Eventually, they found a male nurse who could insert the IV, but it was too late. This shows that HPCC staff lacked proper training in placing IVs. On August 29, I received a call from HPCC saying my wife was unresponsive and waiting for the doctor's orders. My wife is near death, unresponsive, and the nurses are waiting for the doctor. He ordered her to be taken to the ER, where doctors found her severely dehydrated and started aggressive rehydration. Additionally, she had a UTI and pneumonia.

Now, let me explain the potentially deadly complications of dehydration.

Kidney failure:

> When you become severely dehydrated, your blood volume decreases, and your kidneys may shut down to stop further water loss in your urine. If the kidneys remain shut down for too long, they could suffer permanent damage. It is unknown how long the plaintiff was unresponsive before being rushed to the hospital, but it was hours. The plaintiff's kidneys shutting down could have caused damage to her kidneys and contributed to her death from kidney failure.

Brain Injury:

> Rapid blood loss and low blood pressure can harm
> your brain. One reason for HPCC's discharge from
> the hospital was low blood pressure. My wife expe-
> rienced memory loss after aggressive rehydration by
> emergency doctors. I could provide extensive doc-
> umentation showing the harm caused by continued
> catheter use and the severe damage dehydration can
> inflict. However, I believe I have thoroughly addressed
> these topics. My attorney thought it was an excellent
> presentation, but too lengthy, and plans to give a
> shorter case summary to the mediator.

Mediation is scheduled for three hours, with the mediator being paid an estimated $300 to $600 per hour for a minimum of three hours. I agreed that my talking points would take too much time, so I would let my attorney make the opening statement. They provide the clearest description of our case, but the mediator is only there to get a brief background on the subject and not to decide the case's merits. Whether used or not, it helped me to summarize the case.

Many of my points have already been made, but this is my final opportunity to summarize them. As thorough as my summary is, I wouldn't be allowed to present it at trial because only a medical doctor can state what I have just described.

Let me digress here. This case originated as a medical malpractice lawsuit, supported by the HPCC nurses' notes and medical reports that substantiate our claims. Medical malpractice occurs when a healthcare facility deviates from the expected standard of care, either through negligence or intentional acts, resulting in injury to the resident. All care facilities are expected to adhere to this standard.

Deviating from this standard or failing to meet that standard of care usually leads to a medical malpractice claim. Such a claim can be for Medical Negligence, which doesn't require the patient to be harmed, or Medical Malpractice, where the patient has suffered injury. Our claim qualified as Medical Malpractice. We had a strong case and could have secured a fair settlement in mediation.

However, when Beth died, everything changed. The case shifted from a Medical Malpractice claim to a Wrongful Death claim, which is a more challenging lawsuit to win. In the malpractice case, we had all the necessary evidence to support our claim; however, the evidence requirements differed in a wrongful death case.

The Florida Statutes 766.102 states: In any action seeking damages for a person's death, where it is alleged that the death resulted from negligence by a health care provider, the claimant must prove by the greater weight of the evidence that the provider's actions breached the prevailing professional standard of care for that provider.

The general professional standard of care for a healthcare provider is the level of care that, considering all relevant circumstances, is recognized as acceptable and appropriate. If the injury is claimed to have resulted from the negligent medical intervention of the healthcare provider, the claimant must demonstrate a breach of the prevailing professional standard of care.

In any claim alleging a violation of a resident's rights or negligence resulting in a resident's death, the claimant must prove by a preponderance of the evidence that: the defendant owed a duty to the resident, the defendant breached that duty, the breach was a legal cause of death, and the resident's death was a result of the violation. If the plaintiff fails to meet the burden of proof on any of these elements, they will not recover damages.

Here, I am referring to my filing of the quality-of-care complaint with K and explaining why I was determined to prove their conclusions were incorrect. K's decision that the actions of HPCC were within the accepted professional standard of care can be used by HPCC to demonstrate that their efforts did not contribute to the plaintiff's death. We now bear the burden of proving that the medical malpractice evidence we provided was the direct cause of Beth's death.

We lacked sufficient evidence and could only substantiate our claims by hiring doctors, with an estimated retainer fee of $3,000 to $5,000 per doctor. Convincing a doctor to testify against another is unlikely. Now, we essentially enter mediation without a strong case.

Both attorneys knew these facts when the wrongful death case emerged in July 2019 but continued submitting unnecessary court documents for the next two years. After her death, the case could have been settled for a small amount, saving years of litigation.

As mentioned earlier, the defendant had no incentive to settle the case because they were on a retainer. The defense's delaying tactics increased the plaintiff's response costs with each delay, discouraging many attorneys from pursuing a Florida Sovereign Immunity lawsuit and leaving numerous valid medical malpractice cases unlitigated.

CHAPTER 37

Mediation

On August 3, I logged into ZOOM to join my attorney and the mediator for the scheduled mediation. The mediator's primary goal is to help clarify the issue and facilitate communication, allowing the parties to reach a mutually beneficial settlement. The mediator is not there to provide legal advice. He requested a case summary without the defendant attending to update him.

Realizing that my prepared presentation was too long, my attorney provided a shorter version of the case. The mediator clarified that he was not there to decide the validity of our claims but to facilitate an agreed-upon settlement. His primary role was to collect settlement offers and relay counteroffers from the plaintiff and defendant. Then, defense counsel appeared on screen and outlined their case. Although confidentiality rules limit what can be shared about mediation communications, the details of the defendant's case were already known to us, so they are not confidential.

They argued that the plaintiff failed to prove the long-term effects of the catheter and dehydration problems. They cited K's report, which concluded that HPCC's procedures followed the standard of care, and they pointed out that HPCC's two medical experts would support this claim. Their final exhibit was the death certificate, which states that Beth died from Alzheimer's.

One known drawback of mediation is that it rarely uncovers the whole truth of an issue. As expected, because we couldn't challenge their evidence and because the burden of proof was on the plaintiff to show that HPCC's medical malpractice caused the plaintiff's death, our case was weak.

Referring to the confidential clause, let us assume all figures used here are hypothetical. Naturally, the plaintiff will ask for the $200,000 cap on damages, and the defense will either reject the amount or counter it. For the next three hours, the high-priced mediator's job is to facilitate the exchange of demands between the plaintiff and the defendant's counteroffers.

There were many proposals and counteroffers during those three hours, but let's hypothetically assume that the plaintiff's final demands dropped to $20,000, and the defendant's last offer was $10,000.

I want to express my dissatisfaction with my attorney's negotiations. He did not establish a minimum dollar amount for the talks.

Suppose the figure was $50,000, giving us more room to negotiate against the defendant's $10,000 offer, with the potential middle ground being $30,000. When my attorney quickly lowered our demands to $20,000, it indicated he had a weak case, and instead of negotiating, he was capitulating to the defendant. Our strategy of aiming for a midpoint settlement was now limited to $15,000.

Settlement amounts are confidential; however, the reader is aware that the hypothetical settlement fell within the range of $10,000 to $20,000. We should have ended mediation and gone home when negotiations hit this range. Still, we had already committed to a hypothetical $20,000 settlement, which was a great deal for the defendant, so there was no chance we would have succeeded in ending mediation without a compromise. The mediator wanted to settle the case to add to his resume and would have discouraged us from leaving.

One of the main disadvantages of mediation is that it can be challenging to ensure the settlement is fair to both parties. For example, one side might have access to more resources, such as the hospital's medical experts and the long-form death certificate.

In that situation, they might convince the other party to agree to a settlement that isn't in their best interest. During mediation, there is no discovery process, as in a court, and no formal way for the plaintiff to obtain the defendant's information.

Court-ordered mediation often favors the defendant over the plaintiff, especially in cases involving sovereign immunity. The defendant knows that their maximum liability is $200,000, and their attorney's primary goal is to keep that amount as low as the plaintiff is willing to accept.

The plaintiff has limited bargaining power because the goal of mediation is to settle for less than the $200,000 damages cap. The defendant, aware of this, never proposed a settlement during the three years of litigation.

CHAPTER 38

Post Mediation

Knowing that once Beth died, the burden of proof shifted to the plaintiff to demonstrate that the malpractice caused her death, both attorneys could have settled the case two years earlier. Instead, they filed Complaints, Amended Complaints, Motions to Dismiss, and various other legal documents, which increased the plaintiff's legal costs.

Like the military, I decided to conduct an after-action review of the defendant's statements absolving them of any responsibility for Beth's death. My attorney took the wrong approach when trying to find a medical expert who would counter the defendant's use of a Foley catheter.

He should have agreed with the defendant's decision to place the catheter, as long as she medically needed it. The key phrase is 'proving she medically needed it.' None of HPCC's records show that bladder scans were performed, which would justify inserting a catheter. Since the defendant was unable to prove the necessity for the catheter, we would have undermined their medical expert.

Regarding their reliance on K's report, HPCC's actions followed all standard medical practices. According to their Medicare guidelines, we can argue that K depends only on information provided by the provider and does not rely on complaint documentation, which indicates that the data from HPCC was incorrect. Two examples would be.

HPCC's statement claims Beth was transferred from the hospital with a catheter, even though hospital documentation showed the catheter had been removed. The second example involves her being taken to the emergency room in a non-responsive state, and HPCC's records indicate she was sent there due to low blood pressure.

Their reference to the death certificate indicates that the cause of death was Alzheimer's. People usually do not die directly from Alzheimer's, but it is often listed as the primary cause of death on a death certificate for hospice patients. Beth was transferred from an LMHS hospital to hospice after LMHS doctors diagnosed her as being in the final stage of kidney failure.

We had solid documentation to win a medical malpractice lawsuit, but it still does not meet the burden of proof needed to show that HPCC's malpractice caused her death—a hurdle we could not clear. HPCC was guilty of medical malpractice, but only an autopsy would prove it.

By submitting a Freedom of Information Request to the hospital, I was able to obtain a summary of the fee paid to the outside counsel hired to prosecute the lawsuit. He was paid $26,894 for his services plus $579 in legal expenses. My counsel, who spent the same three years preparing meaningless court documents to address the defendant's delays, earned less than $5,000.

Is it clear why attorneys hesitate to accept sovereign immunity lawsuits? My costs deducted from the settlement included a $2,500 contingency fee, $5,425 in legal fees (which was less than

I expected), $2,800 in probate expenses, and $150 for postage and document purchases, totaling $10,875.

Imagine this: The defense attorney earned more money defending HPCC, the medical malpractice defendant, than the plaintiff, whose wife died due to HPCC's medical malpractice, received from the LMHS settlement. I am sure LMHS would not want the public to be aware of this information.

Money isn't the only reason why aggrieved parties file lawsuits. In my case, it was to get HPCC to acknowledge settling a wrongful death lawsuit. I understand that a monetary settlement is considered a cost of doing business; however, I wanted to make it public that LMHS has settled a wrongful death lawsuit.

When a medical facility settles a wrongful death lawsuit, it must report the settlement to Florida's Agency for Health Care Administration so it can be recorded and accessible to anyone researching the facility's lawsuit history. However, this case was dismissed with prejudice and does not need to be reported to AHCA.

My other attempt to promote was through the newspaper. Surprisingly, I was not bound by a non-disclosure agreement. The settlement agreement stated, "The undersigned shall refrain from making any written or oral statement known to be disparaging or negative concerning LMHS's actions related to the alleged medical negligence and alleged violation of resident rights, except the undersigned may provide truthful information in response to a valid subpoena or other legal processes."

Interpreting this statement literally, I once again chose to inform the public through an op-ed about LMHS's wrongful death settlement and to educate them on Florida's sovereign immunity statutes. Aside from the first paragraph, the op-ed was the same as before.

The opening line now states, "After delaying litigation for three and a half years, LMHS, on 3 August, in court-ordered mediation, agreed to a settlement in a wrongful death lawsuit filed against the defendant HPCC. The lawsuit falls under Florida's Sovereign Immunity Statutes. Here, within the 600-word limit, I explained the statute. The op-ed was rejected.

This is my final attempt to inform you about the wrongful death settlement and to educate you on the relevant statutes governing this matter. I recognize that writing a book might not be covered by the guidelines in the hospital release, and I could face legal action.

I also reached out to the Medical Director at K, with whom I had my conference, to see if they wanted to know the final results of the lawsuit. They told me they would, and I sent them the same opening paragraph from my op-ed along with the presentation I had prepared for the mediator.

I am sure you wondered why I was so persistent about criticizing K's complaint investigation process regarding the quality of care. Here's the reason. HPCC is a Medicare facility that knowingly violated Medicare's CMS 20068 mandate on the limited use of catheters, but continues to collect millions of dollars in Medicare reimbursements each year. The monetary settlement for a wrongful death case will be written off as a business expense. This will not motivate HPCC to change their catheter use without medical justification, especially with K's approval that such a practice meets medical standards for future residents.

Your investigation procedures, which accept the records of the charged facility as fact while dismissing the medical documentation submitted by the complainant, are biased against the accused. Your investigation methods are not only unfair to me but will also be unfair to future complainants. According to your stated approach of investigating only one side based on the accused's medical records, I cannot consider K's investigation unbiased.

The only way to stop HPCC from using a catheter without medical justification is through Medicare sanctions. Based on the medical documentation I provided, I expected K to recommend those sanctions. By not doing so, K allows HPCC to continue its practice of using indwelling catheters without documentation of bladder scans. K's response again praised me for my concern about my wife's medical care.

CHAPTER 39

Brief Case Summary

IN JULY 2019, Beth's two years of pain and suffering ended in hospice. After three years of trying to prove the king could do no harm, it concluded in August 2021 with the king paying a minor monetary penalty for Beth's two years of suffering. What did the readers of this story and I learn? We learned that a hospital in Florida, protected by sovereign immunity, can perform surgery to remove the wrong kidney, and the most it can be held liable for in a lawsuit is $200,000.

We learned these facts from Florida's malpractice laws, which are designed to benefit insurance companies, hospitals, and doctors rather than assist kidney patients. These laws make it very difficult to file a medical malpractice lawsuit and even harder to find a law firm willing to take the case, knowing that the compensation recovery is limited.

Medical malpractice cases are often lengthy and costly to pursue, making it impractical for a law firm to handle a case involving sovereign immunity. Usually, these cases are dismissed even when the malpractice is severe and results in someone's death.

The 'same king can do no harm' statute applies to wrongful death. Someone can die during a botched operation, and the same $200,000 pain and suffering maximum damages still apply. Based on articles I researched online, I find that these statements are common throughout all of them.

Because Florida's medical, hospital, and insurance industries are highly politically influential, the law often fails to provide patients with legal recourse when they are harmed by medical negligence. These industries lobby, donate, and receive favorable treatment under the guise of fighting frivolous lawsuits and tort reform. The following is a summary of the wrongful death lawsuit saga that started in May 2017 and ended in August 2021.

It started with her falling and the hospital emergency room failing to diagnose a stable tibia fracture, which resulted in her suffering a shattered tibia and fibula. She was then transferred to HPCC for rehab, where the facility, in violation of Medicare guidelines, embedded a catheter. The catheter then caused her to develop many UTIs, which eventually led to her kidneys shutting down and her subsequent death. This story describes the events between her fall and her death.

I have detailed FSIS throughout my story, so I will not summarize them again. I also documented my efforts to educate Florida residents, especially those in the county using the LMHS, the most extensive health system in southwest Florida, about how the statutes affect their use of hospitals, nursing homes, or doctors affiliated with LMHS.

This effort to educate included three 600-word op-eds and three Letters to the Editor, all of which the local newspaper declined to publish. Their refusal to print probably pleased LMHS, since their inability to publish kept the county's citizens unaware of FSIS.

I also, perhaps excessively, detailed the legal process required to litigate a medical malpractice lawsuit. After the case was assigned a case number, attorneys submitted ninety-nine (99) documents totaling 396 pages of legal text over the course of more than three years. These included Complaints, Amended Complaints, Second Complaints, and Third Complaints, each accompanied by the defendant's Motion to Dismiss. All of these procedures were conducted with the understanding that the case would never proceed to trial due to court-mandated mediation and that the 396 pages were essentially court clutter.

My wife's death in July 2019 ended the medical malpractice lawsuit and changed it into a wrongful death case. Her passing shifted the trial's momentum from the plaintiff's side to the defendant's. There's something wrong with the legal system when a plaintiff's death results in a win for the defendant—so much for equal justice under the law.

Knowing that a monetary settlement made by HPCC would be considered a cost of doing business, I submitted a formal 'Quality of Care Complaint' with the agency appointed by Medicare to investigate such matters. By filing my malpractice complaints with the agency, I intended to convince them that the quality of care did not meet Medicare standards.

Based on my documentation, I expected the agency to recommend Medicare sanctions, a penalty that would be much more damaging to HPCC than a monetary settlement. I was disappointed once again when the agency decided that HPCC's actions met all the standards of acceptable medical care.

According to their investigation, their findings state, "Only the reports submitted by HPCC will be accepted as fact in determining the care given, and it is not up to the agency to determine whether those reports are accurate." It also mentions that despite my documentation of HPCC's misconduct, "the documentation by the complaint will not have a bearing on the vendors' determination whether they followed proper medical practices." Another point against the plaintiff.

Next was the unbelievable situation where Medicare and AARP Insurance told me that I would have to pay $55,000 and $9,000 for medical bills incurred on a conditional basis to LMHS out of any settlement I might receive from LMHS.

Consider this: the money paid by Medicare and AARP to LMHS was meant to be reimbursed by me to Medicare and AARP. To clarify, it is not LMHS, the recipient of the funds, that owes the repayment, but me. Think about this scenario — I might win a medical malpractice settlement from LMHS and then owe Medicare and AARP tens of thousands of dollars. Is something wrong with this picture?

Finally, after years of unnecessary claims, motions, depositions, and other documents totaling ninety-nine, the case concludes with court-mandated mediation. Mediation, which favors the defendant at the plaintiff's expense, is overseen by a mediator earning an estimated $1,800 to facilitate offers between the plaintiff and defendant.

With LMHS, the well-funded defendant, equipped with expert witnesses, reports from the Medicare investigation agency, and a detailed death certificate, along with the plaintiff's need for evidence to prove that the medical malpractice caused the death, can defeat the plaintiff. This mediation process, held in August 2021, could have concluded in July 2019 when my wife died, at which point the attorneys already knew the same facts presented here. It is a long journey through the halls of justice.

Having experienced the operations of five different assisted living and nursing homes, I can share my insights. First, I will comment on the state inspections of nursing homes. It is acceptable to have a detailed review process, but what infractions might occur between inspections, such as using a resident's catheter?

In that case, checks are ineffective unless the issues are caught during the inspection. I was the one who found the unnecessary catheter installation, not any state inspector. How many resident representatives can make such a discovery?

I would also like to emphasize the importance of long-term nursing care insurance. Assisted living and long-term care nursing homes are expensive, and both profit and non-profit facilities face the same challenge: staffing. Usually, the more costly the facility, the higher the quality of care, mainly because they can afford to pay their aides more—who are essential to nursing care—and retain staff members for more extended periods.

Non-profits rely on aides from Puerto Rico, Haiti, Honduras, or other Caribbean nations. Language barriers sometimes hinder communication between residents and aides. Most aides cared for the residents and provided good care, but frequent turnover often prevented a strong connection from forming. I must admit that the theft of my wife's diamond wedding ring did not improve my opinion of some of the aides.

One of the primary factors in selecting a nursing home is the quality of the food and the dining facilities. You might think this is a small detail, but good food is one of the few times residents can really relax and sit with others in a calm setting. The environment and how residents are served can vary from one facility to another.

In one facility, residents select from two meals and sit in a well-lit, colorful dining room with three other residents. The meals are delivered from the kitchen and served on bright, colorful tablecloths. A cheerful dining area allows residents to sit and chat for a while before returning to their rooms. This facility was the best of the five and the most expensive for-profit one. Food was brought into a plain dining room in other facilities and served from a serving cart.

In some facilities, the food was unappetizing and lukewarm, served between 11:00 and 1:00 for lunch and 5:00 to 7:00 for dinner, and the ice cream in a paper cup melted. In these places, residents ate what they could and then immediately went back to their rooms or chose not to go to the dining room.

Finally, I can't praise hospice care enough. The care and service Beth received in her final weeks exceeded my expectations. She couldn't have passed away in a more peaceful setting, and I continue to commend the care and comfort she experienced during those last days.

Yes, I received a damages award against HPCC, but it's hard to see it as a real victory. I view it more as a punishment for LMHS, but even then, how can you punish a firm with monetary damages that are just petty cash to the hospital? It's impossible to truly understand someone's pain and suffering unless you've experienced it yourself.

How can an independent legislature decide that medical misconduct resulting in a loved one's death is only worth $200,000? If this case involved a hospital or nursing home not protected by sovereign immunity, there would be no cap on damages, and a jury would determine both pain and suffering and the loss of a loved one. These caps explain why law firms often hesitate to file lawsuits against the government, which can act without accountability.

Many claims are denied because it is not financially feasible for an attorney to take on a costly FSIS medical malpractice case, even when the malpractice was severe and caused someone's death. The laws should be consistent and treat a sovereign immunity case the same as a lawsuit against a defendant not protected by that statute; currently, the law is unfair.

The law should be consistent, and everyone deserves a fair day in court. Under sovereign immunity, consistency is unattainable and will only change if the Florida legislature recognizes that aggrieved plaintiffs in sovereign immunity cases deserve a statutory change.

While working on this story, I learned about a wrongful death lawsuit in South Carolina where the jury awarded the plaintiff $4.3 million. In that case, the law firm probably spent about the same amount of time as my attorney did on my case.

It becomes clear why attorneys hesitate to pursue sovereign immunity cases and why sovereign immunity entities prefer to settle claims in mediation rather than risk a jury trial. Even the pit bull in St. Louis received $750,000 for his wrongful death lawsuit.

I have clearly documented that HPCC committed medical malpractice by embedding a catheter and leaving it in place for a period that significantly exceeds Medicare guidelines.

Such malpractice caused my wife's death. The unfortunate aspect of this lawsuit is that, despite my documentation of HPCC's misconduct, the case will not prevent the same misconduct from occurring to other residents.

CHAPTER 40

Conclusion

IT HAS BEEN four years since Beth fell, and my journey through the courts seeking justice for medical malpractice has concluded. It could have ended in March 2019, while Beth was still alive, and she could have seen that we achieved some justice for her pain and suffering. Was this journey worth it for me? Not financially, but that wasn't the only reason for the lawsuit. People often start lawsuits for money, but there's more at stake than just money.

The plaintiffs feel wronged; the defendants are insulted. The plaintiff hopes that the financial settlement will motivate the offending party to correct their wrongdoings and prevent similar incidents in the future. In this case, does a small monetary settlement serve that purpose for a nursing home receiving millions of dollars in Medicare reimbursement each year, or will the payment be a negligible amount on the nursing home's balance sheet?

The Florida legislature achieved what the medical profession wanted by passing the Sovereign Immunity Statutes. It clarified that, regardless of the medical practitioner's fault, you, the malpractice victim, will only receive a $200,000 damages settlement, even if the costs of treating the malpractice's aftermath far exceed that amount. For sovereign immunity agencies like LMHS, the settlement is considered a normal business expense.

Getting the maximum settlement is unlikely. During court-ordered mediation, the defendant's attorney aims to minimize the settlement amount while persuading the plaintiff to accept a figure much lower than what is owed. Usually, at this stage, the defense's delays have extended the case beyond its proper resolution, increasing the plaintiff's expenses with each postponement. In this situation, the defendant had deep pockets and was able to pay outside counsel $27,473 in retainer fees and costs.

The plaintiff's attorney must manage these delays while earning only $2,500 for three and a half years of work. A law firm cannot stay in business with a case like this, which shows why so few attorneys are willing to take a Florida sovereign immunity lawsuit. Even worse, the defendant is a public agency, and they are spending my $27,473 to fight against me.

As a side note, LMHS completed its budget year in September 2021, concluding with approximately $160 million in revenue exceeding expenses. Much of this income came from Medicare and Medicaid program reimbursements—the same Medicare mandates they ignored when treating my wife. You can see how, in this David versus Goliath story, Goliath was able to afford bigger stones.

The defendant knew the case would never go to trial because they would avoid the publicity. I attempted to counter this by sending op-eds to the newspaper, exposing the hospital's settlement of a wrongful death suit and educating the public on Florida's Sovereign Immunity Statutes. I also tried the same with a Letter to the Editor, but to no avail.

I attempted to obtain the defendant's report of the wrongful death settlement to the state agency by submitting a Freedom of Information Request for a copy of the documents provided to the agency. However, since the case was dismissed with prejudice, it was not required to be reported to the agency.

Did I have the best legal firm on my side? Who knows, since I had three different attorneys from the same firm. As mentioned, big firms typically won't take a sovereign immunity case because of the tactics the defense can use during the legal process. My third attorney did an excellent job prosecuting the case, but going up against a hospital is like the aforementioned David vs. Goliath story, with Goliath having the bigger stones this time.

I would have loved to take this case to court, especially with a jury of women. Just mentioning how many UTIs my wife suffered would have made the case, I believe, a slam dunk. I knew there was never a chance the defendant would let this case go to a jury trial, so all my and my attorney's preparation was for nothing.

Did the plaintiff conclusively prove that HPCC's medical misconduct was the primary cause of Beth's death? I believe we documented this in the medical records and statements, as noted in the HPCC nurse's notes.

Did I manage to inform the public that the nursing home settled a wrongful death lawsuit? No. Did I succeed in educating everyone about Florida's Sovereign Immunity Statutes? No. Did my lawsuit against HPCC for medical malpractice change their practice of using embedded catheters in the future? We might never know.

Was it worth it? In some ways, yes, because it kept me occupied while my wife was suffering and helped me stay busy after her death. I could use this moment to inform the county's citizens about Florida's Sovereign Immunity Statutes and the injustice they cause to injured parties who may suffer lifelong pain or even death.

However, as I mentioned before, I even failed in this effort. My wife remains gone after years of pain caused by the known negligence of HPCC, and any money I receive will never bring her back.

What did I learn? You'll have a difficult time trying to beat the system. They have no trouble getting expert witnesses to justify their actions, which forces the plaintiff to find witnesses to challenge them. The defendant's goal is to make it so costly for the plaintiff to pursue the case that the plaintiff will drop the case and agree to settle.

Based on all the medical documentation required, we had the 'smoking gun' evidence necessary to establish the defendant's liability for medical malpractice. However, for a wrongful death case, we needed to have the 'bullet' that exited the gun and prove that the bullet caused the plaintiff's death by the preponderance of the evidence.

So much for equal justice under the law.

I did accomplish one goal; I outlived the lawsuit.

CHAPTER 41

Postscript

ON JANUARY 2, 2022, the local newspaper published an article titled 'Dear Readers: Please Write Us.' The main point of the story was that the newspaper staff was frustrated because too many of the Letters to the Editor focused on controversial state and national politics rather than local issues. His plea prompted me to resubmit the following letter.

Over the past few months, I have submitted three op-eds, each time revising the first paragraph to avoid potential legal issues, and two Letters to the Editor on the same topic, neither of which was published by the paper. David says he is looking for more local issues. The subject of my op-eds, Florida's Sovereign Immunity Statutes, affects the entire state but mainly concerns those locally using the LMHS.

I consider myself very knowledgeable about the statutes, having recently settled a three-and-a-half-year wrongful death lawsuit through mediation. This settlement prevents the public from learning about the defendant's settlement. It would have been a front-page, above-the-fold news story if a jury had awarded the compensation. LMHS is a political subdivision of the state, created by the Florida legislature, and is protected by Florida's Sovereign Immunity Statutes.

The statute is too lengthy to explain in a letter, but was addressed in my earlier op-eds. 99% of the county's residents are unaware that they are subject to the statutes when filing a medical malpractice claim against any LH hospital, nursing home, or doctor, and I am sure LMHS would prefer to keep it that way. This letter is not intended for publication, but rather to help David understand that Sovereign Immunity Statutes are a local issue.

This may be my last opportunity to inform county residents that the statutes apply to them. The above letter prompted an email from the recipient, who told me that he was the staffer responsible for the letter to the editor and that my op-eds should be sent to the op-ed editor. Having already submitted my three versions of the op-ed, I decided to try again. Again, I failed to have it accepted.

www.ingramcontent.com/pod-product-compliance
Lightning Source LLC
Chambersburg PA
CBHW030326130626
46554CB00011B/56